RUSSIA UNDER THE AUTOCRAT
NICHOLAS THE FIRST

RUSSIA

UNDER

THE AUTOCRAT,

NICHOLAS THE FIRST.

BY

IVAN GOLOVINE,

A RUSSIAN SUBJECT.

PRAEGER PUBLISHERS
New York • Washington • London

PRAEGER PUBLISHERS
111 Fourth Avenue, New York, N.Y. 10003, U.S.A.
5, Cromwell Place, London S.W.7, England

Published in the United States of America in 1970
by Praeger Publishers, Inc.

Introduction © 1970 by Praeger Publishers, Inc.

Library of Congress Catalog Card Number: 76–109883

Printed in the United States of America

INTRODUCTION

Ivan Gavrilovich Golovine [Golovin] (1816–90) deserves better of history and historians than he has received to the present time. His most important book, reprinted here, is a gold mine of colorful and detailed information about the Russia of Nicholas I, yet it has been overshadowed by the roughly contemporary works of two foreigners, Haxthausen and de Custine. Golovine was one of the first Russians to become a political exile by deliberately defying a Tsar's express order to return home. His publication *Catechism of the Russian People,* issued in Paris in 1849, was one of the earliest uncensored opposition works to appear in Russian. He was a pioneer contributor to the development of dissident political thinking after the Decembrists, distinguishing between the Tsar's Russia and the people's Russia and arguing that the Russian nobility enjoyed an inviolable charter of rights inherited from an earlier period. It was an article by Golovine that moved Bakunin to publish his first public denunciation of the Tsarist regime. Between the early 1840's and 1880, Golovine wrote more than a dozen books, which appeared in English, French, German and Russian, including one that may have been the first volume to give a Russian traveler's impressions of

v*

the United States. In the late 1840's and early
1850's, he was an intimate collaborator of Alexander
Herzen's, an association that gave rise at the time to
the bilingual (Russian and German) pun that Golovine and Herzen were the head and the heart of
the Russian exile movement. Yet, today Golovine is
almost forgotten, and the few references to him in
Soviet and Western publications are mostly con-
temptuous and derogatory.

Born into a noble family, Golovine was educated
at Dorpat University and then entered the foreign
ministry under Nesselrode. He might have risen to
eminence in the bureaucracy, as others in his family
did, but he had literary ambitions and resented being a mere copyist. Nesselrode's criticism of his
handwriting gave him a pretext, in the early 1840's,
for a trip abroad from which he never returned. As
he explains here, he was ordered to return home
when word reached St. Petersburg that he had
written and was publishing abroad a book on political economy. Because he refused to return home,
he was sentenced in absentia to exile in Siberia. In
addition, his property was confiscated and he lost
his title. Outlawed by Nicholas, Golovine turned
into a sworn enemy of the Russian regime and won
considerable attention when this book was published
in French in 1845. English and German translations
quickly followed. From the mid-1840's to the mid-
1850's, he was a familiar and prominent figure among
the political exiles in Western Europe, with highly
placed friends in Britain and France. He published
several books, none of which, however, seems to
have enjoyed any great success. With his fortunes
declining, particularly after his break with Herzen,

Golovine visited the United States for some years, but then returned to Europe. Down on his luck, he sought and obtained permission to return to Russia but never acted on it. Herzen reported that Golovine married a rich German woman at one point and ran through her fortune quickly. The scanty available evidence suggests he lived the last decades of his life in obscurity and poverty.

The obscurity to which Golovine has been relegated arose largely, no doubt, from the devastating and bitter portrait given in the twenty pages devoted to him in Alexander Herzen's memoirs. Herzen paints a damning picture of a scoundrel without redeeming features, a cheat, a liar, a leech, a man without talent, who "thought in minced ideas." Golovine forced the acquaintance upon him from the first, Herzen avers, and Herzen sought in vain to "curb Golovine's friendliness and above all his visits." He accuses Golovine—whom he apparently helped financially at times—of base ingratitude and slander. His description of Golovine is merciless: "The man had not a particle of artistic feeling, no aesthetic requirements, he had no desire to learn and no serious occupation." And Herzen writes mockingly of "the now forgotten contents" of Golovine's writings about Russia, calling them "a hodgepodge of French rhetoric, the liberalism of the Rotteck School, anecdotes flung in pell-mell, platitudes and constant personalities with no logic, no definite view, no coherence."[1]

Nor was Herzen alone in his unflattering opinion.

[1] Constance Garnett, trans., and Humphrey Higgins, rev., *My Past and Thoughts: The Memoirs of Alexander Herzen* (New York: Alfred A. Knopf, 1968), III, 1398-9.

E. H. Carr quotes Bakunin's description of Golovine as a "high-class crook." Other sources indicate that in his later years Golovine suggested to the Tsarist regime that he might be a useful spy, informing St. Petersburg of developments in Russian exile circles in Western Europe.

At this distance in time there is no need to try to defend Ivan Golovine's honor or reputation. As compared with a Herzen or a Bakunin, he was certainly unsuccessful, usually poor, and forced to measures and expedients that a more secure individual would have eschewed. He had to live by his wits and must have been bitterly jealous of Herzen's wealth and enormous literary talent. And no doubt, as Golovine's material fortunes and public reputation declined, he became ever more desperate and ever more willing to attempt even unscrupulous ways to improve his situation.

Yet no one can read this book and easily accept Herzen's diatribe against Golovine as the whole truth. If anything, the thought must occur that Herzen is too bitter and too sweeping in his condemnation, unprepared to say a single kind word about one who was once his boon companion and close collaborator. If Golovine had really been as repulsive, untalented, and abhorrent as Herzen paints him, could the two have enjoyed a close relationship that lasted for roughly five years?

Indeed, the record shows that in the first editions of two of Herzen's most important books, he wrote much more kindly about Golovine. Thus, in 1850, when *From the Other Shore* was first published in German, Herzen wrote: "In the writings of Mr. Golovine, one can find everything that oppresses Russia and must be destroyed, but nothing about that which must be preserved. It is a publication of protest about everything that is hidden in compulsory silence there."[2]

And in the 1851 edition of Herzen's *On the Development of Revolutionary Ideas in Russia,* he hails the book reprinted here as one that brought out into the day's clear light "all that the Russian Government tries to hide. He [Golovine] speaks out in Europe about all that they keep silent about in Russia." Herzen adds that one has to understand how much the Tsar's government fears European public opinion "in order to comprehend the full significance of Golovine's work."[3]

But in later editions of these books, Herzen excised these laudatory references, and there is no hint of them in the bitter anti-Golovine section of Herzen's memoirs. What happened during or after 1851 to change Herzen's attitude so radically? The fact that they quarreled and parted ways seems inadequate by itself. After all, as noted above, Herzen insists in his memoirs that he had never liked Golovine even before he ever met him.

The full explanation may never be known. But Golovine's version of the two men's relationship is worth noting. This was stated in an obscure pamphlet that appeared in 1880, a decade after Herzen's death. The relevant section of this pamphlet is in effect Golovine's refutation of Herzen's description of their

[2] Akademiya Nauk SSSR, Institut Mirovoi Literaturi im. A. M. Gorkogo, *A. I. Gertsen: Sobraniye Sochineniya v Tridtsati Tomakh* (Moscow: Izdatelstvo Akademii Nauk SSSR, 1957), VI, 476–7.

[3] *Ibid,* VII, 401.

contact. Much of it has the ring of truth, with its description of young men spending evenings together drinking, of activities in common, of Herzen's reluctance to share his money as generously as Golovine and other poor exiles would have liked. But the key point is this: Golovine asserts that he himself was directly responsible for Herzen's discovering Natalie Herzen's infidelity, her love affair with George Herwegh, which played so traumatic and shattering a role in Herzen's emotional life. Was this the basis of Herzen's anger at Golovine, or was Golovine, in telling this tale, simply guilty once again of seeking to build up his own importance by twisting the truth?[4]

But enough about Golovine and Herzen, and enough too about Golovine's personal virtues and weaknesses. Whatever one thinks of its author, this book is strong enough to stand on its own feet. One hundred and twenty-five years after its first publication, it still has much to tell us about the Russia that existed a generation before Stalin was born. Here is a Russia ruled with the help of secret police and postal censors, a Russia where the ruler's word on any subject was immediate law, a Russia where men spoke freely only with their closest friends and only when certain that no strange ears overheard them. It is a Russia well worth knowing about even today, if we wish to understand the Soviet Union of 1970.

HARRY SCHWARTZ

---

[4] Iwan Golowyn, *Der Russische Nihilismus: Meine Beziehungen zu Herzen und zu Bakunin nebst Einer Einleitung über die Dekabristen* (Leipzig: Verlag von Louis Senf, 1880), pp. 69–70.

NICHOLAS THE FIRST.

RUSSIA

UNDER

THE AUTOCRAT,

NICHOLAS THE FIRST.

BY

IVAN GOLOVINE,

A RUSSIAN SUBJECT.

———

IN TWO VOLUMES.

VOL. I.

LONDON:

HENRY COLBURN, PUBLISHER,

GREAT MARLBOROUGH STREET,

1846.

LONDON:
HARRISON AND CO., PRINTERS,
ST. MARTIN'S LANE.

PREFACE.

THOMAS GOLOWYN being summoned by
Boris Godunof to return to his country, replied, "I will return when three proverbs
shall have ceased to be current in Russia:
'Everything that is mine belongs to the
Czar;' 'Near the Czar, near death;' 'Do
not fear the judgment, fear the judge*.'"

Above two centuries have elapsed since
these words were spoken, and have effected
but slight alleviations of the misfortunes of

---

* Thomas Golowyn emigrated to Lithuania, where
he died; his descendants still exist in that country.

Russia. Sequestration is still combined with
confiscation, in spite of the laws which expressly prohibit it; the approach of the Czar
forebodes no good to any but the courtiers,
for persecution follows independent and
enlightened men, and, to this hour, a Russian
judge is only an executioner. The proverbs
of that day have been replaced by new
ones, such as: "God is high, and the Czar
afar off;" "He who serves repines," in spite
of the other maxim; "Prayer to God and
service to the Sovereign are never fruitless." Abuses of a different nature have
succeeded ancient cruelties, and had I
chosen to imitate the bold language of my
ancestor, I should have said: I will return
when the whole of Russia shall have advanced to the fourteenth class (persons of
the fourteen classes are not liable to be
beaten); when a German shall not be more
highly esteemed than a Russian, and when

the pen shall have the weight of iron in the social scale.

My happiness could not be complete without that of my fellow-citizens. And as I could not expect to see this wish speedily realized, and was unable efficiently to contribute towards it in my own country, I renounced it with the less regret, because I trusted that I might render it greater service in a foreign land.

I am not the first, nor shall I be the last to deplore the servitude of Russia, and to protest against its oppressors; never shall I attain the energy of the Russian poet who said:

"In Russia the Czar and the knout are honoured; and the Russians, O fools! cry Hurrah! it is time to beat us!" nor do I aspire to the elevation of another who exclaims:

"I have seen enslaved Russia, clanking

her chains, and bowing her neck under the yoke, lying prostrate at the foot of the altar and praying for the Czar."

If I have spoken ill of Russia, it arises solely from the affection which I bear her. We look with comparative indifference upon those faults in a stranger which offend us in our own brethren; and we are more rigid towards those whom we love, than those in whom we take but little interest. Independently of this, I regard Russia as an abstract idea, great and beautiful, which I delight to elevate in the dreams of futurity.

Still less have I thought myself called upon to manifest indulgence towards the Government. As the author of the innumerable ills which afflict Russia, any indulgence towards it would have been an evidence of pusillanimity. Its injustice towards myself has not, however, made me unjust towards it; but, on the contrary, has increased my circumspection by demonstrating to me the iniquity of all injustice.

Men in power dare not, or will not raise their voice. They fish in troubled waters, and are therefore anxious to keep them so. They, in fact, are the traitors and betrayers of their country, and it is they who are the veritable revolutionists. Does not the man who boldly asserts his freedom, and dares to unveil the unworthiness and the ignorance of the Government, call down upon himself only indignation and contempt?

Publicity has this advantage, that error necessarily falls to the ground, while truth survives and perpetuates itself. This will be the case with the present work, and every consequent persecution directed against me will be the offspring of blindness or bad faith, which overlook the motive, and regard merely the present effect.

I have related no anecdotes but such as merit entire confidence, on account of the source whence they are derived. Their authenticity will give them weight with the public, and procure for them even a place in history, for they will tend to illustrate the characters of the individuals to whom they relate. Of great men and good sovereigns, such traits only are recorded as do them honour; whereas of wicked men, and of feeble sovereigns, we have merely statements which it is distressing to relate.

Had I retained what I have thought it my duty to suppress, and were I to acquaint my readers with the rigid scrutiny to which I submitted all I have brought forward, they would not entertain a doubt of the veracity of my narrative; suffice it, however, to declare that I have not invented anything.

On the Emperor Nicholas alone it, however, depends to prove **that** my judgment
of his merits is erroneous, **and** that he
is worthy to reign over the people committed to his care. Let him command
his acolytes. Let him say to Orloff, that
he intends, henceforth, to govern by mild-
ness, sincerity, and confidence, and to
abolish his secret police. Let him say
to Bludoff, that after having collected the
Russian laws he is convinced that they are
only fit to be thrown into the fire, as being
unworthy of the age in which we live;
unworthy of God and of man; and that
in their place he will substitute laws of
justice and equity. Let him say to Panin,
that robbers shall no longer be in power,
but in Siberia. Let him say to Uwarof, that
he will no longer tolerate the charlatanism
of civilization, and that he desires to

render it as pure as heaven. Let him say
to Perowsky, that his name shall be allied
to the greatest work of the age, the emancipation of the serfs; let him declare, that
if the nobles have not enfranchised their
peasants within a specified period, they shall
be compelled to do so by the law, for that
it is an anomaly to have slaves in a christian land. Let him say to Nesselrode, that
France, the centre of civilization, deserves
his high esteem, and can no longer be his
enemy. Let him also say, that the past
sufferings of Poland shall suffice, and that
God, having caused the scales to fall from
his eyes, he at once relieves Poland from
her cruel chains.

And after having said this, let him carry
it into effect. Then will history correct
her sentence; and will say, that, after
having sinned deeply, Nicholas has deeply

repented; and she will place his name by the side of those whom nations love to revere.

Is the unanimous disapprobation which is excited by all his actions, to be counted for nothing? Does he think that error and falsehood exist only in the civilized world, and that wisdom and honour are exclusively on his side? If it be delightful to govern as absolute master, it is surely far more so to give liberty to the nations governed; but this joy is the lot of pure and noble souls alone.

PARIS, 14*th July*, 1845.

RUSSIA

UNDER

NICHOLAS THE FIRST.

MY PERSECUTION.

On the 11th of March, 1843, I was summoned to the office of the Russian Chargé d'Affaires at Paris; I accordingly went thither the next day, and, after being desired to take a seat, his Excellency said:

"Sir, I have received, under the date of the 23rd of February, O.S., the following instructions:

" 'Your Excellency,

" 'It is the pleasure of his Majesty the Emperor, that, on the receipt of these presents, you forthwith send for Prince Peter Dolgorucky, and Mr. Ivan Golowyn, and admonish them instantly to quit Paris and repair to St. Petersburg.

" 'You are not to accept of any excuse whatever, neither sickness, nor other pretext, and you will inform them, that, in case of disobedience, they will be proceeded against as rebels to the Imperial will, with all the rigour of the laws.

(Signed) Nesselrode.' "

After having read this letter, M. Kisselef said, "When shall you set out?"

"I quitted Russia on account of my health, and have always regretted that I could not return thither; but it would be impossible for me to do so at this moment."

"I cannot admit of this excuse."

"I hope that his Majesty the Emperor will have the goodness to accept it."

"You have just heard that I cannot accept of any pretext."

"It is no pretext. I can produce medical certificates of the bad state of my health."

"When do you desire that I should give you your passport?"

"I have already informed your Excellency, that it is impossible for me to leave Paris just now."

"What then, would you have me do?"

"Make your report accordingly."

"I dare not; write yourself."

"I will do so."

"But do you not see that it is the will of the Emperor that you should return instantly?"

"My illness is the will of God," I replied, and bowing to his Excellency, withdrew from the apartment; Prince Dolgorucky entered almost immediately after.

In the course of the same day I sent the following letter, addressed to M. Kisselef:

"YOUR EXCELLENCY,

"It has always been my desire to return to my country as soon as possible. I quitted it only on account of the shattered state of my health, and would gladly have obeyed the summons which I have just received, but my illness will not, at present, permit me to undertake so fatiguing a journey. I trust that my life may yet be useful to his Majesty the Emperor, and that I may not be deprived, by a premature death of the ability to confound malignity and destroy calumny. I rely on the clemency and justice of our most gracious Sovereign, and humbly solicit that my journey may be deferred till my health shall be improved; as soon as ever I am able, I will set out for St. Petersburg. I have the honour to annex a medical certificate.

"*Paris,* 12th *March,* 1843."

I could not divine the cause of my
recall. Every Russian noble is permitted to reside five years in foreign countries, and my passport was dated only
a year and a half back. There was
absolutely nothing with which I could
charge myself. Count Benkendorf, the
Minister of Police, had not even conde-
scended to inform me of the cause which
induced the Russian Government to treat
me thus arbitrarily. He had merely
stated to my brother that the Emperor
deemed my residence at Paris perfectly
useless, and had the goodness to promise
that he would *defend me* on my return, if it
were true, as he had been told, that *I had
a good heart*. Prince Dolgorucky had
shortly before published a little work, entitled, "*Notice sur les principales Familles
de la Russie, par Le Comte Almagro.*"
This pamphlet had excited the indignation
of several nobles, and of some high Russian
functionaries. The Prince had given occa-

sion to his recall by placing a history of
the Romanoffs, which was nearly finished,
under the protection of France, and as I
had myself just put to the press a treatise
on Political Economy, I had no doubt
that offence had been taken at my doing
so, although the contents of my work were
entirely unknown.

Are Russians prohibited from printing
their writings in a foreign country?   Before
proceeding to the publication of my work,
I had sent to the Parisian correspondent of
the Minister of Public Instruction, to ascertain whether I was authorized in doing so.
He informed me that, strictly speaking, it
was prohibited to print anything in foreign
countries; that the engagement which
ought to be signed by those who take out
passports contained this prohibition, but
that passports were generally obtained
without imposing any restriction.   He
further stated that it was an every-day
occurrence for Russians to publish works

out of their country, and that I might consequently do the same without the slightest hesitation. "If your book," he added, "is against Russia, the Government will in all probability punish you; if it is not, it will wink at it; and if it is favourable, it may even reward you." I asked him if I might rely upon his statements? He replied, "You may consider them as official."

I accordingly hastened to communicate to him the news of my recall, and said, "that being convinced of my perfect innocence, I could not account for this rigour, except on the ground of my publication." He had the kindness instantly to write to Count Benkendorf, to tell him that my work was very different from that of Prince Dolgorucky, being entirely of a scientific nature, and rather favourable than otherwise to Russia.

The Russian law is decisive; it commands every subject to return to his country at the first summons; there is, however, ano-

ther law equally explicit, which says that,
after sentence passed, or even *on a mere
order of the Government,* a person may
be exiled to the provinces of the interior;
and those on the confines of Siberia,
namely: Viatka, Perm, and Volgoda,
are generally selected. I was conscious
that I was innocent, but who would say
that I had not been calumniated? Russian spies are very numerous at Paris,
more so than in any other city; and a
slight offence given to one of these gentlemen is quite sufficient to induce him to
inform against the offender to a superior authority, indeed they often gladly seize some
opportunity of this kind to obtain favour,
or at all events to evidence that they have
earned their salary; because those spies who
are too sparing of their reports, are suspected, or dismissed. Informers enjoy the
strictest incognito; they are never confronted with the accused, and their word
has more weight than that of honest men.
Persons, perfectly free from reproach, have

been recalled to Russia on a bare suspicion
of liberalism, and even when they have
wholly escaped punishment, because neither
word nor deed could be alleged against
them, they have nevertheless been shackled
in their future career. A caprice of Count
Nesselrode had already induced me to renounce every branch of public service; and I
was certainly not disposed to subject myself
anew to humiliation. As my recall would
necessarily become public, no justification
could have secured my innocence against
suspicion. My best defence was my book.
I therefore considered it advisable to publish it; besides I could not renounce the
satisfaction of giving to the world the fruit
of many years' study. I loved, and still
love, my country, as much as any man; and
because I loved it, I was desirous to contribute to the utmost of my power to efface
the epithet of *barbarism* by which we are
stigmatised all over Europe.

If I do not here speak of the rights of man,

or of the rights of civilization, which are
superior to all laws, especially to iniquitous
laws, rights which are utterly trampled
under foot, and which I saw shamefully violated in my own case, it is simply because
I am anxious not to soar above the compre-
hension of the Russian Government.

I resolved to use all possible circumspection in order to gain over those, who,
though they did not participate in my
views, merited my esteem. I therefore
saved appearances, by declaring myself ill,
which was in fact the case.

On the 13th I was visited by a secretary
of the Embassy, who requested me, in the
name of the Ambassador, at least to set out
for Germany, in order that his Excellency
might be able to inform the Government
of my departure in obedience to its man-
date. I replied that I had no confidence
in the German physicians; upon which he
begged me at least to fix the time of my
departure; but as it was utterly out of my

power to tell how long my illness might continue, I could not comply with this fresh proposition. On the following day the same gentleman invited me, by a note, to modify my letter conformably to his suggestion. This proceeding on his part met with no better success than the first.

The next day, a person attached to the Legation called on me to say that he had read the draught of the report which had just been prepared respecting my affairs; he added that I must look to the consequences if I did not make some alteration in my letter, because, as Prince Dolgorucky had fixed the time for his return, he was of opinion that the anger of the Emperor would fall upon me alone. Persuaded that I should gain everything by gaining time, and being well aware of the intractable spirit of the Czar, I withdrew my first letter and substituted another, of the following tenor :—

"YOUR EXCELLENCY,

"I should unresistingly have obeyed the direction which I have just received, and have set out immediately, but cannot do so, as the state of my health does not permit me to bear the motion of a carriage; and, as the approaching opening of the navigation will afford me the means of returning more speedily, I intend, as in duty bound, to embark on board the first steamer. I have the honour to inclose the certificate attesting the bad state of my health."

The answer of Count Benkendorf to his correspondent was not delayed.—"As for M. Golowyn," he wrote, "you may be perfectly easy on his account: *nous n'avons pas de corps de délit contre lui* (these are the very words of the letter, which was in French.) In fact, it was only a measure of precaution, and not of repression. This affair will go no farther."

Was not this a plain declaration of my innocence? But, in this case, why should I be persecuted? By way of *precaution?* Would it not be equally reasonable, arbitrarily to lay hold on passengers in the streets and incarcerate them, lest they should commit some crime? Would it not be acting in the spirit of certain owners of serfs, who beat their people in anticipation of the faults which they may hereafter commit; or, who, acknowledging that they have punished them wrongfully, promise to place the castigation to their credit against the next time? Could that be called a measure of *precaution* which would bring confusion and terror into a family, excite a vast sensation in Paris and Petersburg, and in the face of Europe be equivalent to a confession that an author was recalled on account of a work which was still in his desk or in the press? It is true that I had been advised to keep the whole affair perfectly secret. Count Benkendorf

had a two-fold reason for this advice: "the
Emperor's will is that his subjects shall
keep quiet in foreign countries; and we
by no means desire that they should publish anything whatever."

Relying on the letter of the chief of the
gens d'armes to his correspondent, I believed
that, like many other precipitate measures
of the Russian Government, this whole
affair would lead to no result; and especially because there were precedents which
authorized me to arrive at this conclusion.
I sent two copies of my *Economie Politique*
to St. Petersburg, one intended for the
Emperor, and the other for the Minister
of Police; and I then repaired to the Pyrenees for the benefit of the waters. Count
Benkendorf did not take the trouble of
reading more than the Preface, which he
considered very inflammatory, because I
therein claimed the hospitality of France
for my views. He severely reprimanded
his correspondent for having misled him

respecting the spirit of my publication. The censorship of the Press, after a long delay, suffered the book to pass, but cut out several leaves; this, added to the intelligence that Prince Dolgorucky had just been banished to Viatka, was calculated to fill me with well-grounded apprehensions for the fate that might await me on my return.

I was fully resolved not to set out for Russia without a positive assurance that I should not be molested, and as I had not received any notice for several months, I wrote the following letter to the Minister of Police, from Cauterets, on the 15th of August, 1843 :—

" SIR,

"Several months ago I had the honour to forward to St. Petersburg two copies of my last work ; I intended one for his Majesty the Emperor, and the other for your Excellency ; but as I have not received any answer, I fear that ill-founded apprehension may have hindered my brother from sending these books to their destination. In this case I request that your Excellency will have the goodness to relieve my brother from any such groundless fears, and further, to do me the favour to accept one copy, and to present the other to our august Sovereign, with an expression of my extreme regret at being unable to lay it in person at his Majesty's feet, because a serious illness still keeps me at a distance from my country.

" Accept, &c. &c."

On my return to Paris, the Russian Legation transmitted to me a paper, signed " Douvelt," dated 1st (12th) September, 1843, of the following tenor :—

" SIR,

"Count Benkendorf, the Adjutant-General, having been informed that you have ventured, without asking permission, to go from Paris to the Pyrenees, for the benefit of the mineral waters, in defiance of the *supreme* order which you received in March last to return to Russia, and of your own declaration in writing that you would set out at the opening of the navigation by the first steamer, his Excellency has instructed me to acquaint you that he confines himself to repeating, for the last time, the order to fulfil your duty, and to return immediately to St. Petersburg, without availing yourself of any pretext whatever. If you do not comply, his Excellency will make his humble report to his Majesty the Emperor, your very delay in obeying his Majesty's order will be a great crime, and you will have incurred a heavy legal responsibility.

" While I thus obey the orders of Count Alexander Christophorovitsch, I have the honour to assure you of my sincere regard and devotion."

To this I instantly sent the following reply :—

"SIR,

"What answer can I make to the official notice which you did me the honour to cause to be addressed to me under the date of the 1st of September, and which was not delivered to me, by the Legation, until the 22nd of November? If I should speak to you of the cause which detains me here, you have an answer at hand: you will not listen to any objection. My illness, and the course of medicine which I am now undergoing, only excite your displeasure, and this is not calculated to ease my mind respecting the fate which may attend me on my return. Shall I speak of my innocence? You are as fully convinced of it as I am myself; and was I not justified in inferring, from your own words, that 'you had no crime wherewith to charge me, and that the affair would go no further,' permission to go wherever I pleased? Must I assert my devotedness to my Sovereign? History bears testimony that my family has served the throne more than any other, and certainly I have not been an exception. I have only made use of the freedom of the press to consolidate the glory of my country. It is easy to serve it in prosperity; but it is difficult to do so in adversity. My crimes are my illness and powers of mind, and yet you will not leave me, as an indemnification, the faculty which is granted to the meanest subject, that of moving about at will. Nothing, therefore, remains for me but to assure you of my high esteem, and to trust in the clemency and justice of my Sovereign.

"I am, &c., &c."

General Douvelt sent the following reply on the 25th November old style:—

"Sir,

"The Aid-de-camp General, Count Ben-

kendorf, having received your letter of the
12th (24th) of November, has been pleased
to declare that the Government has not had
to accuse you of any crime; but that you
have become culpable *from the moment*
that you refused to obey the order of his
Majesty respecting your return to Russia.
His Excellency, actuated by the kindness
of his heart, has hitherto kept back, and
still keeps back his humble report on the
subject; but it is possible that his Majesty
the Emperor may think fit to inquire whether you have returned from abroad, and
then it will be necessary to lay before him
the particulars of this affair, and, in consequence of your delay in obeying the will of
the Monarch, you will be amenable, as
for a *serious crime*, to all the rigour of the
laws. For this reason, Count Alexander
Christophorovitsch, for the last time repeats his former injunction, and has instructed me to request you to return immediately to Russia, not alleging any fur-

ther pretext; and if you do not comply,
his Excellency will be constrained to lay
the whole before his Majesty.

"While fulfilling the orders of Count
Alexander Christophorovitsch, I have the
honour to assure you of my sincere respect
and regard."

At the same time the Count caused a
letter to be written to me, through a private channel, saying that the Emperor did
not like to be trifled with, and was accustomed to be obeyed; that a single word
from him would suffice to induce the French
Government to oblige me to quit France.
I was incensed at this arrogance, and certainly not intimidated by the reports which
were adroitly spread by the Russian agents,
that M. Guizot had offered to send away
Prince Dolgorucky, escorted by gens
d'armes; I well knew the meanness to which
the Russian diplomacy could resort, and I
was soon perfectly at ease on this point.   I

therefore left my cause in the hands of Providence, and returned the following answer to the Minister of Police.

"Sir,

"In your order of the 25th of November, you admit my innocence and speak of your kindness of heart. I never doubted the former; but the second does not appear in your letter. Kindness of heart and justice require indemnification to those who have wrongfully suffered persecution, and not the continuation of such persecution.

"Besides, you are pleased to announce to me that, in consequence of my delaying to return to my country, proceedings will be instituted against me with all the rigour of the laws, as for a *serious crime*. It would be difficult to find words more plainly conveying an order to obey, and at the same time deterring from compliance with it.

"Being fully persuaded that my cause is

just, I place my hopes on the impartiality
of the Emperor, and beg your Excellency
no longer to delay making your report to
him on the causes which prevent my speedy
return. These I stated to you in my letters
of the 5th of August and the 24th of
November, and are the shattered state
both of my health and of my fortune."

On receiving this letter, Count Benkendorf wrote in the margin, "The young man
will end by ruining himself." He then
sent for my brother, embraced him, made
him sit down, and said, "You know that I
am your friend; but there is no family
without a reprobate, and your brother is
the *reprobate* of your family. Ecce homo!"

On the 8th (20th) of February, the Legation sent to me a letter from General
Douvelt, dated on the 8th (20th) of January, and conceived in the following
terms :—

" SIR,

        " The Adjutant-General, Count Ben-
kendorf, having received your letter of the
3rd of January, (new style,) and finding that
you still delay to execute the Emperor's
order concerning your immediate return to
Russia, has instructed me to inform you
that his Excellency will defer the delivery
of his report to the Emperor four weeks
longer; but if, at the expiration of that
time, (care had been taken to let it expire,)
you have not arrived at St. Petersburg,
your disobedience will be forthwith reported to the Emperor.

        " I beg to assure you of my sincere
respect, and remain, &c."

On the preceding day, M. Kisselef had
communicated to me an order transmitted
to him by Count Nesselrode, dated the
26th of January, which directed that he
should be informed of my decision respect-

ing my return to St. Petersburg. I was
not to be dictated to by Count Nesselrode.
I had received my instructions from Count
Benkendorf. In fact, I had already sacrificed my post in order that I might not be
dependent on the Minister for Foreign
Affairs, for being admonished by him to
take lessons in writing, I thought that I
might be more useful to my country as an
author than as a copyist, and accordingly
withdrew from the service.

I addressed the following letter to Count
Nesselrode, which I sent to M. Kisselef:—

" SIR,

" I thought that I had explained
myself decidedly enough with respect to
my return to Russia, in my letters to Count
Benkendorf, dated the 15th of August, the
24th of November, 1843, and the 3rd of
January, 1844 ; but since your Excellency
condescends to interfere in this measure of

the police, it is my duty to inform you, that
I quitted the service of my country for the
purpose of taking lessons in calligraphy, as
you were pleased to recommend. I have
no protection, and your Excellency cannot
fail to remember that the first Minister for
Foreign Affairs bore the same name as
myself.

" I trust, however, that you will not exercise the full extent of your power, and
cause it to be said, that a Benkendorf and
a Nesselrode have placed a Golowyn on the
proscription list.

" I have the honour to be, &c."

I shewed this letter to the Russian poet
B——, and asked his opinion respecting it.
He urged me to send it off, observing, that
Count Nesselrode was a superior man, who
on calling to mind the injury which he had
done me, would hasten to repair it. Soon,
however, I had a fresh proof of the two-fold

truth, that good men are not always endowed with worldly wisdom, and that great
men frequently harbour petty hatred.

Count Nesselrode, on receiving my letter, lost no time in laying it before the
Emperor, who immediately ordered that all
my property should be sequestrated, that
proceedings should be instituted against me
for the crime of disobedience and high
treason, and that I should be arrested if I
set foot on the Russian territory.

Prince Dolgorucky was recalled from his
place of banishment at Viatka, and the
Emperor issued a decree prohibiting Russian subjects from going abroad before
they had attained the age of twenty-five,
and imposed a tax of 800 francs a year on
their passports: none but invalids and merchants were exempt from this measure.

At length, one evening, his Majesty did
me the honour to read my letter to a small
circle at court. "Who would have thought
it," he cried, "that the brother of our

Golowyn should be the author of such a letter? And who will venture to say that this man writes well? I leave you to judge for yourselves, gentlemen, is this letter well written?" And immediately, the gentlemen present bowed their heads, saying, " Certainly not, Sire, the letter is very ill written."

Thus condemned by the court, I was very shortly sentenced by the senate, which pronounced against me the penalty of banishment to Siberia, the privation of all my civil rights, and the confiscation of my property.

Chapter 1.

HISTORICAL NOTICE OF THE REIGN OF NICHOLAS I.

It is no part of my design to dwell at length on the history of a reign which is distinguished only by acts of cruelty and violence; acts which will, however, be useful, inasmuch as they will serve to fill up the measure of iniquity, and hasten the coming of a better order of things.

Alexander, who died at Tagenrog on the 19th November, 1825, carried with him to the tomb many generous plans; his death excited both regret and apprehension; but the regret was lessened by the administration of Araktshêief, into whose hands he had suffered the reins of government to fall, when overcome by feelings of disgust; while the apprehensions were increased by a storm which was rising in obscurity, but of which there was a general presentiment. The nation was far from being comfortable respecting the fate which the brothers of Alexander were preparing for Russia. Constantine, at the most, was calculated only to act anew the reign of his capricious father, who was good and bad by fits and starts; it was out of the question to expect from him an equable and intelligent exercise of power; and as for Nicholas, he was scarcely known. Constantine had, besides, renounced the crown, by his marriage with Princess Lowitz, the daughter of a private Polish gentleman named Grusinsky. The act of his renunciation of the crown, and the manifesto of Alexander, nominating Nicholas for his successor, were deposited in the church of the Assumption at Moscow, and entrusted to the care of the three highest authorities of the empire, — the Synod, the Council, and the Senate. The Grand Duke Constantine, in his letter to the Emperor, dated 14th January, 1822, declared, that " in case he should ever be invested with the high dignity to which he was called by his birth, he did not believe himself possessed of the talent or energy indispensable for the performance of its duties."

Nicholas sported with the crown; he offered it to Constantine, and made the troops take the oath: " thus though he pretended the contrary, he left his beloved country in a state of uncertainty, respecting the person of its legitimate sovereign." Constantine again reiterated his refusal, and Nicholas then required the oath to be taken to himself. This was the signal for an insurrection, and it broke out almost instantly.

The flower of the nobility and of the Russian army, mostly young men distinguished by their education and talents, who were ill at ease amidst institutions which bore heavy on them, and impelled by ardent love for their country, had resolved to remedy its evils. Since the year 1817 they had formed several societies, similar to those in other countries, especially that of the German *Tugendbund*. The object of these associations was to diffuse knowledge by the establishment of public schools, particularly on the Lancasterian system; to labour in favour of the emancipation of the vassals by the promulgation of liberal ideas and examples of generous enfranchisement; to remedy the abuses in the administration of justice, by not refusing the functions which might be confided to their members*, by encouraging upright judges, and even affording them pecuniary assistance. It was their desire thus to aid the

---

* Ryleief and Pontshine, among others, had filled, with great credit to themselves, offices that were far from agreeable.

efforts of Government, which they considered to be insufficient; and so far from thinking that their views were blameable, they frequently wished to ask its assent and countenance, and were withheld only by the fear of not being adequately supported by its philanthropy.

A petition demanding permission to open a subscription for the emancipation of the vassals was, in fact, presented to the Emperor, though without leading to any result. The names of the most respectable men, such as Count Woronzow, Prince Menchiskof, were found among the petitioners. M. Wasiltschikof, now President of the Council, first gave his assent, but subsequently withdrew it; several of those who signed the petition fell into disgrace in consequence of doing so.

The association, which was at first formed under the name of *The Union of Safety*, subsequently assumed that of *Union of the Public Good*, or of the *Green Book*, from

the colour of the binding of its statutes.
It was divided into the Society of the
North and that of the South. The first had
its sittings at St. Petersburg, the latter at
Tultschin. In 1823 the latter joined the
Society of the United Sclavonians, and
Moscow served as their rallying point.
Constitutional ideas were then in vogue,
and had spread among the enlightened
classes, after the campaigns of 1813—15.
The organization of society necessarily
became the object of the deliberations of
these meetings, and was the subject of
frequent and warm debates, which, however,
rather resembled private conversations than
formal deliberations.

The existence of these societies was
denounced, in 1820, to the Emperor Alexander, who did not think it necessary to interfere openly. In June, 1824, a subaltern
officer, named Sherwood, directed the attention of the Government to what he called
a plot; and on the 1st December Captain

Mayboroda, of the regiment of Viatka, addressed a letter to the Emperor Alexander, impeaching the association of which he was himself a member. The sublieutenant Rostootzof also wrote a letter to the Grand Duke Nicholas, of which Ryleief obtained a copy. On showing it to his brethren, on the evening of the 13th December, he exclaimed, "You see that we are betrayed: we must act—we must die in one way or other." "The scabbards are broken," cried one of the members, "our sabres can no longer be hid."

On the 14th (26th) December, when the guards had just taken the oaths to Nicholas, the conspirators dispersed themselves among the ranks, telling the soldiers that they had been deceived; that Constantine had not abdicated; that he was marching to St. Petersburg, and would punish the traitors. Prince Stepine Rostowsky wounded General Fredericks and General Shenshine, who attempted to interpose his authority. He seized the colours, and four companies of the regiments of Moscow marched in open revolt against the palace. Lieutenants Southof and Panof brought up a detachment of grenadiers of the guards. "Do you hear that firing," cried Nicholas Bestuchef to the Imperial marines: "they are assassinating your brethren;" and the whole battalion instantly rushed to arms.

On the other hand, General Alexis Orloff, whose brother was among the conspirators, advanced at the head of his cavalry to the defence of Nicholas. Thirteen hundred men were drawn up under the walls of the Senate-house; Miloradovitch, Governor-General of St. Petersburg, endeavoured to induce them to return to obedience, but he was killed by Kahovsky.

The Metropolitan, attired in full episcopal robes, advanced and raised his voice to stem the tumult, but it was drowned by the noise of the drums. Nicholas ordered a squadron of horse-guards to charge the rebels, but the guards were repulsed; cannons were then brought up, and a general conveyed cartridges in his carriage. The artillerymen refused to fire, upon which he lighted the match himself, and the insurgents were dispersed. Several balls were fired into the city in different directions, and a great number of the inhabitants were killed or wounded. Next day (the 26th of December) the dead bodies were taken away in a barge, and order was completely restored.

Colonel Pestel, the President of the Southern Society, of which he was the life and soul, was arrested the same day. Sergius Muravief, having received timely warning, escaped till the 29th, but his comrades rescued him as well as his brother; they excited the regiment of Tschernigof to revolt, and marched against Belaïa-Tzerkof. They were, however, attacked on the heights of Ustinovoke by a detachment of the corps of Geismar. The soldiers rushed towards

the cannon, and the grape-shot thinned
their ranks. Hippolytus Muravief fell dead
upon the spot; Sergius was wounded; the
cavalry charged them on all sides, and they
laid down their arms.

A minute inquiry was instituted at St.
Petersburg, and the Grand Duke Michael
was among those who took part in the
examinations. Vast numbers of persons
were arrested on the slightest suspicion;
their papers were diligently examined, and
if no overt acts could be found against
them, words, which might have been spoken
ten years before were laid hold of, though
perhaps scarcely remembered either by those
who were accused of them, or those who
professed to have heard them. Even sup-
posing that calumny had not induced some
of the impeached to make false declarations,
fear may have led them to charge others, in
order to extenuate their own faults; words
were wrested from their true acceptation;
comments made upon them, and, consider-

ing *the serious nature of the facts,* recourse was had to *extraordinary measures;* persuasion was employed in some instances, and in others intimidation. Several of the unfortunate victims were loaded with chains; some were made to confess inaccurate facts, others to sign pure fictions; and both times and events were confounded.

"Fear," says a Russian proverb, "has large eyes;" and the commission of inquiry converted facts of small importance into a monstrous affair, while it at the same time endeavoured to ruin the conspirators in the public opinion. It attacked their personal dignity, called their courage in question, loaded them with the grossest epithets, and ridiculed their political views as *vulgar philanthropy,* or *the attempt of scoundrels.*

A careful examination of the acts of accusation will show at a glance the contradictions and nonsense with which they abounded, and the total absence of all proof. Defence was out of the question; the conspirators were impeached by prejudiced accusers, sentenced by servile judges, and were without the benefit of counsel. For instance, Mr. Jakuschkin had offered to assassinate the Emperor with his own hand.— When?—In 1817! But he yielded to the arguments of Von-Viesen and Sergius Muravief. At a meeting, held at Kiew in 1823, a motion to exterminate the Imperial family could not be adopted according to the act of indictment itself. Sergius Muravief declared that he would not consent to regicide. Bestuchef-Rumin maintained the same opinion in a letter to Juschinski; with respect to the letter which he was accused of having addressed to the Secret Society of Poland, and in which he was said to have demanded the death of Constantine, it was never dispatched. It was said, that it was intended to seize the person of the Czar at Bobruisk; who can prove that the means were wanting and not the will? Jukof exclaimed, that if the lot fell on him to assassinate the Emperor he would kill himself. Nikita Muravief desired only the propaganda: and declared the plan of exterminating the Imperial family to be barbarous and impracticable.

Matthew Muravief, in a letter of the 3rd of November, 1824, to his brother Sergius, demonstrated the impossibility of any revolutionary convulsion. Yakobovitsch, it was said, wished to revenge himself on Alexander and to kill him; but he denied the accusation, and the commission ascertained that the other members of the Society endeavoured to hinder the execution of this menace, which was nothing more than bravado. With respect to the assassination of Nicholas, the commission itself ascribed to Yakobovitsch the following words: "I will not undertake it; I have an honest heart and cannot become an assassin in cold blood." Bestuchef having, as it was said, expressed, an opinion that they could *penetrate into the palace*, Batinkof exclaimed,

" God forbid !"   If we may give credit to
the report of the commission, Kahofsky
imputed to Ryléiéf the intention to murder
Constantine, but Bestuschef and Steinhell
denied this charge.

The accusation of regicide being disposed of, we now proceed to that of attempting a Republic.

Ryléiéf stated that a Republic is a folly;
that they ought to strive for limited Monarchy, although this was not favourable to
the development of great characters.   He
would not allow the Society the right of
establishing a new order of things without
the concurrence of the representatives of
the nation.   Batinkof even said, that the
prayers which were put up at mass for the
Imperial family, rendered a Republic impossible in Russia.

The projects of a constitution alone remained.   But who at that time had not
drawn up some sketch according to his own
notions?   There was not a man capable of

thinking, who had not the draft of a constitution in his pocket, in his desk, or in his
head. The Emperor Alexander had three,
that of Navosiltzof, that of Speransky and
that of Mardvinof. No one thought of
using violence to impose this constitution,
which was in fact not one; for, according to
the very words of the commission, " Projects
without connection, without a basis, cannot
be called plans." The parties concerned
desired to avoid shedding blood, and were
persuaded that the Emperor would make a
concession, and would cause deputies to be
convoked; and it was with this understanding that they had repaired to the place of
meeting.

After more than five months' investigation, the Commission of Inquiry completed its labours. The Emperor appointed
a supreme tribunal, composed of the Council
of the Empire, the Synod and the Senate, to
decide on the fate of the accused. To
these three public bodies several military

and civil officers of high rank were added. This tribunal decided that, according to law, all the prisoners, one hundred and twenty in number, deserved death; but it appealed to the Imperial clemency, and classed the criminals under eleven heads, making an exception of five of them, whom, it set apart, on account of the enormity of their crime. These were Pestel, Ryléiéf, Sergius Muravief, Bestuchef - Rumin, and Kahofsky, who were condemned to be quartered. Thirty-one individuals of the first category were sentenced to be beheaded; those of the second to incur political death; those of the third to undergo hard labour for life; those of the fourth to serve as private soldiers, retaining the rights of nobility, &c., &c.

The Emperor granted a commutation of these punishments. The five individuals condemned to be quartered were sentenced to be hanged: thus an indignity was put upon them even in the kind of death which they were to suffer. Those of the first category were condemned to hard labour for life; and the punishment of the remainder was mitigated in proportion.

On the 13th (25th) July, the execution took place on the *glacis* of the citadel. The condemned were compelled to look on for a whole hour while the preparations were going on for their execution; and their less wretched companions were forced to march round the gibbets; their swords were broken over their heads, and their epaulettes and military decorations thrown into the fire. The ropes to which Ryléiéf*, Muravief, and Bestuchf-Rumin were suspended unhappily broke, and these men were led to death a second time. Orders were given to erect gibbets instead of crosses on the graves of the officers killed at Ustinofka.

* The Commission of Inquiry has thought proper to designate Ryléiéf as a sub-lieutenant and *journalist*. He was at the head of an office, and a poet.

On the following day the square in front of the Senate-house, where the revolt had taken place, was purified by a religious and expiatory ceremony. The Emperor sent one of his aid-de-camps to the wife of Ryléiéf to assure her of his protection; he presented 50,000 rubles to Pestel's father, and to his brother he gave the epaulettes of an aid-de-camp in his service, which gave rise to the saying, that he wore the rope with which his brother had been hanged. Rostofzof's fortune was made; and Sherwood, the informer, received 50,000 rubles, a house, and the title of Faithful, which, however, did not save him from being subsequently expelled from his regiment for misconduct.

A manifesto of his Majesty of the 13th (25th) of July, informed the world that he had seen with pleasure " the nearest relations renounce and give up to justice the wretches who were suspected of being accomplices."

The soldiers who had taken part in the insurrection were sent to Georgia, and in the war which broke out soon afterwards, they were employed in the first line against the Persians. The regiments which had remained loyal received rewards: to one of them was given the uniform of Alexander; to others, his initials; and to the Don Cossacks, his sword. Fortunately, we need not go far to look for a criticism on all this proceeding. Facts, analogous to those which we have related, had just taken place in a neighbouring country, tributary to Russia, but enjoying a more enlightened administration. They had results which unanswerably condemned the arbitrary proceedings of despotism, and proved, incontestibly, the superiority of a constitutional government. The inquiry, instituted at St. Petersburg, shewed that there were in Poland secret societies which had even been connected with the Southern Society. The attention of the Government was naturally

turned to them, and an investigation was
ordered to be made at Warsaw. It was
ascertained, in fact, that ever since 1821
there had existed in Poland the *National
Patriotic Society;* and that, in the following year, Mazefsky had organized the
Society of the Templars, on the model of
that of Scotland. Uminski, Jablonowski,
Soltyk, Krzynanowski, were members of
these societies, the principal object of which
was the restoration of Poland. The Commission of Inquiry classed the accused
under five categories, and the Senate was
charged to decide on their fate. It appointed advocates as counsel for the prisoners; the proceedings were public, and
lasted a month; after which the supreme
court ordered a new act of accusation,
which, with the exception of one dissentient
voice, that of General Count Krazynski,
unanimously set aside the charge of high
treason, acquitted the greater part of
the accused, and condemned the others

to some months' imprisonment. The Emperor ordered the judges to be reprimanded, a thing before unheard of; and he consoled himself by confining the accused in the dungeons of St. Petersburg: this was a violation of the constitution, and was one of the grievances subsequently alleged in defence of the Polish revolution.

But to return to Russia:—

On the 3rd of September (22nd October),* 1826, the coronation of the Emperor took place at Moscow, in the midst of such pomp and ceremonies, that a handsome woman exclaimed, "How vexatious it is that such fêtes are so rare!" The people were invited to a monster feast at Devitsche Polé, but when the crowd fell on the viands which had been prepared for them, they were driven away by the fire engines. A manifesto reduced, by five years, the term

* One of these dates must be wrong; perhaps they should be 20th September and 2nd October.

of imprisonment to which the political prisoners were condemned.

On the 16th (28th) of September, an imperial manifesto declared war against Persia. The Treaty of Gulistan of the 26th of October, 1813, had left an opening for inevitable disputes by stipulating, that either of the two contracting parties should have the power of enlarging its territorial possessions according to circumstances, on condition of indemnifying the party injured. By virtue of this stipulation, Russia had occupied the coast of Lake Goktcha, offering to Persia, by way of indemnity, the territory comprehended between the rivers Capunaktchay and Tschudow; but the Shah declined accepting this arrangement.

Prince Menchikof, who was dispatched by the Emperor to settle the difference, was refused an audience. The Khan of Talychyn massacred the Russian garrison of Erivan, and Abbas Mirza, heir to the Persian throne, invaded the province of

Elizabethpol, at the head of 50,000 regular troops. The Musselman tribes of the Caucasus rose at his approach. On the 2nd (14th) of September Madatof defeated the vanguard of the Persian army, on the Schamkhor, and occupied the town of Elizabethpol. On the 21st Paskewitsch joined with his division of 9000 men, and defeated Abbas Mirza, on the banks of the river Djeham, two leagues from Elizabethpol, from which place this battle took its name. The Persians repassed the Araxes, and Grabbe obtained some advantages on the coast of the Caspian. Paskewitsch was appointed Commander-in-chief in the room of Yermoloff, and Benkendorf succeeded Madatof in the command of the vanguard. Etchmiadzin surrendered without resistance, in April, 1827. Paskewitsch crossed the Araxes, and defeated the enemy's army in the battle of Djwan-Bulak; the *victorious standard* of the vanquished, fell into the hands of the Russians, and Abbas Abad surrendered to them on the 19th (31st) of July.

These successes did not, however, hinder the Persians from besieging Etchmiadzin. Krassowsky in vain endeavoured to make them raise the siege, and Paskewitsch was obliged to repair to his aid. The Persian Prince again crossed the Araxes, and Sardar Abbas surrendered to the Russians, and Erivan was occupied on the 13th of October, after six days' siege. On the 25th, Tauris, the capital of Adzerbadaidjan, and soon after, Ali-jar-Kan, shared the same fate. The Persians sued for peace, and conferences were opened on the 2nd of November. Russia demanded the cession of the provinces of Erivan and Nakitchevan, and an indemnification of twenty millions of silver rubles. Abbas Mirza accepted these conditions; but the Shah's ratification was delayed for three months, which obliged Paskewitsch to resume hostilities. On the 15th (27th) of January, 1828, he occupied Urmiah; Souktel entered Ardebyl, and on the 10th (22nd) of February the treaty was signed at Turkmantchai. Paskewitsch received, as a reward for his conduct in this campaign, a million in money, and the title of Count of Erivan. Russia acquired two provinces by this war, which cost her more labour than men.

The war with Persia was scarcely ended when that with Turkey broke out. On the 14th (26th) of August, 1828, a manifesto of the Emperor was published, followed by an explanatory declaration, to which the Porte replied on the 4th of June. The two parties accused each other of not having observed the treaty of Bucharest. Turkey reproached Russia with having countenanced the insurrection of the Greeks, with having supported and received Ypsilanti, and fomented troubles in Moldavia and Wallachia. Russia, on her part, accused the Divan of having stimulated the Circassans to revolt, of having fettered the commerce of the Black Sea, violated the amnesty which had been granted to Servia, supported the resistance of Persia, and retarded the peace which had just been concluded with that power.

Immediately after the declaration, Field Marshal Prince Wittgenstein placed himself at the head of an army of 105,000 men, and on the 7th of May crossed the Pruth at three points; Jassy and Bucharest were immediately occupied, and the administration of the two principalities was given to Count Pahlen. The third corps passed the Danube on the 8th of June, and besieged Kustendji. The Zaporogue Cossacks, who had been subject to Turkey for two centuries, returned to the dominion of Russia, and their example was followed by those of Neckrazow. The Grand Duke Michael besieged Brailow, at the head of the seventh corps, and the Emperor repaired thither in person on the 20th of May. On the 15th of June an attempt was made to take the place by storm, but it failed; one mine blew up too soon, another did not explode at all, and no practicable breach was effected. The troops rushed to the ramparts and sustained great loss, and the Grand Duke was compelled to give the signal for retreat. In the course of the next day the mine which had not previously exploded, made a considerable breach. The Turkish Pasha surrendered the place on the 18th of June, and withdrew with the honours of war. The Emperor conferred on the Grand Duke Michael the order of St. George of the second class.

Menschikof took Anapa on the 11th, Kustendji submitted on the 20th, and Bazardschik was occupied without resistance on the 6th of July. An engagement was fought under its walls, which was disadvantageous to the Turks. A severe contest took place on the 20th of July, in the direction of Schumla; the Turks retired to their camp, and the Russians erected some

redoubts. Count Soukheln advanced
against Varna, and was repulsed. Uscha-
kow came to his aid, but could not prevent a Turkish reinforcement from entering the town. General Roth invested
the fortress of Silistria, and Geismar was
ordered to protect Wallachia. A very
smart action took place before Schumla, on
the 28th of July, but which did not lead to
any important results. Menschikof had
taken the command of the siege of Varna,
and Admiral Greig blockaded the town by
sea.

In Asia, General Paskewitsch opened the
campaign on the 7th of July, and on the
15th he took Kars. The fortress of Poti,
the only one possessed by the Turks on the
east coast of the Black Sea, surrendered on
the 26th to a detachment of the troops of
Georgia. On the 4th of September, Paskewitsch gained a complete victory under the
walls of Akhalzik, which surrendered on
the 8th, after a vigorous resistance, in

which the Russians suffered considerable loss.

While the Emperor went to Odessa, to hasten the arrival of reinforcements, and to order a new levy of recruits, the Sultan was actively preparing measures of resistance; he caused the Bosphorus to be fortified, the ships of war to be repaired, and troops to be armed and exercised at Constantinople. The Seraskier, Hussein Pasha, was shut up in Schumla with an army of 60,000 men. Joussuf and the Captain Pasha were gone to defend Varna. The Grand Vizier had repaired in person to the camp. The plague, which had broken out at the opening of the campaign, extended its ravages more and more in the ranks of the Russians; provisions and forage were becoming scarce; the cavalry was visibly losing its horses; and the population flying at the approach of the enemy, left the country a desert. The presence of the Emperor, far from being a stimulus and an advantage, was only a restraint, because it checked the authority of the general-in-chief; but unhappily this was not understood until it was too late.

The Pasha of Widdin proceeded to offensive measures, and forced General Geismar to retrograde and to abandon his camp; but an energetic movement gave him the victory, and compelled the Turks to fly beyond the Danube, leaving in the hands of the Russians 24 standards and 600 carriages loaded with ammunition. This was on the 26th of September. On the 5th and 6th, General Roth gained some advantages before Schumla; but the Russians had sustained a shock on the night of the 25th of August.

The Turks attacked them at three points. On the first, they carried a redoubt commanded by General Wrede, who was killed, with all his men; at the second point, they obliged General Rüdiger to destroy his intrenchments at Eski-Stamboul; and at the third, they captured a piece of cannon.

On the following day they occupied Eski-Stamboul, which restored the communication of the Turks with Adrianople. These successes permitted a Turkish detachment to go to the aid of Varna.

On the 7th of August, Admiral Greig seized 14 Turkish vessels, and then caused the magazines and the arsenal of Neada to be destroyed. Captain Kritzki took 12 pieces of cannon, spiked the others, and blew up the arsenal.

On the 21st of August, Prince Menschikof was wounded before Varna, and was succeeded by Count Woronzow in the command of the siege. The imperial guards arrived to reinforce the army, and on the 12th of September, General Golowyn occupied the heights of Gulata; but having sent the regiment of chasseurs of the guard to reconnoitre a Turkish corps which was advancing on the road from Aidos, that regiment was cut to pieces, and General Hartung was killed in this action. On the

28th of September, General Freytag lost
his life in a desperate combat, in which
both parties claimed the victory. On the
30th, a Russian brigade, having ventured
too far, was roughly handled, and General
Jarnow was killed.

The works of the besiegers being far advanced, the brave Lieutenant Zaitzewsky,
at the head of some marines, reinforced by
the volunteers of the guard, entered Varna
by the breach, on the 7th of October. He
took possession of a bastion, and penetrated
into the town, but not being supported, he
was obliged to retreat, after having spiked
seven Turkish guns. The next day, Joussuf
Pasha sent a secretary to open a confer-
ence, and on the 9th he came himself on
board a Russian vessel; on the 10th he
surrendered, and soon afterwards went to
the Crimea to receive the guerdon of his
treason. His people followed his example,
and laid down their arms; the Captain
Pacha obtained permission to rejoin the

Turkish army. On the 12th he left Varna at the head of three hundred men; and the Russians entered the town immediately afterwards. The Emperor sent twelve Turkish guns to Warsaw, in memory of the death of Wladislaus VI., who was killed in 1444 under the walls of Varna, which were reputed to be impregnable; but these guns did not reach their destination; they were cast on shore during a storm, and fell again into the hands of the Turks. The property which Joussuf possessed in Turkey, as well as his harem and his family, were sequestered. The Captain Pasha took the place of the Vizier, who was exiled to Gallipolis. At the same time the siege of Schumla was raised, Silistria abandoned; the Russian army retired to Jassy, in a complete state of disorganization, and the Emperor returned to St. Petersburg.

On the 25th of January, General Langeron took Kalé after two days' fighting; Turnow surrendered on the 11th of February, and thirty Turkish ships were destroyed before Nicopolis.

On the 18th of February, Diebitsch was appointed commander-in-chief in the room of Prince Wittgenstein, who took leave of the army on the 27th. Count Toll was placed at the head of the staff; President Pahlen was recalled to St. Petersburg, and Langeron took his leave. The Russian army was augmented to the number of two hundred and forty thousand men; and twelve ships of the line were stationed in the Black Sea.

On the 27th of February, Rear-Admiral Kumani took the town of Sizeboli, twenty-five leagues from Constantinople. The Turks afterwards made an unsuccessful attempt to take possession of the redoubt, which the Russians had thrown up in haste.

On the 7th of August the Russians were attacked near Silistria by a part of the garrison, which was repulsed, and the city besieged. On the same day, General Roth

had an engagement, near Pravady, with
the new grand vizir, Reschid Pasha, and
being reinforced by General Wachter, he
obliged the enemy to retreat: but the latter
being succoured on their return, rallied to
the charge, and did not desist till the evening, after both parties had sustained considerable loss. Major-General Rinden was
killed in this affair. The Russian commander-in-chief marched on the 1st of June
to succour Roth, and surrounded the Grand
Vizir. On the 11th of June the battle of
Kulewtscha took place, which lasted four
hours, during which the Russians, notwithstanding the superiority of their number,
suffered severely; the Grand Vizir forced
his passage through the Russian army, and
occupied a strong position, which he was
obliged to abandon the next day, with
a loss which was estimated by the Russians
at five thousand killed and one thousand
five hundred prisoners. The official bulletin
compared this battle to those of Kagul

and Rymnik, leaving it to history to place Diebitsch by the side of Romanzoff and Suwarrow. The General-in-Chief then caused proposals for peace to be made, which however came to nothing.

The news of this victory affected Silistria, the entire fortifications of which had been at length demolished. Some shells, which were thrown into the town, caused great terror; a mine, which opened a breach in the heart of the fortress, completely discouraged the besieged. The two Pashas capitulated, and, together with their garrison, surrendered as prisoners of war. The Russians entered the place on the 1st of July.

In Asia, the opening of the campaign was retarded by a crime committed against the Ambassador at Teheran. On the 12th of February, the Russian legation attempted to detain an Armenian woman, who was a Russian subject; this circumstance excited the indignation of the populace, who proceeded in arms to the hotel of the legation. Some of their party having been killed by the Cossacks, the crowd massacred all the persons attached to the legation, with the exception of the Secretary, who was absent at the time. The Shah, to prevent any disagreeable discussion, punished the guilty, and sent his grandson to St. Petersburg to express to the Emperor his regret at the occurrence. Being released from all apprehension on that side, Paskewitsch resumed hostilities in Asia where Akhalzik was besieged by the Turks. On the 13th of May, General Bourzof defeated Achmet Khan. On the 1st of July, Paskewitsch, anticipating the junction of the Seraskier of Erzerum with Hagki Pasha, in the valley of Zevine, marched against the former, whom he put to flight, and on the next day defeated the latter whom he took prisoner; thirty-one pieces of cannon, nineteen standards, and fifteen hundred prisoners were the trophies of this two-fold victory. On the 5th of

July he took Hassan-Khale, the key of Erzerum, the capital of Turcomania which surrendered on the 9th.

After the taking of Silistria, General Diebitsch resolved to cross the Balkan, while the Grand Vizir expected him under the walls of Schumla. The three corps formed into two columns, passed the river Kamtshik, and easily carried, or turned the little posts which the Turks had opposed to them. The Vizir attacked Rüdiger, near Aidos, on the 21st of July, but was repulsed, and the Russians in consequence of these advantages took possession of Aidos and Karnabach. Halœ Pasha was not more successful than the Vizir in his attack at Jamboli and Selimno, which the Russians took by storm on the 11th of August.

On the 19th the Russian army was in sight of Adrianople, which opened its gates the next day; thence it marched on to Eynos. Meantime, its rear under Generals

Sturmur, Geismar, and Krussowski continued to be severely harassed.

The Prussian general, Baron Müffling
urged the Divan to conclude peace, conformably to the instructions which he had
received from his Government, after a visit
which the Emperor Nicholas had paid to
Berlin. On the 28th of August, two Russian negotiators, Count Alexis Orloff and
Count Pahlen arrived at Burgos, and the
Turkish envoys, Mehemet-Sadi Effendi and
Abul-Kadir-Bey repaired to the Russian
head-quarters for this same purpose; other
negotiations commenced on the 30th, and
the treaty of peace was signed on the 14th
of September. Russia retained the conquered territory bordering on Imeritia and
Georgia, Anapa, Poti, Akhalzik, &c., &c.,
and the Dardanelles were thrown open to the
commerce of all nations. The Porte engaged
to pay eleven millions and a half of Dutch
ducats in the course of eighteen months,
and give its assent to the treaty of the 6th

of July, 1827, concerning Greece. Lastly, it bound itself to restore to the Principalities, the establishments on the left bank of the Danube. The hospodars were to be appointed for life, and the taxes hitherto paid in kind, were henceforward to be paid in money.

On the 24th of May the Emperor was crowned at Warsaw. He pronounced on his knees a prayer, in which we observe the following words, " O my Lord, and my God, may my heart be always in Thy hand, and may I reign for the happiness of my people, and to the glory of Thy holy name, according to the charter granted by my august predecessor, and already sworn to by me, in order that I may not dread to appear before Thee on the day of the last judgment."

From Warsaw the Emperor and Empress proceeded to Berlin.

Khosrow-Mirza, the son of Abbas-Mirza, came to St. Petersburg to implore pardon for the crime of the 12th of February, 1829.

In February, 1830, two Turkish ambassadors arrived, who obtained a deduction of three millions from the contribution imposed on their country.

On the 28th of May the Emperor opened the Polish Diet, with a speech in the French language, and in a very lofty tone. Some complaints were heard in this assembly, to which the Czar paid little attention. These complaints related to the suppression of publicity for the discussions of the Diet, to the restrictions on the press, the vexatious conduct of the police, and the cruelties of Constantine.

The news of the revolution of the 30th of July was the spark that kindled the elements of discontent which existed in Warsaw. On the 29th of November the standard-bearers forced the entrance of the Belvidere palace; Gendre and Lubowicki were killed; Constantine escaped by a secret door, and took refuge in the ranks of his guard. The Polish hussars flew to arms, and seized on the arsenal. Constantine had 10,000 men, and might have crushed the revolt in the bud; but his courage failed him, and he preferred evacuating Warsaw. A provisional administration was instituted in that city, of which Prince Adam Czartoryski was president, and Clopicki received the command of the troops. The new authority sent proposals to the Grand Duke's camp, to which he was not authorized to accede. He retired into Wolhynia. Clopicki was nominated dictator, and the Diet was convoked for the 18th of December. It continued Clopicki in his post, and formed a national council, to take the place of the provisional government.

On the 24th of December, Nicholas published a manifesto againt "the *infamous treasons*, which employed *lies*, threats, and delusive promises, in order to subject the peaceable inhabitants to a few rebels."

"The Poles," says the manifesto, "who after so many misfortunes enjoyed peace and prosperity under the shadow of our power, precipitate themselves anew into the abyss of revolution and calamity, are *an assemblage of credulous beings,* who, though already seized with terror at the thought of the chastisement which awaits them, dare to dream for a few moments of victory, and to propose conditions to Us, their lawful Sovereign!"

On the 10th of January, 1831, the Poles published a manifesto, stating their grievances. It contains the following paragraphs. "The union of the crown of an Autocrat and of a constitutional King is one of those political anomalies which cannot long exist. Everybody foresaw that the kingdom would become the germ of liberal institutions for Russia, or succumb under the iron hand of its despotism; the question was soon decided. Public instruction was corrupted; a system of obscurant-

ism was organized; the people were shut
out from all means of obtaining instruction; an entire Palatinate was deprived of
its representation in the Council; the
Chambers lost the faculty of voting the
budget; new burthens were imposed; mo-
nopolies were created, calculated to dry up
the sources of the national wealth; and the
Treasury, augmented by these measures,
became the prey of paid hirelings, infamous incendiary agents, and despicable
spies."

"Calumny and espionage had penetrated
even into the privacy of families; had infected with their poison the liberty of domestic life, and the ancient hospitality of
the Poles had become a snare for innocence. Personal liberty, which had been
solemnly guaranteed, was violated; the
prisons were crowded; courts-martial were
appointed to decide in civil cases, and imposed infamous punishments on citizens,

whose only crime was that of having attempted to save from corruption the spirit and the character of the nation."

All the proposals of Poland having been rejected with contempt by the Emperor of Russia, war became inevitable. Clopicki, doubtful of success, resigned the office of Dictator, and entered the Polish army as a private volunteer. He was succeeded in his post by Radzivill, and afterwards by Skzynecki.

On the 25th of January, 1831, the Polish Diet, on the motion of Prince Roman Soltyk, declared that the Emperor Nicholas had forfeited the throne; and in consequence of this bold step, the Russian army invaded Poland in the month of February.

The particulars of this heroic conflict are well known; such as the drawn battle of Grochow of the 19th and 20th; the sanguinary combat of Praga of the 25th of the same month; that of Ostrolenka of the

26th of May, in which the Poles so obstinately disputed a victory, which the Russians did not turn to account. The laurels which General Geismar had gained in the war with Turkey, were blighted in this campaign; for on the 14th of January, Dwernicki took from him eleven pieces of cannon; on the 19th he was beaten at Waver, and together with Rosen, was defeated at Dembewilkie. Nevertheless, all the attempts of the Poles to raise an insurrection in Lithuania and Wolhynia were ineffectual, and only caused the loss of the troops which had been sent to those provinces. On the 17th of April Kreutz defeated Sierawski; Rüdiger discomfited Dwernicki, and obliged him to retreat into Austria, where his corps was disarmed; Chrzanowski and Jankowski, who seconded kim in Wolhynia, shared the same fate. Clapowski and Gielgud, having been beaten at Wilna by General Sacken, took refuge

in Prussia, where they also were disarmed.
Dembinski alone was able to preserve his
troops, and take them back to Warsaw.

Diebitsch died on the 10th of June, and
the Grand Duke Constantine sixteen days
after. Paskewitsch took the command of
the troops, passed the Vistula on the 29th
of July, and on the 6th of September made
the memorable attack on Warsaw, which he
entered on the 8th. The vengeance of
Nicholas was fearful. The vanquished were
treated as criminals; patriotism and independence, virtues which we should rejoice
to see possessed by the Russians, were imputed as crimes to the Poles. Siberia, the
Caucasus, and the army, were filled with
these unhappy beings; Poland was incorporated with Russia, and, contrary to all
treaties, became a province of that empire.
Every species of punishment was inflicted;
and neither property nor the ties of family
were respected.

Europe, to which Poland had in vain

stretched out her arms, saw these enor-
mities without protesting, and suffered
all these cruelties to be exercised with
impunity; but Heaven visited Russia with
its chastisements. Revolt, stifled on one
side, rose in the very heart of Russia
herself. Two hundred officers perished at
Novgorod and at Staraia Roussa. The
ravages of the cholera were succeeded by
famine in 1833 and 1840. The public dis-
tress was extreme. The winter palace at
St. Petersburg was destroyed by fire in
1838; death deprived the Emperor of a
beloved daughter. History in short, the
supreme judge of kings, has not waited till
Nicholas has ceased to live or to reign, to
accuse him of tyranny.

Chapter II.

GENERAL VIEW.

Those who speak against Russia are greatly mistaken.   Men there enjoy a large share of freedom, and life upon the whole is not without its attractions.   What is there that men are not free to do?   Take tea in the evening or in the morning in a cup or in a glass, with or without cream; take one, two, three, or forty cups if you have a mind; put sugar into your tea or hold it in your hand, (*v prikouskow,*) or hang a piece to the ceiling, and let each of the company taste it by turns; do, in this respect, just as you please.   Mix water with your wine or

not, nobody will interfere with you. Drink
French or Spanish wines as you choose, or
even Portuguese, if you please. White
wine or red, you have your choice. You
need be under no apprehension of spending
all your fortune: for the paternal Government of Russia has guardians for spendthrifts. Ride in a droshki or in a chariot,
with one or two horses; nay, even with four
if you are a noble: you have a right to do
so, unless it be true, as is pretended, that
the Emperor Nicholas, offended at the luxury displayed by some young people without titles, has limited the prerogative of
driving with four horses to the dignitaries
of the first four classes: let your horses be
of the same or of different colours,—the
choice is yours. Drive slowly or at full
gallop, provided you do not run over
anybody, and if such a misfortune should
happen, you will escape with the loss of
your horses, and some *coups de bâton* to

your coachman*. But you must take care not to pass the Emperor; courtesy prescribes this as a law, and propriety, in this instance, is in accordance with the regulations.

Do you prefer a brunette or a fair lady? pay your court to her who takes your fancy. Keep one woman or two clandestinely, but do not commit adultery; punishment awaits you, even though there should be no complaint on the part of the husband: this is justice. Do not seduce a maiden, you will be compelled to marry her. Beware

* Baron Dellinshausen, Adjutant-General to the Emperor, one day broke the file of carriages in a public promenade. The Police laid the blame on his coachman, and the Baron wrote a virulent letter to the Governor-General of St. Petersburg. On Easter day, when he went in his turn to compliment the Czar, the latter put him aside, saying, that he did not embrace the disturbers of public order. The General tendered his resignation, and the Emperor sent him the ribbon of the White Eagle, which restored him to the service. This is the way in which family quarrels are generally made up.

also of meddling with the pupils of the
theatre, unless you have a mind to pass
some months in prison, as happened to
Prince V.: the Emperor is very strict on
this point. Do not elope either with a single
or a married lady, if you do not choose to lose
your rank, like Count F., who, for having
married without the consent of his wife's
parents, lost his rank in the guards, and
was transferred to the army. That he has
since become Equerry to his Majesty is
owing to the circumstance of his having led
the ass which carried the Empress across
the mountains of Saxon Switzerland, a
chance which not every one is likely to
meet with. Notwithstanding all this, you
may still act the part of a Russian *Faublas.*
Without drawing down upon yourself any
inconvenience, you may marry ten times in
your life, provided you ask for your bride
only such as have not attained the legal
age for marriage. A divorce will be
granted you as often as you have become

a husband, and your children cannot even bear your name. The innocent always suffer for the guilty.

Do you love the theatre? You have every variety: the French, the German, the Russian, and the Italian, the opera and ballets at St. Petersburg, Moscow, and even at Odessa. If you prefer the French theatre, you must take care to put on a proper dress, because the Emperor often frequents it. Do not remain seated when he stands, nor applaud when he does not: it would be at variance with decorum.

Employ whatever tailor you prefer; dress as you please, provided that there is nothing in your dress which may offend the Emperor. Beware of wearing a beard; you would be politely invited to shave, for the sight of a beard affects the Emperor's nerves. Do not wear your hair too long: the Emperor is bald!

"Marry, you will do well!" as the Grand Duke Michael says. Do not marry, and

you will do better. If you espouse the
daughter of some great functionary, you
must first have the consent of his Majesty
the Emperor. This is logic.

Retire to rest at what hour you like:
pass the night in gambling if you please,
only do not play at forbidden games, nor
stake too high: your own servant might
denounce you to the police. Consult whatever physician enjoys your confidence, if
you are so happy as to find a good one.
Read the books which you prefer, even
such as are prohibited: they are easily
procured. Write and publish, but strictly
observe the existing laws on the subject,
and conform to the ideas of the Government. The censorship would not exempt
you from responsibility for articles which
it may have suffered to pass unnoticed.
When you walk abroad, bow to the Emperor if you meet him, because he is extremely tenacious on this point; bow also
to the Grand Duke Michael, even though

he should never return the compliment.
Do not assume the character of a brawler
or a bully; the capital is the property of the
Emperor, who insists on the observance of
good manners and the public peace. Do
not smoke in the streets, for fear of setting
something on fire. You must be in the
public service, or at least have been so;
this is an established rule, and you are
looked upon with an evil eye if you are
not. You have a variety to choose out of,
from the jacket of the hussar to the cuirass
of the horse-guard, and the dress of a civil
functionary! Choose that branch of the
service in which you have some relations or
some connexions that may aid your promotion.

Travel, if that kind of life suits your
taste. Every well-educated man ought to
visit other countries. Go even to France;
the Emperor does not like it, but he winks
at it; but when there, conduct yourself
with prudence: do not meddle with writing,

—do not connect yourself with any association; do not have any intercourse with
ultra-liberals. If you are recalled to
Russia, return immediately; your obedience
will mitigate the rigour of the banishment
which awaits you, and will shorten its
duration.

What a happy lot is that of the Russian
nobles! they live like kings or demi-gods!
A noble retired to his estate with a handsome wife, at the head of some thousands
of peasants, with large revenues, passes
days of delight, and enjoys an existence
which has not its parallel in the whole
world! You are absolute sovereign on
your own estates: all cringe and bow before
you; all crawl in the dust, and tremble at
the sound of your voice. If you order a
hundred or two *coups de bâton* to be inflicted on Peter or John, your order will be
executed, and his back will immediately
become as black as a coal. You have
merely to throw your handkerchief to any

woman who pleases you : you are not a
sultan for nothing. After all, let us not
mind those philanthropists who come to us
from Europe : we have seen some, and the
most distinguished of them, who openly
reproached us with our rudeness, our
cruelty, and who, having married noble
Russian ladies, and become the lords of
their estates and of their vassals, then say
that there is nothing to be compared to
the life of a Boyard. Go, speechifiers,
we know your value, and we know ours ;
preach morality to others : we have our
own.

This is a complete picture of Russia.
Men vegetate here ; they seek excuses for
everything, and say that the end makes
amends for all. The noble imagines himself free, and thinks that he has only to
blame himself if he exchanges his liberty
for offices, for distinctions, and becomes a
servant instead of a sovereign master. He
has his court, his residence, his estate—let

him remain there. The serf thinks tha
his condition is natural, fixed by the decrees
of Providence, and that he would be infi-
nitely more wretched if he were free. The
military man thinks of nothing : he has no
time left to do so, and he is kept in perpetual exercise to fill up his leisure. The
civil officer thinks only of adorning his
button-hole, or filling his pocket, and all
move by the force of the iron will of the
Sovereign.

But in what direction are they moving?
Towards a revolution? This will long be
impracticable, for the materials which constitute a revolutionist are not to be met with
in Russia. The few liberal-minded men
who are found there look at their bayonet,
but let all go on in the old way; and it will
be long before the army revolts. No revolution is possible in Russia, except in the
palace, and only with the consent or by the
command of the heirs to the Crown themselves. Thus Iwan V. and Peter III. dis-

appeared at the sole order of Catherine II.; thus Alexander, having to choose between his own exile and the forced abdication of his father, decided for the latter; but those appointed to execute the plan went beyond his intentions. To judge by all appearances, one generation, if not two, must pass before there can be a revolution in Russia. But the decrees of the Most High are inscrutable!

With respect to probabilities, however, calculations are often erroneous. How frequently does a tempest break out when it is least expected! The earthquake, the inundation give no previous indications of their coming, and men often perish when they think themselves the safest; revolutions have always taken kings by surprise. The great mass of the people is excessively inflammable; a spark coming perhaps even from the Government itself, will speedily kindle a conflagration. The Government is already uneasy; it is disquieted about everything, and makes everybody unquiet, and thereby does itself infinite harm. A mustachio on the lip of a citizen, a beard on the chin of a civil functionary, a merchant without a beard, suffice to inspire it with apprehension. It sees in them indications, harbingers of civilization, of liberalism, of the storm which is brooding. It pursues them without mercy, and its poor subjects enclosed, hemmed in on every side, begin to think of liberalism, of which previously they had not the least notion.

Meantime all is quiet, men do not complain openly, except where they are not afraid of being overheard,—at home, or in some desert spot; they lower their voice in the towns; they do not breathe a syllable in the capitals; they groan and writhe under the Imperial rod; they beat or are beaten; are either hammer or anvil; nay, they are both at the same time. Happy those who can choose! The Emperor abuses his courtiers, and they revenge themselves on their subordinates, who not finding words sufficiently energetic, raise their hand against those, who in their turn, finding the hand too light, arm themselves with a stick, which further on is replaced by the whip. The peasant is beaten by everybody; by his master, when he condescends so far to demean himself; by the steward and the *starosta*, by the public authorities, the *stanovoi* or the *ispravnik*, by the first passer by, if he be not a peasant. The poor fellow on his part has no means to indemnify himself, except on his wife or his horse; and accordingly, most women in Russia are beaten, and it excites one's pity to see how the horses are used. At St. Petersburg there is a continual smacking of whips, and all the blows fall on those poor animals. Peter I., in his ardour for reform, ought to have substituted for the Russian whip, a long lash, in using which the coachmen would lose their love of whipping, because they only beat the air.

Will you attend the levée of a Russian petit-maître, not exactly one of the old school, but of a gentleman belonging to the class of frizzed and perfumed fashionables, who talk to you of philanthropy in three or four languages, all very prettily mangled; who dance more or less agreeably, and even sing the Marseillaise? Let us begin with the *petit lever.* He commences with questioning his valet about the weather, the day of the week and month; and his valet must answer off hand. The latter then prepares to dress his master, putting on his socks and drawers while he is still in bed; then his pantaloons, which he fastens very carefully, his robe de chambre, and his slippers. After an innumerable quantity of pipes, filled, lighted, and washed down by an infinite number of cups of tea, the *grand lever* commences. Here the poor valet de chambre is certain of committing some blunders, for which he receives as many, or a hundred times as

many, cuffs and kicks, applied indifferently
to every part of his body. If he makes no
mistake in any part of his waiting, his own
toilette is sure to be attacked, and with
this his master now begins to cheer his
heart and to divert his mind, as well as to
have an opportunity of being set a-going.
"You are always as dirty as a pig; your
coat is out at elbows and threadbare ; your
linen is slovenly;" and lo! a shower of
blows fall heavily upon the unfortunate
valet. No inquiry is made whether the
poor wretch has the means of attiring himself more seemly, and it is well known that
handsome clothes are forbidden him. If,
through some unexpected good fortune, no
fault can be found with his costume, exception is taken at his face; either it is dirty,
or it is melancholy, and, in either case, he is
beaten, pinched, and knocked on the face
and head, and handfuls of hair are torn out
by the roots, by his indignant master.
" Why do you look so sulky—lift up your

head—look your master in the face? Are
you afraid of him? I do not like that
gloomy air; any one who saw you would
suppose that I tyrannized over you; that
you are unhappy with me. Are you so?
Let us see!" And the crouching valet is
obliged to answer, " No, my Lord, I am
very well satisfied with your service!"

If a lady wishes to chastise a man, she
calls for another, and orders him to box
the culprit's ears in her presence.

The master of the police beats the commissary of the quarter; he again the police
officer, who, in his turn, takes revenge on
the soldier of the city, who vents his ill-
humour on the first individual with whom
it is possible for him to find the most trifling
fault.

" Naturam expellas furcâ tamen usque recurret."

The Russian imbibes the mania of beat-
ing with his mother's milk, and this mania
does not leave him on this side the tomb.
" The first blow with a fist which I received

in a foreign country for a stroke of the whip, was my first lesson on liberty," said Prince K* * * *; and if I were permitted to speak of myself, I would say, that I do not pass a day out of my country, without better understanding the rights of liberty and of humanity, without more duly appreciating the worth and the dignity of man; and if I remain abroad, it is precisely because I perceive that I grow better by doing so.   What shall we say?

There are things which seem to pervade the air itself: the tastes, the habits of a country are acquired involuntarily. The Marquis Custine, after a residence of three months in Russia, grew so cruel, as to suffer a foal to run for a whole stage by its mother's side. Europeans have become cannibals by living among savages. Let the Russians be allowed to become free with free men; and if I now write, it is that there may be no remains of all the atrocities which are continually committed

in Russia in the face of day. There is a
national proverb, which says, "Do not throw
the dust out of doors," and hence the house
becomes and remains dirty. We should
reverse the phrase, and say, "Sweep your
room as often as possible." "Wash your
dirty linen at home," it is said; but, if
the family neglects this duty, ought not
strangers to be called in to help; publicity
and exposure to the light of day will do
far more than Imperial decrees. It is
through their feelings that even the ignorant must be gained. Men are much more
easily corrected of their faults when they
have been obliged to blush for them, than
when they have only had to suffer for them.
Publicity is the salvation of the world, and
would be that of Russia, if it were suffered to
penetrate there. Open the doors of the
tribunals, and justice will take her seat
there. Publish the acts of the Government, and it will become better; let it be
well understood that supreme justice, which

nothing escapes, exists not only in the other world, but also in this. There is a tribunal, at the bar of which we must appear, even during our life,—it is the tribunal of public opinion: let the wicked tremble, and let the good rejoice!

Such are not the thoughts of the Russians of the old school. Foreign countries have nothing to teach them, and the residence which they make there cures them of their notions of liberty which they may have taken with them. In France, they say, they can get none to serve them, for all act as masters, and treat them like equals; there is no obedience, and consequently there can be no order. "We will have none of this regime. The Government is weak, despised abroad, little respected at home, whereas all tremble at the name and sight of our Czar. Immorality is at its height in France, everything is venal, peculation is universal."

"There is almost as much despotism here

as among us; despotism runs in the veins
of the French, and wherever the law leaves
him some arbitrary power, the agent of the
Public Adminstration indemnifies himself
for all the checks on his will, which he otherwise meets with.   Interest alone guides
France. See how the shopkeeper humbly
bows to a customer in a carriage, he who
behaves so proudly when he goes to visit
some unfortunate wretch who lives in a
garret. It is interest again which sits in
the Parliament; we there hear only the
declarations of those who desire to rise, or
of those who have lost all hopes of doing
so. Public opinion is in the hands of a
few private individuals, who deal with the
press as with a piece of merchandize, and
sell themselves to the highest bidder. If
the Emperor pleased, he might have the
whole of the press on his side, and the
Parisian journals would combat each other
to obtain his rubles. They live only on
gratuities from the Government; and serve

their subscribers at the expense of the Government which pays them."

Is it worth while to refute attacks of this nature? Foreigners are wrong thus to calumniate France; they ought to recollect that if they eat, drink, and clothe themselves, it is thanks to that country, which has taught and still teaches them the true enjoyment of these trifles, which constitute the sum of life. French cookery is without dispute the best in the world, and that which foreigners prefer; French wines are superior to all other; fashions, furniture, &c., are everywhere brought from Paris; and when other nations shall desire to be free, it is from France again that they will have to learn the lesson.

"Never write against Russia. Whoever uses his pen against his country is a murderer." Thus one of the most distinguished men of that country, once caused me to be told. This he said at a moment when the Government had ordered the sequestration

of my property, and endeavoured to deprive me of every means of subsistence.
Patriotism, even in the opinion of this eminent man, was superior to the love of truth,
and the fear of making known in foreign
countries the faults of his own, surpassed,
in him, the desire of seeing them remedied.
Must we wait till truth finds her way to Russia?   Our generation will not see the liberty
of the press established there.   Foreigners
have too many means of knowing our defects, either by visiting our country, or by
learning our language, and the imperfect
knowledge which they thus acquire, is frequently more unfavourable to us, than the
naked truth itself could be.

We, more than any other nation, have a
lawful title to the indulgence and the respect of Europe.   Scarcely emerged from
barbarism, we are proceeding with rapid
strides in civilization ; and in part, at least,
we may console ourselves for our faults, by
looking at the defects of others.   I should

be unpardonable if I took pleasure in exhibiting the Russian nation in an unfavourable light,—far from it; it is a very painful task to me, and one which I perform with reluctance; but I regard it as a sacred duty, which no consideration must deter me from performing. Few persons, I am willing to believe, will find themselves in my position, and as a compensation for all the evil which results from it, it would be madness not to profit by the only good which can be derived from it. I have not called down persecution on myself, as the friends of the Government think fit to say; quite the contrary, I have done every thing to avert it; but as the forlorn hope of civilization, it is my duty to defend it at all risks.

I love my country as much as any man, but I love mankind more; and should I even make enemies of my dearest friends, I shall not cease to oppose everything which is a violation of the universal and imperishable laws of social order.

Chapter III.

ASPECT OF THE COUNTRY.

I QUITTED Russia for the first time in the spring of 1836. The road from Moscow to St. Petersburg was covered with snow, which was falling there though it was the 21st of May, (O. S.) We had a speedy and pleasant voyage across the Baltic, and in three days and a half we landed at Travemunde. I fancied that I had trod on another planet ; the almanac indicated a distance of twelve days between the two countries, but to judge by the appearance of nature, there was a difference of months. The grass was as green in Germany as it was yellow in

Russia; the wheat, which I had left just springing up, had here almost attained its full growth; the trees appeared clothed with all their beauty, whereas in Russia there were neither fruit nor leaves, and we ourselves arrived here, wrapped in our warm furs.

The happiest day in the life of a Russian is incontrovertibly that on which he journies from Travemunde to Lubeck. Nothing can be compared to his happiness; his curiosity is highly excited, everything gives him an agreeable surprise; he leaves frost behind him; a brilliant sun shines over his head, and effuses rays which are all rays of hope. He enjoys life, in the full sense of the expression; he has no longer reason to desire Paradise, for he has seen it here on earth. It would be difficult to find expressions adequate to the enthusiasm which the Russians feel and manifest, more or less openly, under these circumstances.

This sentiment is modified according to

the age, character, and preceding experience of each person, and assumes as many different forms as there are individuals; but in all, it resembles a kind of intoxication. These new pilgrims are almost ready to kiss the ground they tread, like navigators who discover new lands; they can hardly refrain from adoring the sun which they salute as the star of another world and the prophet of another life—a life of happiness and joy*.

A year and a half afterwards I returned to my country by way of Prussia. I approached it with a trembling heart, fearing that it would bear no comparison with the lands which I had visited, not knowing whether I should find indemnification sufficient for the deceptions which I expected. I was like one who is going again to see his betrothed after a long absence. Will she love me? Shall I love her? Shall we suit

* I expressed these ideas on my return from abroad in a Russian Review, 1838.

each other? What can I do for her? What will she be inclined to do for me? Such were the questions which agitated my mind.

At every step that I proceeded, I found more and more indications that I was approaching my native home. The Duchy of Posen offers a pretty decided foretaste of it. I again saw the grey caftans worn by the Russian peasants; the cold became more intense and the snow deeper and deeper. It was in the month of March; I had quitted the opening spring and was proceeding to the depth of winter. It was the reverse of what I had experienced at my departure.

We courageously met the custom-house officers and encountered nothing unpleasant; they made me pay heavily for the importation of gloves and cigars; but they suffered a smelling-bottle and a collection of handkerchiefs to pass, and above all they had the courtesy not to touch my papers. Thus far I was satisfied, but some foreigners who accompanied me did not fare so well, for the officers disputed about everything, and even found fault with their linen and their clothes, which they declared were too new.

I entered the country at day-break, and the first incident which attracted my attention was a blow with the whip, which my postilion gave a peasant who was passing harmlessly along in a low sledge. My heart was wounded; the peasant said not a word, and received the blow on his back, taking care to stoop a little. The postilion was satisfied with himself, and a complacent smile passed over his countenance. For a moment I thought of turning back again. " It is still," exclaimed I, sadly and thoughtfully, " the country of the knout!" A succession of painful ideas rose before me, while the sledge glided rapidly along over an ocean of snow, which offered not the slightest diversion to my melancholy thoughts.

Lithuania spread before me in all its monotony. I entered dirty and infected

villages, inhabited by Polish Jews. I saw
them wearing strange Turkish-looking tur-
bans, and dressed in long tunics. I seemed
to be transported into Asia. Thus another
foretaste realized my project of a journey to
the East. "The barbarism which we cannot avoid," said I, "is surely quite sufficient;
its aspect has nothing so attractive nor so
interesting as to encourage us to brave, for
its sake, the dangers of such a distant journey. An hour's conversation with civilized
men is much more desirable than years
spent in studying savage manners and rude
customs. Let others pursue the study of evil,
I have enough to do to fathom the good."

The cold continued to increase, and I
soon felt a difficulty in breathing; the wind
stifled my breath, and hindered me from
speaking. I had taken the precaution to
provide myself with an excellent bear-skin
pelisse, but my shoes being too thin, my
feet were soon frozen; I will say no more
of the remainder of my journey. It is

pretty well known what travelling in Russia
is. With the exception of the road from St.
Petersburg to Moscow, which is the finest
causeway in Europe, and where there are very
handsome hotels at almost every stage, we
no where find roads worthy of the name,
or any kind of resource for travellers. On
the south the causeway does not go beyond
Tula, and on the road towards western Europe, it stops at Narva, which is only forty-
five leagues from St. Petersburg. It is difficult to obtain provisions sufficient to satisfy
even the most moderate appetite, except in
the government towns; the postmasters can
indeed provide *bouillotte,* but seldom tea;
also a bed, but sheets are an unheard-of
luxury, save in the German provinces.
Accordingly, the traveller, who has any
regard to comfort, is obliged to drag with
him all the requisites of a household, from
the cook to the kitchen utensils, and even
to the sheets on his own bed. The hotels,
even in the capital towns, are filthy beyond all

conception, and swarm with vermin, and even those which receive travellers are not free.

The rapidity of travelling post in Russia is great, but it has often been exaggerated, for it by no means exceeds that of the French mails. Private persons obtain the privilege only by means of money or blows, and they lose the advantages of it by the delays which they experience at the stages where they change horses. This is an operation which is performed very leisurely: the ropes of the harness frequently break; sometimes there are no horses; nay, perhaps just as you are stepping into your carriage, your horses are taken away to be harnessed to that of some person high in office, who has arrived unexpectedly. There are no public diligences, except on the roads to Moscow and Riga, and a wretched vehicle is the only accommodation that the postmaster is able to place at the disposal of travellers.

No idea can be formed of the petty vexations which strangers experience on their
arrival at St. Petersburg, and the French
are more exposed to them than any other
people. After very long and very circum-
stantial declarations on a variety of topics
which they give in writing, they are subject
to an inquisitorial examination by the chief
of the secret police, of which the following
is a specimen:—

"What are your intentions in coming to
Russia?" said General Duvelt, to a Frenchman of my acquaintance.

"I wish to become acquainted with the
country."

"You have chosen a very bad season for
that purpose."

"I thought that winter was the best time
to study Russia."

"I beg your pardon; summer is the best.
You have been in the army, Sir?"

"Yes, I have."

"And of course you are anxious to make yourself acquainted with all that concerns our army?"

"I do not aspire to that; I have long since left the service, and have not retained much taste for anything relating to it."

"Do you think of making a long stay in Russia?"

"Some months."

"And by what route do you intend to leave it?"

"I intend to return by way of Odessa and Constantinople."

"Shall you enter into the French service?"

"My past and present affairs may be in your province, the future concerns myself alone."

"I am really ashamed of having asked you all these questions, but my duty required it."

Pushkin has well described St. Petersburg in a few words: "A sumptuous city,

a poor city, the appearance regular, the fir-
mament of heaven of a pale green : gloom,
cold, and granite."

The houses look handsomer at a distance
than close at hand; they are of brick instead of stone or marble; the buildings are
constructed for show, rather than for dura-
bility, and fall to decay as quickly as they
spring up. Nor is there any taste in the
general arrangement. The squares are
large wastes, and verdure and fountains are
things unknown. While at Berlin you have
the Thiergarten, at Vienna the Prater, at
London a number of parks, at Paris Les
Champs Elisée, at St. Petersburg you have
nothing but a mean summer garden. The
appearance of some parts of the city, especially the quays, is imposing, and there are
fine churches, bridges, and monuments. The
reigning Emperor has largely contributed
to the embellishment of St. Petersburg,
but this he has done in common with great
monarchs, as well as with great tyrants.

The ostentation and vanity which they display strikes every eye; the letter N. appears on all the bridges along the causeway to Moscow.

St. Petersburg is a foreign city, a complete imitation; Moscow is a national, and altogether Russian capital; the former is the Imperial residence, the latter the metropolis. Petersburg is a motley collection of citizens and courtiers, of strangers and men in office; Moscow is the residence of the nobility, and the seat of manufactures. Here the streets are narrower and more varied, the inhabitants are more sociable, less distrustful, and more engaged in serious and really useful occupations. Provincial gossip is a good substitute for the intrigues of the court, but the immorality of the latter does not spread its snares here. The absence of the military adds to the tranquillity of life, while it lessens the attractions of fashionable society, and the pomp of processions. The various

branches of the police, official and secret,
are less prominent, and even escape the
eyes of the inhabitants. All this powerfully
contributes to the charm of life, and makes
Moscow the quiet retreat of those who have
other notions of happiness than promotion
in the Imperial service.

The thousand and one churches, which
are all built in the national style of architecture, and the convents, equally rich
and numerous, tend to keep up the genuine
Muscovite piety. The historical reminis-
cences which float over Moscow recal days
of trial and of suffering, of trouble and
of discord, and bind to that city all truly
Russian hearts. They hold out to them
the promise of fair days of future liberty,
and console them for the want of the
splendour which they have at St. Petersburg, by the remembrance of the tyranny
which they would rejoice to see entombed
in the marshes of that capital.

With the exception of Odessa, which is

entirely an Italian city, and the most advanced point of European civilization on the Russian soil, the other towns of the empire resemble rude villages, which differ only in their extent. The principal, and almost the sole ornaments of all the cities of the interior, are the churches, which are more or less handsome, and always very numerous; and government buildings some of which are fine, standing in very spacious and uniform squares. The towns are ill-paved, scarcely lighted by night, and contain a far greater number of wooden houses than of stone buildings.

The *Gastinoï-dwor* (the Russian bazaar) is the indispensable ornament of all the towns. It is composed of a file of shops adjoining each other, and comprised in one edifice, distinguished by a variety of rich merchandize. It breaks the monotony of the town by the perpetual cries of the shopkeepers, who seize upon the customers, or dispute with the purchasers.

The Russian villages are exclusively composed of wooden huts, covered with thatch or planks, and form one street, which is often excessively long, intersected by sheds and ornamented with one or two churches.

This mode of building renders fires frequent and dangerous.

The almost total absence of mountains imparts a wearisome uniformity to Russian landscapes ; the only ones in the interior of the empire are sufficiently characterized by their name, *Elevation Plate.* Scarcely any trees flourish in Upper Russia, except the pine, the fir, and the birch. There the towns and villages are very rare, and even isolated habitations are scarcely to be met with. The desert commences at the gates of St. Petersburg, and extends, with few interruptions, in all directions, although under a variety of names and partial changes of aspect. Sand and morass dispute the possession of the soil. Even agriculture leaves a third part of the cultivated ground fallow, and half of the land uncultivated. To the south, on entering the government of Orel, the face of the country changes, and the climate at the same time sensibly improves. Vegetable mould succeeds to the clay and sand which predominate in the northern provinces; the vegetation becomes manifestly more rich and vigorous, and the air milder, but the wealth of the people does not keep pace with these improvements in nature. The want of communications, and the distance of the centres of commerce, deprive the country of markets, and keep down the price of provisions, which is so much the lower in proportion to their great abundance.

The climate in the north of Russia is extremely rigorous; in winter the thermometer is often broken by the effect of the cold, and leaves no means of ascertaining its intensity. Winter begins in October, and ends in April; all the other seasons are comprised within five months, which justifies the proverb, that in Russia there are two winters, one white and the other green. In fact, there are frequent frosts during the night, even in summer, and the temperature suddenly changes from one extreme to the other. At noon the heat is quite African, and at eight o'clock in the evening you are forced to wrap yourself up in a cloak.

There is no other country where the number of ugly women is so great, and of pretty women so small, as in Russia. In the higher ranks of society only, and in the provinces, at a distance from the great roads, we find models of real beauty. In general the women are very robust, while the men are remarkable for their beauty. Civilization, education, and sensibility are almost the exclusive portion of the women, and their superiority to the men is incontestible in everything that regards the cultivation of the mind. This phenomenon is accounted for by the different mode of life pursued by the two sexes. The intellectual faculties of the men are absorbed by the ambition of rising, of decorations, and *tshinns;* while contempt of learning, especially in the army, is fashionable; but happily this fashion does not extend its influence over the ladies.

CHAPTER IV.

CHARACTER OF THE PEOPLE.

THERE is no task at the same time more complex, more embarrassing, and more ungrateful than that of drawing the character of any people. It is often difficult to define the character of an individual: how much more so, then, must it be, to delineate that of a whole nation, and especially of a nation like Russia, which is a compound of so many races. As men of genius and idiots are found among all people, whence none can pretend to a monopoly of the one or of the other, so cold hearts are found in hot countries, and impassioned men and women in frigid climates. We are therefore authorized to say, that capacities and sentiments are not regulated by the geographical position of a country, or by the origin of nations, but rather by individualities. Vanity and pride, duplicity and falsehood, egotism and avarice, are vices common to all men, and it would be very difficult to say whether they are more general in one nation than in another. We perceive, also, that all nations, from the French and the Russians, to the Chinese and the Jews, are, or may be almost equally courageous and moral; these qualities only vary according to circumstances, or assume different forms as applying to diverse objects. Civilization, besides, fills up, more and more, the distance between nations, smoothes the differences which distinguish them, and tends to generalize their characters. In Russia it has this effect more than elsewhere, because it did not arise there spontaneously, but was imported from foreign countries, and inoculated on the people at one stroke. But as its work is not complete, the character of the people is not yet definitively formed, and its actual state is one of transition. In order thoroughly to appreciate it, we must study it in all the shades caused by the differences of origin, of classes, and of occupations. But as there are, nevertheless, several general points common to all these varieties, and others which are peculiar to the Russian nation, we will endeavour to lay hold of them, though fully aware how thankless such an undertaking is; for we never praise a nation sufficiently to please it, and the blame which* we lay upon it, however well founded it may be, invariably wounds its susceptibility.

The Russian is naturally good and mild, more so than other nations: this is a point which is generally conceded. He still retains something of his primitive barbarism, as he has already borrowed some of the defects of modern civilization; but, on the whole, he merits esteem in more than one respect, and if he does not decay before he is ripe (a puerile and absurd fear), if the Government does not cause him to receive an impression which it would afterwards be too late to efface, he may in time rise high in public opinion.

A bad, and unhappily too common penchant, in this people, is that of cheating. Not finding a worthy and sufficient occupation for his mind, the Russian turns his attention to fraud, which he considers as an easy means of rising in the world. This is an effect of the want of civilization and the fruit of slavery. Not feeling his strength, or not daring to make use of it, he has recourse, in most instances, to craft. This is also a proof of his misery, not knowing any remedy for his sufferings, and unable to escape the evils which overwhelm him, he is more liable than another to fall into fatal derelictions, such as cheating, drunkenness, and general debauchery. But the very abberrations of mind, may serve as a criterion of his ingenuity; the Russian sharper may rival the most adroit in the world, and surprising instances of his knavery are adduced.

An officer being warned that robberies were committed in the steamers, on their departure for foreign countries, carefully kept his hands in his pockets while chatting with a friend of whom he came to take leave. The bell rung; he embraced his friend, and immediately put his hands into his pockets, but found them empty.

Another laid his eye-glass on the counter of a refreshment room at a theatre, and watched it very attentively, but when he raised a tumbler to his lips, the eye-glass vanished.

Not to repeat facts which may have happened in other countries, or which occur everywhere, without our being able to determine the place of their origin, I will

mention one that happened to myself.
Being on my way from Twer to Moscow, I
hired a coachman who was to drive me by
a certain time to the latter city. On the way
thither, during the night, he asked me for
part of the money agreed upon. Being
awakened on a sudden, I gave him eight
rubles more than he was entitled to, and
which I did not perceive till the next day.
A fortnight afterwards he saw me on the
same road, recognised me, and came up
holding his hat in his hand. I thought he
was going to return the rubles, and was
delighted at having met with such an
honest man, but how great was my surprise,
when I found that he came to demand
eight rubles more, saying that, in my sleep,
I had made a mistake in the reckoning.
The trick was so absurd, that I could not
be angry, and the man actually made no
difficulty in acknowledging that he was
wrong, as soon as I gave him credit for
his ingenuity!

Cheating is carried to such excess in Russia, that one might be tempted to say, it is in the air or in the blood. Russian commerce and manufactures are unquestionably the most dishonest in the world. China and England have had equal reason to complain of it. The Chinese, who are too suspicious to receive, without examination, the rolls of Russian cloth, find pieces of wood inside; the English receive grease instead of tallow. Their Government has in vain repeatedly protested against these abuses, and the Emperor has in vain issued decrees to suppress them. A Frenchman, who was appointed by the Government to unmask all this fraud, was well nigh killed by the manufacturers; and the officers have evidently not been proof against the seduc-- tions which he resisted, for his denunciations have had no effect.

The petty shopkeepers live only by plunder: you purchase an article in a shop, and take a different one home with you;

you must be always on your guard. All servants are notorious thieves, especially the cooks and coachmen. It may be pretty much the same every where, yet it is never carried to such excess as in Russia: there the officers, even of the public administrations, seize eagerly with both hands; they do not wait till you give them something, but they beg and bargain with you, accept large presents, and do not disdain the most trifling. Drunkenness is no where so common as in Russia. This may be traced to various causes: such as poverty, despair arising from the precarious state of things, the want of security for property, the uncertainty of the future, and, above all, the lack of education. Time, and the Government, may do much to remedy these evils; the first, by enlightening the masses, and the second, by seeking more honourable sources of revenue than the distilleries, of which it retains the monopoly, by making itself the first tavern-keeper in the country.

Manual skill is a talent peculiar to the Russians; without any instrument, save his hatchet, the peasant succeeds in the most complex constructions and delicate carving in wood. The intrepidity and dexterity of the journeyman masons is really surprising: they are seen suspended at immense heights working with great precision.

The Russian possesses, in a very high degree, the faculty of imitation, and it is unjust to refuse him that of invention. Hitherto, he has had enough to do to reproduce what has been done by others; when he has no more to imitate, he will be able to create. In point of intelligence, as well as in the general traits of character, the Russian holds the middle place between the Frenchman and the German; he has, at times, the profoundness of the one and the brilliancy of the other. He is less phlegmatic than the German, and less sparkling than the Frenchman; more practical than the former, less inconstant than the latter;

and less a slave to routine than either. Russian, or rather Sclavonian intellect, unites in itself both these elements, and conciliates the two characters. I am not one of those who think that he has the vocation to regenerate the world, for I do not believe that the world is disorganizing and approaching its destruction; but I am of opinion that he is destined to reconcile the French and the German intellects, to complete the one by the other, to blend and combine both, and in time, perhaps, to extend the sphere of their action.

As I have before observed, it is very difficult to define the morality of any people, and especially to state in this respect, its superiority or its inferiority, in juxtaposition with another. When compared with his European neighbours, the Russian has less of that immorality of mind which is the fruit of advanced civilization; but he has also less of that morality, founded

on principle, which only a solid and prudent education can give. His sensual
immorality has neither for its cause, its
excuse, or ornament, that imagination
which explains and redeems that of polished
nations. If he is debauched, he is so, even
to brutality, through the heart rather than
the mind; and the seductions which he
finds in his country are not of such a nature
as to cause or to extenuate his aberrations.

The woman, (I speak of the woman of the
great world,) is more refined in her licence,
thanks to the bitter-sweet fruits of French
romance; but she does not take sufficient
pains, or has not sufficient tact to veil her
intrigues; and the want of reserve on the
part of some Russian ladies has obtained
for them European celebrity. This laxity
is more fatal, because, as it spreads, it
undermines domestic happiness, which is the
only refuge of the Russian, who is so poor
in pleasure and comforts, and contributes to

destroy family ties, which other causes render very insecure.

The Russian has great strength, both of body and mind; he readily endures fatigue and privation, and could easily bear all kinds of suffering if his moral were equal to his physical strength; his equanimity and perseverance often give him an indisputable superiority over other nations; but his nonchalance and his carelessness are perfectly Asiatic. They are the effects of the want of civilization, and, in their turn, one of the causes which check improvement. The Russian has zeal and application only by fits and starts, and his idleness is one of the chief obstacles to the development of the powers of the country.

He is more ambitious than men of other climes; the political organization of his country makes it imperative on him; but as it at the same time paralyzes his zeal and represses the exercise of his capacity, there is no country where there are so many instances of persons who have failed in their career, or been disappointed in their ambitious projects, or where discontent, unable to find vent in legitimate and open opposition, terminates in melancholy apathy or inevitable ruin. It is, however, consolatory to see that while some sacrifice everything to their career, their honour, and even their relations, there are others who do not think that the gifts of Goverment can compensate for the humiliations, with which its favours are accompanied.

The Russian is pious, hospitable, and generous; qualities which are common to primitive nations, and which civilization unfortunately tends to weaken. But his piety is closely allied to superstition, and consists almost entirely in the scrupulous observance of religious forms. I have seen a thief with with one hand pick the pocket of a passenger, and with the other make the sign of the cross at the sound of the vesper bell. The Russian perpetually makes the sign of

the cross; he does it in front of every
church and every image, when entering a
room or leaving it, when sitting down to
table or when rising from it, when retiring
to bed, and when getting up.

Next to the King of heaven the Czar is
the object of the adoration of the Russian.
He is in his estimation the representative
and the elect of God, as he is the head of
His Church, the source of all the beatitudes,
and the first cause of all fear. His hand
distributes as bounteously as his arm strikes
heavily. Love, fear, and humble respect, are
blended in this deification of the monarch,
which most frequently serves only to mask
the cupidity of some and the pusillanimity
of others. The Czar is the centre of all the
rays, the focus to which every eye is directed; he is the *red sun* of the Russians,
for they thus designate him; while they
call the vestibule of the Kremlin, where the
ancient Czars showed themselves to the people, the Red Vestibule; *Krasnoïé Kryltzo.*

In public every eye is directed towards the Emperor; in the drawing-room the conversation turns solely upon him and his family; even in private, men's thoughts are chiefly engaged about him. All that he does is well done, and worthy of imitation; everybody walks in the promenades at the time that he walks; everybody loves dancing because he is fond of it; and there is no person who does not admire the military service, because the Emperor is a zealous advocate for it. The Czar is the father of the whole nation, and no one has any relation that can be named in the same day with the Emperor. When his interest speaks, every other voice is hushed.

The relations of the conspirators of 1825 were dancing while those unfortunate men were made to pass through the city, and it is difficult to say whether the mother, who accepted 300 rubles as a reward for having given up her son, who was a deserter, or the Emperor, who gave them to her, acted the

most like a Spartan.   There is abundance
of liberalism with closed doors, but stones
are thrown at him who revolts, and a liberal
who is compromised is shunned like a leper.
Those men who at different times have
sacrificed themselves for the public good,
have reaped more indifference and hatred
than sympathy.   Instances are not wanting
of relatives who have abandoned their sons
and their brothers in Siberia without an
attempt to save them, and then enjoyed the
property, to which they had become the
heirs by their condemnation ; nay, and who
afterwards were reluctant even to carry on
a correspondence with them ; and whose
unfeeling conduct has been the severest
part of the fate of these poor sufferers.
Mr. L. having one day brought letters from
these exiles to their relations, they refused
to take them, because they had not come
through an official channel.   It is consolatory, however, to say that such has not
been the line pursued by all ; and history

will religiously preserve the memory of Princess Trubetzkoi (née Countess Laval); of Madame Larischkin (née Naryschkin); and of Madame Rosen, who refused to separate their fortunes from those of their husbands. France can boast of having at all times and in all places taken a noble share in acts of similar devotedness. A French lady, the companion of Madame Ivaschef, after having concealed from every eye her attachment to the son of that lady, went to Siberia to offer him her hand, where from the rank of a distinguished officer of the Guards, he had been reduced to the condition of an unhappy slave. She gladly lightened the burden of his sufferings and has just returned with him to Russia.

Nothing is comparable to the happiness of a Russian when the Emperor condescends to speak to him. It is in truth curious to see how the courtiers are on the watch for every word that falls from the Imperial lips. They stand waiting for a word, quite motionless, listening with the most eager attention and riveted looks, instantly crowd round him who has been so fortunate as to receive it, or withdraw with long faces and chagrined looks, when they have been disappointed in their expectation. The Commandant Baschutzky asked the Emperor Alexander as the only favour he wanted, that every time he saw him at Court, he would whisper into his ear the word "imbecile."

A French Ambassador, being desirous to speak to Paul I., and vexed at seeing him continually address one of his favourites, said, "Sire, that is apparently some great man of your empire?" "Know," replied the Czar, "that there is no great man but he to whom I speak, and that only as long as I speak to him!"

There is still something which surpasses the honour of a conversation with the Sovereign, namely, one of those *liasons* which seem to approximate to his family those

who are *honoured* by it; but it is not
everybody that can obtain it. If they do
not go so far at Court as to congratulate
the husband who has been deceived by a
member of the Imperial family, it is as
much from jealousy as from decorum; but
they seldom fail to envy his lot, and he
himself is so little master of his happiness,
as openly to boast of it.

Barbarism, tyranny, and immorality are
born and thrive in unworthy promiscuous-
ness. They are so closely allied, that it is
difficult to distinguish the mother from the
offspring; the one produces and maintains
the other. Tyranny is established, and
subsists by means of the barbarism which
it propagates, and sustains in its turn;
while immorality necessarily succeeds and
crowns the work. To study the melancholy
effects of this combination of these three
elements, we must go to Russia. The Russian does not understand how to stop at the
limits of obedience, he confounds it with

servility, and order with slavery; he sees in liberalism a want of calculation and good sense, whenever he does not dare to designate it as treason. Few persons are to be found in Russia capable of comprehending that liberty is a condition and an effect of the dignity of man, and the Russian is generally ignorant that moral and civil courage are fully as difficult to acquire, and equally as honourable as purely physical courage. The great majority of Russian liberals are merely malcontents, and thanks to the fatal conviction that an absolute Government is the only Government which is at present adapted to their country, enlightened men contrive to live at peace with their conscience. They will not understand that even if it were so, it is the sacred duty of an honest man to contribute, to the utmost of his power, to the spread of civilization, and to hasten the order of things, from which it necessarily flows; for if a free Government be an effect

of civilization, it is likewise a cause of it,
and I believe that we might as well begin
with the one as with the other. Russia is a
land of serfs and men in office; the virtues
which accompany or flow from liberty are
unknown here. It is the Government
which makes the Russian what he is, and
which ought to bear the responsibility of
all his defects. It is to the Government,
much more than to the character of the
Russians, that we must attribute the hatred
which is felt towards them as a nation;
and this hatred is so strong, so general in
foreign parts, that I have met with some
of my fellow countrymen who did not dare
to confess to what nation they belonged.

It is an error to believe that hatred of
slavery, love of liberty, and contempt of
tyranny are exclusively the effect of civilization; they arise solely from a sentiment
of dignity, and are met with among savage
races, as well as among the most civilized
people.

CHAPTER V.

MODE OF LIFE.

THE Russian is very sedentary, for the climate compels him to be so, and his manners are in consequence as indolent as those of the Oriental. He prefers lying down to standing, and riding in a carriage to walking on foot. Idleness is a general defect of the nation. An equipage is an article of the first necessity; fashion prescribes it as a law, and the great distances to be traversed in the towns, render it almost indispensable; while the cheapness of horses and of forage, and the facilities which the nobles have of taking their coachmen from among their serfs, makes it very inexpensive to keep a carriage. Accordingly, there is no gentleman, however small his fortune, who does not sport a carriage, and no wretch, however poor, who cannot boast of a vehicle. The number of carriages on the public roads is therefore positively countless; but for that very reason they are seldom worth looking at. The horses are scarcely ever well matched, and certainly the Russian coachmakers cannot yet rival their foreign neighbours.

At St. Petersburg the number of droshki and hackney sledges is incalculable; besides those which are stationed at certain stands, and which are the best, thousands circulate in all parts of the city. In the winter, all the peasants who have no work in the country, come with their horse and a wretched sledge, to drive the inhabitants of St. Petersburg, on excessively moderate terms. There is not any fixed scale of prices for these hired carriages, which gives occasion to perpetual disputes, altercations, and even blows.

The long droshki are the rudest carriages imaginable, the lightest and the most inconvenient. They consist of a long plank placed on springs, borne on four wheels, close to the ground, covered with a cushion, and flanked with lateral boards, which afford but slight protection against the mud; sometimes there is a small seat in front for the coachman, but oftener there is none. In this case the driver seats himself astride on the droshki, twisting his robe round his legs, and supporting his feet by the side of the wheels, which splash him unmercifully. The master likewise sitting astride, takes the place behind him, and may, in case of necessity, place another person between himself and the coachman. This man holds on as tightly as he can, at the risk of being thrown out at the first jerk.

The round droshki is an approach towards the cabriolet. There are likewise covered

droshki, which are a shade more respectable, but they are going more and more
out of fashion, whereas they are becoming
more common at Berlin and at Paris.

The houses are seldom kept in good condition, especially in Moscow, and you are
sure of finding some dirty hole in almost
all of them. Comfort and elegance, taste
and luxury, are, however, making great
progress in the furniture. The number of
domestics is overwhelming; but they are
for the most part ill-fed, ill-clad, and badly
paid. The antechambers are crowded with
them, and they contribute rather to the
filth than to the neatness of the house.

It is easy to protect yourself from the cold
in Russia, thanks to the abundance of furs
and the cheapness of firewood. St. Petersburg is indebted for the latter advantage to
the great number of barks which arrive
from the interior, and which, when they are
unloaded, are broken up to serve as fuel for
the city. Hence fuel is only half as dear

as at Moscow, which has no inland navigation.

In the winter the doors are double, and
well listed; the stoves are of immense size,
and constructed upon a system which so
thoroughly condenses the heat, that it is
sufficient to make up a good fire once in
the day constantly to maintain a very high
temperature. Some persons believe that
the great heat which prevails in the Russian
apartments is unfavourable to their health,
especially in the bed rooms; others think,
with M. Virey, that it is the cause of their
passionate dispositions! What is more
injurious to health than the heat of the
houses is undoubtedly the humidity of the
marshy tracts which surround St. Petersburg. It is presumed to be the first cause
of the scrofulous affections to which the
people are subject.

Carpets and chimneys are a luxury which
has not yet become general. The pelisses
afford complete shelter against the rigour

of the climate; whence you are better protected here from the effects of the severest frosts than in other countries, where the cold often takes the inhabitants by surprise.

The Russian cookery is very indigestible, and, with the exception of some dishes, cannot be touched by delicate persons. It is therefore banished to the inferior classes, and is replaced among the nobility by French cookery.

Two or three kinds of soups, gruel, and Russian cakes, are the only dishes which retain their privilege of appearing at the best tables. Generally speaking people live very well, and the meals are numerous and sumptuous. The consumption of champagne is immense. It is said that more champagne is drunk in Russia than is made in France; and the Russian infant learns the name of cliquot at the same time as the words father and mother. This wine costs, however, twice as much as at Paris, because the Russian exchequer takes a glass for every one drunk by a private person.

The best Bordeaux wines are sent to Russia; but Burgundy will not stand the passage by sea. Several wines of the Crimea rival those of France, and might prove a great resource, if proper advantage were taken of them. Nevertheless, the use of wine is not yet general; *kwas* and brandy supply its place in moderate establishments.

Tea is a favourite beverage of the Russians, and some people drink it all day long, just as the Spaniards do their chocolate. A German tourist remarked, that "while civilized Europe loudly calls for gold, the Russian calls for tea."

The Russians are much addicted to smoking, and their tobacco is of a pretty good quality, the excise not having yet interfered with it. The young men carry the mania of smoking to a great excess, and have valets in their service, specially appointed to fill and light their pipes. If the master

enters, or rings his bell, they do not ask
what he wants, but immediately hasten to
him with his pipe and light. Formerly
there was much ostentation displayed in
their pipes, and in the amber mouth-pieces;
now quantity has supplanted quality; and
the cigar is already beginning to assert its
right over the pipe.

The vapour baths are nearly the same as
they have been from time immemorial;
they are at once a luxury and a pleasure,
promoting cleanliness and health. The use
of linen is not so general as might be
desired; nay, it is still a mark of distinction
of the higher ranks. Many persons change
it only when they go to the baths—once,
or at most, twice a week.

"So you put on clean linen every day,"
said a Russian officer to his comrade, who
had been accustomed to Parisian habits.
"And you?" inquired the latter. "I keep
that for Saturday," replied the other, with
great naiveté. In fact there are persons

who prefer coloured linen, because it is less liable to become dirty, or at least to appear so.

Cards are the usual resource and amusement of the Russians, and fill up their evenings more than dancing and conversation. Whist and *Préférence* have superseded Pharao and Lansquenet; and the civil officers, in particular, have acquired great skill in these games.

Economy is a thing unknown to the Russians; they are either covetous or avaricious, and the former more often than the latter. Some merchants deprive themselves of every pleasure in life to hoard up their wealth, and succeed thereby, rather than by successful speculations, in amassing immense fortunes, which the sons squander away more rapidly than their fathers have acquired them.

The nobles, on the contrary, generally live far beyond their income, and consequently contract immense debts, of which

L 2

they defer the payment till the time of their marriage, or their promotion in the service. It is considered fashionable, and a mark of good breeding, to get into debt, and to send the creditors about their business if they venture to apply for their due. The public service creates a kind of right in this respect, by securing the military and civil officers against certain legal annoyances; and, accordingly, there is no country in the world where it is more difficult to get paid, and where credit is less extended. Those who are wise withdraw betimes to their estates, in order to repair the breaches which a residence in the capital has made in their fortunes.

The nobleman may choose between entering the public service, living on his estates, and going on foreign travel. He who enters the service must renounce all individuality and independence, arm himself with patience, indifference, and insensibility, and hope for promotion only by

perseverance in all these melancholy elements of success. He must always flatter
and cringe, but never complain; still less
may he allow himself to have, or to give, an
opinion of his own.

No person can reside at St. Petersburg
without being in the service, at least for
form's sake—that is to say, without being
inscribed in some branch of the Administration; but in the Provinces it is extremely
difficult to escape serving in elective offices.

The life of the landowner is monotonous
and insipid in the extreme; winter especially is insupportable in the country, and
everybody in tolerable circumstances spends
it at Moscow, or at least in the capital of
his province, where he has the resource of
clubs, of some balls given by the nobility,
and of gambling. The country seats lie very
scattered, and their owners see each other
but seldom, and whenever they do meet,
they always pass several days together.
Hunting and fishing parties are rare; the

newspapers go round in a limited circle, and conversation languishes or turns only on uninteresting subjects.

The most civilized, the most discontented, or the most wealthy, go to amuse or to console themselves in foreign countries, where a residence seldom fails to be of great advantage to their minds, even though, on their return, they resume their former habits.

Travelling is, however, often resorted to by the Russians as a source of economy as well as of luxury; but this does not prevent the Czar from using every effort in his power to hinder the visits of his subjects to foreign countries. The difficulties which he throws in their way enhance the temptation, and the emigration of the Russian nobles has become quite systematic. They save up money only that they may be able to go abroad, where they remain till their resources are wholly exhausted, or till the expiration of the term for which their passport is granted, viz., five years for the nobleman, and three years for the citizen. The latter is presumed to be more diligent or more dexterous in his affairs, or to have less important business than the nobleman, who, in fact, has no business save his pleasure. The mania for travelling is stronger in the courtiers than their complaisance for their Sovereign—nay, the Grand Duke Michael himself said, that if he were merely a Russian general, he would not fail to go to Paris.

The life of the merchant is very different from that of the nobleman. He plays at draughts instead of cards, rides in a car instead of a chariot, and has the liberty to wear a long beard, an ornament which no nobleman is permitted to indulge in. He is faithful to the Russian cookery, drinks his champagne, and sips his tea in the saucer instead of the cup. He employs his superfluous wealth in ornamenting the images of his patron saint, and in adorn-

ing his wife; the whole in the worst taste
imaginable. His children have nothing
more at heart than to throw aside the national costume, and to dress like *petits
maîtres*.

The vanity of the peasant is displayed in
the ornaments of his cottage. The Russian huts have a great resemblance to the
Swiss cottages; the handsomest are two
stories in height, and are covered with a
great profusion of carvings in wood, and
sometimes they are painted with very brilliant
colours. Those peasants who are in tolerable circumstances preserve very great
neatness in the interior of their dwellings,
and this extends even to the *Tarracans*,
which a popular prejudice has stamped as
guests that bring good fortune. The stove
and the bed are curious articles; the former
occupies the middle, or the largest part of
the room, and the bed is a wooden stage
on tressels, and forms a kind of second
ceiling where the whole family sleeps, nay

sometimes several families sleep under the same roof, by the side of each other.

The Russian peasant likes to marry while young; indeed a wife is indispensable to him. She is his workwoman, his servant, and his housekeeper. He does not absolutely insist on her virtue, and hence the young villagers almost always have lovers before they have a husband. There is something extremely pleasing and delightful in the politeness and candour of a Russian peasant; he salutes all he meets, and has a kind word for everybody. If he finds a man at work, he says "May God assist you;" and if he sees any one eating, he cries "Bread and salt!"

On holidays the villages present a very animated appearance, the people dress themselves in their best, the grey caftan is superseded by the blue, and the bark leggings are laid aside for the boot or shoe. The women put on their smartest cap, or

chacot of stuff, more or less fine, ornamented with ribbons and beads.

The assembled population amuse themselves with singing and dancing, to which
gambling is sometimes added. The songs
are of a rather melancholy cast, and of an
equivocal character, but the choruses are
very agreeable.

The *ba-la-laïka* supersedes the guitar
as an accompaniment both to the voice and
the dance, in which the heels and arms of
the performers act the principal part. The
garcilke is a very general and very innocent game; the dancers arrange themselves
in two rows behind each other, the men
giving their hands to the women. At the
head is the principal person, who *burns,* as
it is called, and hence the name given to
this game. The last couple separates and
runs forward, he who burns must endeavour
to catch the woman before her partner, if
he succeeds, the latter takes his place, and
so on.

The Russian mountains afford a never-ending diversion in the depth of winter. They are built by the street boys with the first ice, and during the carnival, are erected even in the capital towns for the use of the populace. At Easter, when the ice has disappeared, they are made of wood. The bon ton have mountains of their own at St. Petersburg, which they call *English*, because an English club has the direction of them.

The Easter holidays are celebrated in a singular manner, and continue at least for a week, which is called Holy week. The people then greet each other, according to establish-ed custom, and embrace three times; some, however, do not content themselves with exercising their privilege on their acquaint-ances, but select pretty women in preference, who cannot refuse with a good grace, unless they belong to a higher class of society, where foreign manners have acquired an ascendancy over the national usages and religious habits. The Emperor embraces

all his court, and all the officers of the
guard, on the first day of the holidays, and
the Empress allows them to kiss her hand.
On these occasions it is the custom to say,
"Christ is risen," and to answer, "Risen
indeed!" One day, when the Emperor
Nicholas thus saluted a Jewish sentinel,
the latter replied, "It is a terrible lie!"
The Czar very considerately ordered that
the Jews should not again be made to
mount guard on those days.

Painted eggs and imitations of them
in china, sugar, and wax, are offered and
received in profusion. The people amuse
themselves in breaking them, one against
the other, and making them roll in tubes:
the winner in the first case is he whose egg
breaks the other; and, in the latter, he who
touches it.

Russia is very rich in game of every
kind, and the chase is excessively easy;
with the exception however of bear-hunting,
which is as dangerous as it is diverting.

This animal, which is peculiarly national, has very singular habits, with which the natives are perfectly acquainted. He is very fond of wheat, and often goes into the fields by night. The strawberry is his favourite fruit, and more than one woman has found herself face to face with a bear while gathering strawberries. A woman was once surprised at seeing a bear just opposite to her, she was excessively alarmed, and gave him a violent blow on the head with her basket. The beast, taken by surprise, was seized with a panic terror, and fled as fast as he could. It is said that he was found dead at some leagues' distant, and this is by no means improbable, for other facts of the same nature prove that this animal is subject to sudden terrors which are capable of causing his death.

In winter the bear covers himself with dry leaves, and remains lying on the same spot, sucking his paws, which in fact is all the nourishment he gets. A solitary pea-

sant sometimes ventures to attack this animal, armed only with his hunting knife.
He quietly allows him to place his front
paws on his shoulders, in order the more
easily to plunge the knife into his belly.
At other times, two men go together, armed
with forks, and seek out the bear in his
retreat. They salute him in a friendly
manner, call him by his name, Michael, and
walk composedly for some way by his side.
Suddenly, one of them makes a movement
as if to attack the beast, which instantly
falls upon him, leaving his side exposed to
the other hunter, who plunges his fork into
his loins, and with the assistance of his
comrade easily overpowers him.

Sometimes the bear is taken by means
of his defects, which are obstinacy and glut-
tony; snares of this kind are particularly
successful with the cubs. Thus for instance, balls stuck with nails are thrown at
them which they persist in endeavouring to
crush, and the more pain the nails give

them, the closer they drive them into their paws ; or a barrel smeared with honey is thrown to them, which easily sticks fast to their head, and they are thus taken alive by the huntsman.

When the bear is wounded, he becomes furious, breaks the trees, or if there are none, tears up heaps of earth, which he tosses into the air. Whenever he throws down a man, he cleaves his skull, and consequently, if any one is so unfortunate as to be without defence, he takes care to fall before him in such a manner as to expose the less noble part of his body to the bear's claws.

Wolves are very common, in consequence of the want of regular battues, but in the western provinces, which are the most void of wood, they, as well as the bears, are becoming more and more scarce. They are inoffensive and timid in summer, but in winter they approach the dwellings and attack man and beast. They always fall

upon the latter rather than upon the former,
and above all, devour any of their own
troop that are killed or wounded. The
parts which they prefer, are the calves of
men and the breasts of women. They are
attracted by the squeaking of a pig, and
whenever a peasant goes out to hunt them,
he fastens sucking pigs to his traineaux,
whose squeaking allures them.

The moorcock is the principal game in
Russia, which it never leaves, and it is
hunted both in winter and summer. In
winter, a sort of tent of boughs is built in
the forest, at the top of which the sports-
men place impaled cocks, that serve to
attract the game. The habits of these
birds deserve to be attentively studied.
They have scouts which warn the band of
the approach of the hunter, upon which
they instantly flee away, but do not fly;
they have leaders, which are the oldest and
most experienced among them, and which
it is extremely difficult to kill, for they are

the last that suffer themselves to be caught in the trap of the impaled cock.

The deaf heath cock is two or three times as large as the common cock. It is remarkable that he is deaf only while he is crowing, and that as soon as he stops, the slightest noise scares him away. The hunter is therefore obliged to attack him while he is actually crowing; as long as it lasts he is quite at liberty, and may even miss the bird without being heard; but he must refrain from the slightest movement when the cock is silent.

The woodcock is found in great profusion in Russia, and the snipe exists in all its varieties. The red partridge and the pheasant are met with only in the south, and are very numerous in the Caucasus. The white partridge is as common as the grey; and there is an abundance of hares and foxes, whereas rabbits and goats are extremely rare.

Chapter VI.

THE RUSSIAN GOVERNMENT.

THE distinctive characteristics of the
Russian Government are despotism and
rapacity. It has never conceived the possibility of reigning without oppression; nor
has it been able to comprehend that gen-
tleness secures the happiness of the people
and the security of the Government, more
than cruelty, which in Russia, is called just
severity, while tyranny is confounded with
power.

The Emperor Nicholas is the declared
enemy of liberty, and his entire policy is
concentrated to persecute it to the utmost.

He believes that liberty is equivalent to disorder, and cannot comprehend that order cannot exist without it, and that there are no abuses of power under the regimen of slavery. Nicholas has stifled liberty in Poland; and has done everything he can to crush it in Russia. In a letter which he wrote to the Emperor of Austria, at the opening of the second campaign in Turkey, he told him, that " in order to assist him against liberalism, which was raising its head even at the foot of thrones, and which he deplored as much as himself, it was necessary that Francis II. should not encourage the resistance of the Sultan, which required the employment of all the forces of Russia."

When will sovereigns be convinced that their interests, and those of their people, are identical? That without liberty there is neither wealth nor civilization? That to suppress it is to commit robbery, and that to give it is to acquire the highest title to

renown, and to the gratitude of the world.
It is not necessary to be a Washington for
the accomplishment of this; it is quite
enough to be an honest well-intentioned
man. It is the duty of a Government, not
only not to restrict the liberty of its people,
but to elevate them, and qualify them for
the enjoyment of it. Nicholas often makes
a show of frankness; he says that "a constitutional government is repugnant to his
honourable feelings, because it commands
plots and intrigues, of which he dis-
approves." What is there in this to call
for our admiration? The frankness of
despotism is only the impudence of
vice.

The peculations of persons in office are
beyond all conception. All the functionaries, high and low, steal openly and with
impunity, from the amunition to the ra-
tions of the soldiers and the medicines of
the hospitals. Will it be believed that they
actually conceal the number of men who

fall in every action till the end of the campaign, and thus continue to receive the provisions and equipment of those who have disappeared from the ranks, but who nevertheless remain on the lists till the end of the war? In the Caucasus, where hostilities are incessant, this abuse had risen to an enormous excess; the ranks were thinned, yet the lists were full, as also were the pockets of the officers*.

The captain lives on his squadron or his company; the colonel on his regiment; the general on his brigade; and so on. On giving up the command of his corps, the general comes to an understanding with his successor, and nothing more is said†.

---

* In 1813 and 1814, Colonel P. took care to indicate among the dead, the soldiers who prepare the gruel for their comrades, because they carry the iron pots used for this purpose about with them, the loss of which it was necessary to replace; all this was so much gain for their insatiable chief, who had besides acquired a large fortune with his wife.

† Endeavours are now being made to remedy these

The officers of police who receive salaries of 1000 francs, have cloaks and horses worth many thousand rubles. The heads of the police have houses, and the governors hotels. Persons in office make their fortunes much quicker in Russia than in other countries, and in some departments sooner than in others. One hand washes the other. The officers, high and low, share their gains, and woe to him who shall pretend to act with probity; the poor innocent sheep would speedily be devoured by these rapacious wolves.

By the aid of money the worst causes are gained in the tribunals, and money will purchase indemnities for every crime. Does any one desire to institute a law suit? He does not inquire whether he has better rights than his adversary, but merely examines whether he is richer. In that case,

abuses, by depriving the military chiefs of everything relative to the administration of the corps, and to entrust it to a special commission.

being certain of having the judges on his side, he proceeds to act. The Emperor himself declares that he is powerless against this scourge, and it is well for him if his own fortune is not stolen*.

On the other hand, he has confiscated the estates of the Poles for the benefit of the Crown, and this refinement of cruelty

* During my stay at Berlin, a characteristic anecdote was in circulation.

The Emperor, during one of his visits to that capital, showed Prince Augustus a snuff-box, which his Majesty intended for M. Krüger, and which the Prince greatly admired. After it had been given to the artist, his Royal Highness expressed a wish to see it again, and great was his surprise on finding a very ordinary snuff-box in place of the one which had been shown him. He spoke of it to the Emperor, who, perceiving that he had been robbed, replied that he should have too much to do if he attempted to eradicate this vice.

This did not prevent the degradation and banishment of the contractors, who had so badly provided the Russian corps at the reviews of Karlisch, in 1835, and afterwards Prince D———— was deprived of his epaulettes as aid-de-camp to the Emperor in the Caucasus, which were bestowed on his brother-in-law, the Baron Rosen.

cannot be justified in our days. M. Gejelinshky made a trade even with the Emperor's signature. He was at the head of the Chancery of the Committee of Ministers, and, on the receipt of large bribes, effaced or altered the Imperial decisions which were written in pencil. He was informed against by a clerk whom he had dismissed, and was accordingly summoned by the Emperor, who promised that he would be lenient to him if he confessed his crime. He did so, and was brought to trial, but when before the Court, he denied the confession which he had made to Nicholas. He was degraded to the rank of a private soldier, upon which the Emperor, yielding to a culpable weakness, had him admitted into the 14th class, in order to enable him to enjoy the property which he had amassed so illegally. Since this affair the decisions of the Emperor, written in pencil, are covered with a kind of varnish, which prevents their being altered.

The main spring and sole object of the Russian Government is its own interest; the happiness of the people it regards as of secondary importance. Their physical wants are all that it endeavours to provide for, and as this is impossible, without the civilization which it dreads, because it does not comprehend it, it finds itself condemned to the punishment of the Danaids. "What I desire above all things," said the Emperor Nicholas, "is to secure the tranquillity of my son's reign:" and this son, on hastening to meet and congratulate him on having escaped the mysterious musket-shot at Posen, which, according to all appearances, proceeded from a carriage in his own suite, the Czar reprimanded him severely. "We must not," said he, "make the people entertain the idea that it is possible to fire at the Czar."

One day Count Benkendorf said to the Russian author B——, whom he lectured for a patriotic article, "You must not instil such notions into the people : they are the cattle which serve to draw the car."

In this Government the Emperor is everything: all moves and lives only through him. From the colour of a dress and the button of a coat, to the most complex law-suit; everything passes, or is supposed to pass through his hands, and nothing can be done without his orders or his sanction. His interests ought to be the rule and the primary duty of every person in his service, and the Russian Government has the simplicity to write at the head of its legislation: the Emperor of all the Russias is an autocrat monarch, whose power is unlimited. God himself orders all to obey his supreme will, not only from fear, but from conviction.—Swod., vol. I., sec. i., art. 1*.

* The catechism used in the Polish provinces speaks of the homage paid to the Emperor: it says, that " People must submit to the decrees of his justice, according to the example of Christ, who died upon the cross." M.

" The power of the Government," says an article of the same code, " belongs, in its full extent, to the Government." It is the Government which makes and which changes the laws. The 60th article lays it down as a rule, that the laws have no retrospective force, but the following article excepts all those in which it is expressly stated that they apply to times anterior to the publication. The 70th article formally states, that " every distinct or special ukase, applying to a certain cause, or to a certain order of things, deprives the general laws of their force for these same causes;" and it adds, that " privileges granted by the Emperor to individuals or to societies, may contain clauses contrary to the general laws, which lose all their effect as far as those cases are concerned." Everyday exceptions to the general laws pass under

de la Mennais exclaimed on this subject, "It has been given to this man to enlarge the limits of blasphemy!"

the egis of these words, " *ne v primer drougnim,*" without application to other cases. Tyranny has never held more frank language, nor shewn less reserve in plainly expressing her meaning; far from blushing at herself, she believes, and would have you to believe, that she is the guardian angel of Russia.

The interest of the Sovereign is the clue which runs through the labyrinth of Russian legislation. It is this which the Governors of the Provinces are to attend to in the first place: the interest of the country is a secondary consideration. The censorship is enjoined to attend to it above all things. In the churches, the Emperor is placed on an equality with God. The Czar is prayed for more than the human race and the spread of the Gospel of Christ; and the liberty of religion is inscribed in the laws, only that God may be prayed to for the happiness of the Sovereign, in all languages and according to all religious forms*.

The judicial power appertains to the Czar as much as the legislative and the executive. The Emperor may suspend, modify, revise, or quash every kind of sentence, mitigate or aggravate a punishment, and unhappily, Nicholas more frequently uses the latter than the former of these privileges. Prescription is a mere illusion. Baron B——, an aid-de-camp of General Diebitsch was recommended to the Czar by the Field Marshal, respecting an affair which had been terminated more than fifteen years before, and the Emperor ordered

---

Swod., vol. I, art. 45. " Religious liberty is given not only to Christians of different sects, but also to the Jews, the Mahometans, and the heathens, in order that all nations residing in Russia, may glorify Almighty God in their different languages, according to the law and the rite of their ancestors, *blessing the reign of the Russian monarchs,* and imploring the Creator of the universe *to increase the prosperity and the power of the empire.*

that it should be reversed in the full Senate. The bills of exchange which had led to the sale by auction of an estate belonging to his father, were declared illegal, because they had been given to courtesans, and the person who had bought this estate at the auction was deprived of it without any indemnification.

The Czar is President of the Council for the Empire, but his vote is not only reckoned as two when there is a division, but it avails even against the majority, however great that may be. The will of the Council has no effect except it be unanimous. It is sufficient for one member to express an opinion, at variance with the other, for the Emperor to give it the preponderance. "There is no evil without a compensation," say the Russians, who find an apology for every abuse; and whenever the majority is in error, the Emperor does well to decide against it; but when he desires to favour a courtier, or to punish an adversary, he has no difficulty in finding at least one voice, to express the opinion which he desires to prevail.

"There is no law in Russia," says Puschkin; "the law is nailed to a stake, and that stake wears a crown." The Russian lawyers have no idea of justice, and magistrates do not believe in the sanctity of the law. There are as many laws as there may be particular cases, whence the Russian legislation is as elastic as the conscience of a jesuist. There are no laws in Russia: there are only ordinances, ukases, emanating from the caprice of the master, or dictated by isolated circumstances, and such decrees do not merit the name of laws, save when they have the force of such*. Law has a moral and reasonable basis; it flows from acknowledged

* The Empress, Catherine II., having convoked Deputies to proceed to draw up a code of laws, one of them inquired if there would be any ukases, and being answered in the affirmative, exclaimed, that " In that case there was nothing to be done," and immediately returned to his own province.

facts, which frequently recur, from ascertained wants, and is the expression of indisputable utility; ordinances, on the contrary, are only the inspirations of an isolated will, of a transitory want, real, or imaginary. Confiscation of property was abolished by Catherine, but it has been reestablished by Nicholas, in consequence of the Polish revolution. Emigration was tolerated on condition of a certain payment to Government; Nicholas has caused it to be assimilated to high treason, in consequence of a Polish subject going to settle in Switzerland. Two charters, those of Michael Romanof and of Catherine II., permitted the nobles to reside in foreign countries; Nicholas, from antipathy to liberal ideas, limits their residence abroad to five years, imposes a tax on their passports, and submits the delivery of them to all kinds of difficulty.

The Russian Government is perfectly aware that the unworthy proceedings in which it takes pleasure, cannot subsist except under the shelter of the grossest ignorance and the deepest immorality : and, accordingly, the main secret of its policy is to brutalize and demoralize the people. It is wholly ignorant of the dignity of man, which it makes to consist in a blind obedience to its decrees, and whoever has a sense of his individual worth is considered by it, as a rebel. It desires to command despotically and to be servilely obeyed. M. Kukolnick brought out a play, called "The Hand of the Most High," which was replete with classic Czarism. The delighted Czar sent for him ; the poet, who had a brother implicated in the revolt of 1825, trembled when he appeared before the Sovereign, who inquired the cause of his fear, and encouraged him by saying, " It is an every day occurrence, that of two brothers, one is base and the other honest." M. Polevoï who ventured to find fault with this famous play was arrested at Moscow, torn from his family, dragged to St. Petersburg, and escorted by a gen-d'armes in a courier's car, and this shock had so great an effect upon him, that the liberal author was transformed into a fulsome parasite of the Court. On this occasion, some verses of the following purport were made.—

"The Hand of the Most High" has accomplished three prodigies,—it has saved the country, elevated Kukolnick, and ruined Polevoï.

No body in Russia dares to differ in opinion from the Emperor, even on the most trifling subject; on a question of art, or of literature. When he has once given his opinion nothing remains but to accede to it or to remain silent. I one day asked a journalist if he would give a review of the History of M. Buturlin, Adjutant-General to the Emperor? he answered with much simplicity, "I have not got two heads upon my shoulders."

The Russian Government is a military

government: strong and resolute, but brutal
and precipitate, ignorant and cruel. The
forms, which are otherwise observed, are
superfluous, and would, in fact, be ridiculous
the moment they seemed only to mask its
cruelty. The politeness of M. Douvelt had
made him the buffoon of the secret police,
and the Emperor whenever he wishes to
be polite puts a constraint upon himself:
like the sea and like Mirabeau, a handsome
man is never so handsome as when he is
angry.

Under the reign of the sabre and the
mustachio, the peaceful citizen feels ill at
ease. Talent is out of place where brutal
force prevails; while the latter, though
blushing at itself, fears, hates, despises, and
persecutes it. Civilization cannot be regulated by beat of drum; this noise is hate-
ful, and it shuns it, withdraws in despair,
and pines away in melancholy inactivity.
"Persecution," says a German proverb, "is
the fate of talent in Russia." Persecution

might be endured, and talent might consider it as a crown of laurels whenever its
power is thus acknowledged and honoured;
but when barbarism sways the sceptre, it
affects contempt for talent, as a futile object and the source of deception, rather
than as a means of success. It encourages
only those who amuse it, and, at the most,
endures him who gives it no umbrage.

In Russia, the term "learned man," is
equivalent to an odd man, a poor devil, a
sort of labourer;—a professor is on a par
with domestics; a literary man, one who
has mistaken his vocation. If an artist is
welcomed and received, it is for the most
part with an excess of enthusiasm or indifference which exceeds the limits of propriety. The singer loses his voice in Russia; the artist can paint only soldiers or
portraits; an architect of genius cannot get
one plan adopted which does not resemble
some edifice already known. The Emperor
effaced a portrait by Krüger, because he

found eight buttons to his uniform instead of nine, and sent it back to the artist at Berlin! Count Benkendorf would not permit a celebrated painter to set out for Italy. "What would you do there with the peasants?" said he; to which the artist, being closely pushed, replied, "And what have I to do here with servants?" The President of the Academy of Fine Arts invited M. B—— to go and study the style of an obscure artist at Dusseldorf; to which the other answered, "There is nothing in common between us; he drinks water, and I drink wine." Another Russian painter presented some pictures for churches, which had been ordered, and the Emperor not only would not receive them, but had him expelled from the Academy, which did not afterwards dare to give him much employment as a drawing-master.

M. Petscherin, one of the most distinguished pupils of the Institution of Professors, went to Naples after having completed his course of study at Berlin. The Secretary of the Russian Legation at Naples had the imprudence to write a letter by the post to a friend at St. Petersburg, telling him that he had just become acquainted with Petscherin, a man of talent, but a violent republican. The letter was of course opened and read at the post-office, and orders were given instanter to place M. Petscherin under the inspection of the secret police. On his return to fill a Philological Chair at Moscow, he perceived a spy attending his lecture. Indignant at such a proceeding, he asked leave of absence to go abroad, and went to settle in Switzerland. M. Strogonof, the Curator of the University of Moscow, wrote to him, inviting him to return, and promising to forget what was past. M. Petscherin replied, that he knew the fate which awaited him in Russia; that he should have gold and decorations lavished upon him; but that to such a condition, he preferred poverty and independence. His melancholy forebodings were more than realized. His relatives quickly abandoned him; his father, who held the rank of General, had already refused him any support, from the moment when he would not be prevailed upon to embrace the military career. His profound and various knowledge failed to furnish him with means of subsistence; he made an unsuccessful attempt upon his life; and at length shut himself up in a Belgian monastery, where he now languishes. May peace follow him there, and may his name be branded on the forehead of the Russian Government!

The countenance of the Sovereign, and long continued public services, far from securing a man against arrogance, only expose him the more. "Is it your decorations that make you so proud?" said the Emperor one day to one of his Generals; "it was I who gave them to you, and I will take them away." "You cannot make your Cadets march," said the Grand Duke Michael to General Sch* *, and made the veteran place himself in the ranks, and march with the standard-bearers. Very recently, in 1843, the Emperor having entered the tent of the Prince of Oldenburg during the exercise of the troops, and perceiving on the carpet a spot of oil, which there had not been time to remove, wrote in the order of the day, " I thank the Prince of ———— for his uncleanliness," which induced the Master of the Horse to tender his resignation. The Prince, though he retired from the service, could not overcome his taste for the Court, and asked the Emperor for permission to retain the carriage and livery of the Court. Nicholas replied, that he had not expected such meanness in the Prince of ————.

It is difficult to decide whether brutality and despotism exceed the baseness and servility of the Russian courtiers; as they mutually support each other, they are necessa-

rily equal, and deserve to be equally con-
temned.

It is considered a mark of particular
favour if the Emperor condescends to address any of his subjects in the second
person singular; and his confidants imitate
their Sovereign in speaking to their subordinates, who do not venture to use the
same familiarity.

Can we be astonished after all this that
a Minister should with impunity, and with
his own hand, strike a postmaster? Everybody in Russia has done the same, more
or less, in the course of his life; but it was
for the heads to set the example.

A general aid-de-camp to the Emperor
was very near proceeding to similar acts
of violence towards a postmaster in Germany, who, however, cooled his courage
by threatening to treat him in the same
manner.

All the evil committed in Russia is laid
to the charge of the Emperor. This is

a necessary result of an absolute Government; good or bad, example is always contagious when it comes from an august personage; but, it is no less true that, where the good is not executed in consequence of the negligence of the functionaries, cruel orders and injudicious measures may often be indefinitively deferred. "Abuses," said an ingenuous man, "are the salvation of Russia; it is very common for unreasonable orders to be disobeyed."

The friends of justice and of the country, frequently excuse every abuse that is committed, by the want of superior men. Such men have, however, never been lacking to great sovereigns. Peter I. knew how to find in the streets a Menschikof, to raise a Schafirof, to employ a Dolgorucky, to distinguish a Scheremeteff, to honour a Golovine.

Catherine had a Potemkin, an Orlof, a Rumanzoff, and a Suwarof. Genius and talent crowd round a throne which gives them distinction, but they shun that which does not appreciate them. It would not be very difficult for Nicholas to find men of talent, if he knew how to make use of them. But they avoid the service, and bury themselves in their estates, or spend their leisure in foreign countries, because they are men who require honourable treatment, and will participate only in meritorious actions. The German party is all-powerful in Russia, and if the Baltic Provinces are in the proportion of three to fifty, with respect to the Russian governments, the functionaries of German origin, who surround the Government, are, with respect to the Russians, in the inverse ratio of fifty to three. They fill the great dignities of the empire; the parts of ministers, ambassadors, generals, and superior officers, are given in preference to Germans. When Peter conquered the German Provinces, he little thought that he was subjecting his own country to them. If he was fond of foreigners, it was not those with whom he peopled Siberia. The Germans, more civilized than the natives, conquered Russia, while they suffered themselves to be conquered. This same circumstance has taken place in China with the Mongols, in Italy with the barbarians, in Greece with the Romans. The savage conquerors impose their yoke on civilized people, only to submit in their turn to be vanquished. But here policy has done more than civilization. The secret of the success of the Germans is not their intellect; the Russian has a hundred times as much as the Finn, and the education of the Russians, though less varied, is not less solid than that of the Germans. The latter owe their success to their characteristic perseverance, and this is accounted for by the state of destitution which nails them to their post, a species of capacity which is admirably expressed by the German word *sitzfleisch*.

The secret of the systematic preference
which the Government, calling itself Russian, gives to the Germans, is the confidence
which it has in them; for, animated by a
devotion to the throne, which is proof
against every trial, they feel only indifference
for the country, and hatred or contempt
for the people. "I do not serve Russia,"
said a foreigner of distinction; "I serve
my master, Alexander Paulowitsch." Hence
we may readily understand the hatred which
the Russians bear the Germans. "Make
me a German," said Yermalof, to the
Emperor Alexander, who offered him the
choice of a favour. "Your *Tschinn?*" says
an actor in a play. "German," he replied.
"Before thinking of entering a civil or military service, one thinks of becoming a German," said a father to his son, and, when
the latter returned to his country with all
his German erudition, he everywhere found
the doors closed against him. And why

was this? Because the virtue indispensable
to success under the Government was not
possessed by him—it is an inheritance
dependant on the blood, and not on the
intellect.

The throne of Russia is open to both
sexes, but the males have precedence of the
females, and the elder sons of the younger.
At the death of the Emperor, the sceptre
descends to his eldest son, or if he dies without male heirs, to a younger brother, and
so on, till the entire extinction of the male
branches, after which the empire falls to
the female line, nearest to the last Czar.
The husband of the Empress enjoys the
rights belonging to the wives of the
Emperors, except the title of Imperial
Majesty.

If the Crown should fall, by inheritance,
to a Princess who is sovereign in another
country, she would have to choose between
the two thrones and the two religions, if

she professed one different from that of Russia. The reigning Sovereigns can profess no other than the Greek religion.

The issue of the marriage of the Imperial family, and an individual not belonging to any reigning house, cannot ascend the throne.

No heir to the Crown is at liberty formally to renounce it.

The Sovereign has attained his majority at the age of sixteen. The minor who is called to the throne is under a tutor and a governor, which offices may be held by one individual, or by two different persons. The choice of them belongs to the Emperor, who may nominate them in his lifetime.

If not otherwise provided for, these functions belong of right to the father or the mother of the young Sovereign, and in default of these, to the uncle. The Regent must be assisted by a council of six persons of his own appointment. The members of the Imperial family may be admitted to it, but they are not an integral part of it.

The arms of the empire of Russia are a black eagle with two heads and three crowns, on a field of gold, holding a golden sceptre in the right claw, and a globe in the left. The shield bears the arms of Moscow; St. George on a white charger, piercing the dragon with his spear*. The right wing of the eagle is adorned with three shields, emblazoned with the arms of the three kingdoms of Casan, Astracan, and Siberia, and on the left wing are those of Poland, Taurida, and Finland. On the breast of the bird hangs the chain of the order of St. Andrew.

The Empress receives 600,000 rubles a year, besides what is requisite for the maintenance of her household. She has this

---

* This is a false and arbitrary imitation of the primitive arms of Moscow, which represent only the Czar himself, for whom St. George has been gratuitously substituted.

sum so long as the Emperor lives; after the death of her husband, she enjoys this income while she resides in Russia, but if she quits the country she has only the half.

The heir presumptive, besides the maintenance of his household, receives 200,000 rubles a year; his wife 150,000 rubles during the life of her husband, and double if she becomes a widow. Their children have 50,000 rubles each, till their majority, or their marriage. His daughters and grand-daughters receive a million rubles as their portion; the great grand-daughters 300,000 rubles, and the more remote descendant 100,000 rubles each, &c.

Chapter VII.

ON THE RUSSIAN POLICY.

The corner-stone of the Russian empire, of its power, its riches, and of its policy, is Peter the Great. He is met with at every step, and everywhere he is sublime and admirable. While, with one hand, he dispersed the Swedish fleet on the Baltic, with vessels which he had created out of nothing, and, having conquered at Pultowa, erected upon impenetrable morasses, a marvellous city, he indicated with the other hand the road to Calcutta, founded settlements on the Caspian and the Black Seas, the currents of which, ever since, have borne the

Russian ships direct to the walls of Byzantium. He failed, indeed, at Khiva, and was reduced by the Treaty of the Pruth, whither he had been led by the pride of victory, to raze Azov, which he had just before taken from the Turks; but he conquered an entire province from Persia, and covered the Caucausus with a network of fortresses so placed as to check the incursions of its hordes of banditti. Standing with a firm foot in Europe, on the ruins of the Swedish power, he opened in Asia a vast field of material and moral conquest to Russia, and advanced the first step towards universal empire. His successors followed his policy, but it was too gigantic and too much beyond their measure, and therefore, to this day, as in the time of Peter the Great, Russia is still two steps from Constantinople and Calcutta, those main points of universal empire, those roads which lead to the tomb or to conquest; two steps, formidable to take, and which, perhaps, Russia never will achieve.

It has obtained some conquests by arms; diplomacy has undermined the ground which separates Russia from the Mediterranean and the Pacific Ocean, but it has hitherto wanted the power to spring this immense mine. Having once entered on this course of conquest, Russia can hardly go back; it is a rapid declivity which it is now more easy to descend than to reascend. To conquer or die, has hitherto been the only alternative of conquering Powers, and all those which have aspired to universal empire have failed, when they had reached only half their course. Will Russia be an exception to this general rule?

Considerable progress, it is true, has been made on the road pointed out by Peter the Great. Poland no longer separates Russia from Europe; Turkey, stripped of several parts of its territory, is no better than a corpse; and, with some military talent, the occupation of Constantinople might be easily effected. Persia is subject to the will of the Russians; the Caucasus, which still mocks at their power, so blindly expended in that country, is not an insurmountable obstacle. Khiva and Bochara feel the Muscovite influence, so that when Russia moves, Asia trembles, India is agitated, and London in consternation. It is to the East that all the great questions of policy converge; there, once more the fate of the world must be decided. Petersburg cannot remain the capital of Russia; it is an advanced camp, the founder of which never intended to make it a permanent residence. Constantinople or Calcutta, these are the natural capitals of empire. The Colossus is checked in its steppes, without sea, and extends its arms towards the ocean. Will it ever reach it? If Russia invaded the East, Germany would remain plunged in its lethargic slumber. France could do nothing without England, and would besides have only to chose between the possession of Asia by the English or by the Russians. England and Russia therefore may divide the world between them. The first seriously threatened in India would easily leave the second to establish itself in the Bosphorus; but then Austria would claim her share; France would oppose her *veto,* and, if she were indemnified by the cession of Egypt, it would be necessary to cede Poland to Germany, which would be an exchange altogether to the advantage of Russia.

Hitherto the Court of St. Petersburg has endeavoured to sever France from England, through mean and personal views. It succeeded for a moment; but having no mind to attach itself to France, its work has come to nothing. It may find occupation for France, and lull or intimidate Germany; but England is always awake, and the genius of Peter the Great is not inherited by his descendants. All these questions are therefore adjourned, and Russia would have done better if she had suffered them to lie dormant till the advent of the man who shall be able to solve them at once. The unchangeableness which distinguishes the Russian policy is rather adverse than favourable to it; by directing the general attention to it, secresy and surprise, which are the first conditions of success in politics, are rendered impossible.

The danger is, nevertheless, considered great and urgent. In fact, if Russia were once established in India, the political balance would be destroyed; the conquests which she makes in Asia are advantages gained over Europe. Without doubt Asia ought not to be tributary to Europe, and we must earnestly desire to hasten the subjection of barbarism to civilization. Without doubt Asia would gain by the conquest of Russia; but what then would be the fate of the world—what the fate of liberty? Slavery, and, above all, military slavery! As long as Russia shall serve under this banner, the friends of liberty cannot wish her success in her warlike undertakings. The day when she shall sway the sceptre of the universe, the liberties of the world will be at an end. Even then there might be glorious wars, for their object would be independence; but the issue would be fatal to their noble cause. Even after having triumphed abroad, Russia will succumb at home. It is not with the evil which ferments in her bosom, and which, though latent and dormant, is nevertheless terrible, that she can venture to hazard new conquests. Her noblest conquests are at home. There she may increase her population tenfold, civilize and enrich it. Under the effect of a great internal shock her parts will become dislocated, and the conquered nations would avenge themselves by cruel reprisals. Whereas, after having triumphed over intestine dangers, after having solved the questions of internal life, she will be able, with less apprehension, to brave external dangers. The part which Russia is destined to act in Asia is secured to her by the power of circumstances, even by her geographical position alone : it is noble, it is great and sublime; but in order to accomplish it conformably to the laws of equity and perfectibility, she must herself have progressed in the course of civilization, that she may not by new conquets, commit acts of spoliation on her masters in knowledge and liberty.

Such is the ideal, and it is always encouraging to have such a vast horizon before you, even though you never reach the bounds; but it is not the reality;—this is gloomy and humiliating.

In this point of view, Constantinople and Calcutta are but chimeras, and Warsaw is the chain of the galley slave which binds Russia to a volcano, ever on the eve of an eruption. Constantinople is to her what

Alexandria is to France, and Rome to
Austria. As for Calcutta, its occupation
exists only in the imagination of English
agents, who would veil their own intrigues
by disquieting public opinion with the projects of an empire which is vain enough to
suffer such reports to gain credit, and un-
wise enough not to contradict them.

In order to reach Calcutta, the Russians,
to whom heat alone is an invincible enemy,
would have to traverse countries unknown
and unhealthy, and to combat warlike nations, who have often withstood very formidable attacks.   For such an enterprise,
which demands more wealth than they now
possess, they would have to sacrifice entire
armies.   They want money, the very sinews
of war, and will long want it.   Even sup-
posing that Russia could conquer India,
what advantage would she derive from it at
this moment?   Her manufactures and her
commerce are absolutely null; the first cannot even supply the wants of the country,

and the second is in its infancy: and it is
notorious that it is manufactures and commerce alone that render the possession of
India important to England.

Europe, then, may turn her eyes from
Calcutta, for it is evident that there can be
no ground for serious alarm in that quarter.
To seek Russia on that side, renders one
liable to miss seeing her in other quarters
where she more nearly threatens the future
condition of the world. When politicians
ascribe to Russia a systematic tendency
towards the Pacific Ocean, and admirable
perseverance in overcoming the obstacles
which separate her from it, they do more
honour to her policy than it deserves. I
ask no other proofs of this than the unhappy end of M. Witkewitsch. England
imagined for a long time that at Cabool
and Lahore he had acted conformably with
his instructions, and yet, on his return
from the East, after an audience of Count
Nesselrode, he blew out his brains. The

Minister had told him that he should be compelled to set him aside for a certain time, and assuredly he did not add, that it was to please England, or at least to lull its suspicions, otherwise the young officer would not have shot himself. The Government took much pains to conceal this event, and the remains of Witkewitsch were disposed of like those of a private.

Thanks to the vigilance of Europe the project of occupying Constantinople, if not wholly abandoned, is at least adjourned *sine die*, and we even saw Nicholas, in 1833, support the power of the Sultan, which he could not destroy, at the moment when it threatened to crumble to pieces under the attacks of Ibrahim. Did he desire to attach to himself by gratitude, those whom he could only half conquer by force of arms, or did he fear to see the Ottoman Empire consolidated under the sceptre of the Pacha of Egypt, and thus enabled to brave his power? But the gratitude of the

Turks is by no means equal to their inveterate hatred of the Russians ; it will never
stifle the voice of their well-understood
interest, and the ancient policy which
would leave an enemy to ruin himself by
intestine discord, is still the best.

As for the foreign influence, which it
might have been wished to annul in Turkey,
if it sufficed to prevent Russian interference, it will be able to render ephemeral
any alliance between the two Emperors.
However this may be, the chivalaresque proceeding of Nicholas ended only in a sterile
manœuvre, and in a Protectorate, which,
at the best, is only illusory. It was not
otherwise in 1840. At the moment when
the Russian troops were about to enter
Syria to support the decisions of the Allies
with regard to Mehemet Ali, England,
jealous of all Russian intervention, had
rendered it unnecessary by her splendid
successes at sea.

It is an evident fact, that since the commencement of the reign of Nicholas, Russian policy has become weaker and weaker. It never was more unpopular, or more discredited in public opinion, that arbitress of our age, whose power is continually increasing. It is detested in Germany, abhorred in Italy, ruined in Greece, exiled from Spain, mute in France. The antisocial principle, and its hatred of enlightenment, undermine its strength and future prosperity. It destroys itself by its tendency to absolutism, and by its haughty language, which its power by no means justifies, and the vanity of which is now fully understood. Reduced to the friendship to Austria which, though uneasy at her encroachments, unites with her, on account of the dangers which threaten absolutism in both empires; looked upon with dislike even in Prussia, she maintains her ground in Germany only, by the alliances which exist between the Courts : family alliances which are always ephemeral. She is as unpopular

among the Sclavonian nations as Austria is
welcome; they prefer the Austrian to the
Russian Government, and the conformity of
religion and language is not calculated to
overcome the repugnance with which the
latter inspires them. Nicholas, by carrying
the misfortunes of Poland to the utmost,
has alienated all hearts from Russia, and
has thus created a formidable support to the
cause of liberty, which will not fail to bear
its fruit.

The dignity and the resolution of Russian
policy are lauded, and indeed, it would be
surprising if its language were not explicit
and decisive, with a nation of 60,000,000
men, bent under the yoke of absolute
power, supported by a numerous army,
which may be recruited *ad infinitum*, without exciting any serious opposition, seated
on a soil which tempts nobody, for nobody
desires to conquer snow and sand; not
constrained in its movements by national
control, the Russian Government, which

knows the warlike temper of its people, which has issued victorious from so many struggles, and little disposed to endure any compromise with the enemy, cannot and ought not to suffer itself to be intimidated by any menace, and is able to menace in its turn. But what gives true dignity and real force to a political system is its object, its tendency, and in this respect Russia has not always been free from reproach. As for its means, she does not invariably prefer the most moral, and her perfidy passes improperly for ability.

Her diplomatists have the reputation of being able men, thanks to traditional qualities which they acquire in the long course of service, and which consist in an habitual craft, a kind of coin which wears away with every dupe. Russian diplomacy is certainly that which has most contributed to injure its cause, for none any longer believe its necessity, and all dislike its proceedings. It is difficult to conceive the little kindness which the Russian legations manifest towards their fellow countrymen, and, it is affirmed, that it is in order to disgust them with visiting foreign countries that they refuse to show them the least complaisance. One is repairing his apartments, another his fortune, and they cannot give *fêtes;* a third announces his intention of giving one, only when he foresees the death of some great person, which will oblige him to countermand his invitations. A fourth says, to whoever will hear him, that his relations with the Court at which he resides, are too precarious for him to venture on asking it for the slightest courtesy. Arrogance is the general rule of all, and politeness only an exception.

Chapter VIII.

ON THE RUSSIAN POLICE.

I FIRST became acquainted with the police of St. Petersburg in the autumn of 1840. I had made an excursion to the baths at Reval, and returned by a steamer which goes to Sweden; we were therefore detained at Cronstadt for two tedious hours, before all the absurd formalities to which foreigners are subject on entering Russia were completed. On our arrival at St. Petersburg, while we were at dinner, a barrier was put up to prevent our leaving the boat till the coming of the officer whose business it was to distribute the passports.

Notwithstanding the difficulties and the accidents of the voyage, we were punctually at the rendezvous; but the officer was not. There is a Russian proverb which says, "Seven men must not wait for one;" and we were at least seventy, many of whom were rather higher in office and rank than the police officer, not to speak of other distinctions, which are held in less estimation in Russia. His arrival was the signal of our deliverance; he was immediately assailed by the most urgent, who availed themselves of their titles, and were, of course, attended to before the rest. Prince T——, a gentleman of the chamber, obtained his passport first of all, and then the whole of his suite. The officer indeed made some objection to the latter; but the Prince persisting, he called Lafleur and Frontin before the other passengers. Then came a tailor, begging the officer not to make a countryman wait; the officer was a Finnlander, and the tailor a Jew. I was

more inclined to laugh than to be angry at
this scene, when an incident forced me to
become an actor, instead of a mere looker-
on. M. R., the councillor of state, came
up to me, and entreated me to procure his
passport for him, as he was attending upon
his wife, who had been confined to her bed
during the whole voyage, in consequence of
an operation which she had undergone at
Reval. I did not doubt that such serious
reasons would enable me to obtain the
desired favour for Madame and M. R——;
and accordingly I approached the officer,
hat in hand, and as he spoke French, which
generally passes in Russia as an indication
of some education, I calculated upon meeting with a courteous reception.

"Sir," said I, "would you have the great
complaisance to give me the passport of
Madame R—? She is very ill, and it will
therefore take some time to convey her to
her residence."

"Sir," replied he cavalierly; "your lady
may wait."

Being thus disappointed, I replied that this was consulting his own ease. Immediately the other passengers, especially the ladies, who were present at this scene, expressed their regret, and the interest which they felt for the invalid lady. One word led to another, and one of the ladies observed, "We have now been waiting four hours;" upon which the officer exclaimed, "It is not true that you have been waiting four hours."

I lost patience at this impertinence, and exclaimed, "Nobody spoke to you, Sir."

"What does that mean?"

"That means that you have no right to mix in conversations that do not concern you."

"Who are you?"

I mentioned my name.

"Where do you serve?"

"Where you do not serve."

"I forbid you to go away without my permission."

Foreseeing that this permission would be delayed, I went away immediately; and on the following day was invited to wait on the chief of the police, Major-General Kakoschkin.

"Sir," said he; "your first step on *your return from abroad* has been characterized by a want of respect to the officers of the Government."

"I have been only to Reval," I replied, overturning by this one word the whole edifice of incendiary ideas which are supposed to be imbibed in foreign countries.

"Your permit mentions Helsingfors."

"Even if I had gone there, General, I should not have gone beyond the limits of the Russian empire."

"No matter whence you come, you ought to respect the functionaries."

"I assure you, General, that I am never wanting in respect towards those who merit it."

" And what did you say when you were asked where you served?"

"This question was perfectly superfluous; your officer had our passports in his hand, and might therefore have known precisely where I served; besides, I only answered what was quite correct; for, in truth, I do not serve where he serves."

"Do not you think that that is very offensive?"

"I have always thought, your Excellency, that every kind of service was equally honourable; but the manner in which we acquit ourselves in it imparts to it its dignity; and, if your officer has complained of my words because he took them for a reproach respecting the manner in which he performed his duty, I will not be so impolite as to contradict him on this point. Will you allow me to explain what passed between us?"

"I will not hear any excuse."

"You have, however, received his complaint."

"Yes; and I shall not show it to you."

"But I may have reasons for complaint on my side."

"Complaint? I desire, then, that you lay it before me in twenty-four hours."

"I can do it sooner." And I was about to withdraw when he cried—

"Where are you going?"

"What is your pleasure, General?"

"Go about your business."

Just as I was opening the door, he called out to the clerks in the chancery that they were not to draw up any kind of complaint for me.

Some hours afterwards I was visited by two of these gentlemen, who offered me their services on condition that I should not betray them.

I delivered to them a statement which I had drawn up; I paid one of them, and thought it unnecessary to give anything to the other; but as I held out my hand, he imagined that it contained a fee, and almost tore off the skin as if he expected to find a bank note beneath it. I afterwards met with one of these officials, who told me, with a most mysterious air, that M. Kakoschkin had required the Governor-General to have me put under the surveillance of the police. I thought that this man wished to fleece me anew, and thanked him for the interest which he testified for me. I, however, never learnt the result, or indeed heard anything more of the matter.

On another occasion, at the fête of Catherinenhof, where everybody is allowed to smoke, just as I was lighting my cigar, a police-officer, half drunk, came up to me, apparently in the act of striking me on the fingers, and said, "How do you dare to smoke in a place where the Imperial family intend to walk?" An officer of the guards, who was with me, saved me the trouble of being angry, for he warmly took my part;

but he could not discover the name of the officer, who observed a prudent silence.

One evening, as I was quitting the French theatre, and drew near towards the door, a cold wind met me, and accordingly I put on my hat just at the entrance of the corridor. The police-officer who was on the spot said, " Sir, you put on your hat too soon."

Another time my pelisse was stolen at a private residence. The master of the house immediately sent his servant to the police-office, where he was detained several hours, waiting for the return of the commissary. On the following day, the servant was again dispatched, and brought me the following answer: "Tell your master, that since he did not think fit to wait for me yesterday, I am not inclined to make any inquiries." I must confess that a suspicion afterwards crossed my mind that the servant himself might have been the thief, and, in that case, would naturally have invented the proceedings at the police-office.

One day, when I related a number of these petty vexations to a public officer, he answered, that I had really been unlucky, for that nothing of the kind had ever happened to himself. It is possible, in fact, that being destined to unveil the infamies of the Russian Government, it may have been the will of fate to make me know them by personal experience; but to prove that others are not exempt from similar annoyances, I will mention the following facts, which have come to my knowledge, among a thousand others.

The young Prince V * * * had kept a French mistress, on whom he had settled an annuity after his marriage. This lady subsequently resided in the street of Vonessenkaia, in St. Petersburg, and had the misfortune to please the police officer of that quarter. His assiduities having been rejected, his anger was excited, and he persisted in persecuting this unfortunate lady. The wretch bribed the grocer at the corner of the street, the porter of the house, and her own maid, to act as spies. The servant soon after was afflicted with sores on her body, in consequence of a malady brought on by a dissolute life. The police officer immediately informed against her mistress for having beaten her so severely as to inflict wounds. He obtained an order to arrest her, and presented himself to his victim, offering her two ways to escape persecution : either to yield to his wishes, or to pay 10,000 rubles, and, as she indignantly rejected this base proposal, he had her seized in her bed, and carried in her sheets to the police office, where she was entered on the list of prisoners. She wrote many letters to Count Benkendorf, who, however, was not in the habit of reading those which were addressed to him. She languished in a filthy dungeon, where she remained, till at length her maid, who was a serf in the government of Twer, impelled by remorse, went and confessed the whole to her lord, who succeeded in obtaining the deliverance of the innocent lady, but without procuring the punishment of the guilty.

A young man, on his wedding-day, hired some diamonds for his bride which were stolen during the night. He waited on the commissary of police, who, after having heard his complaint, opened his desk and showed him the jewels. The young man hastened to take them. " There are 6000 rubles to pay," said the commissary. The poor young man observed that, as he lived on his salary, he could not procure such a sum; upon which the commissary quietly locked the drawer which contained the diamonds: The bridegroom immediately hastened to General Kakoschkin, and gave him the particulars of what had just transpired.

" I have no such officers," said the chief of the police; and dismissed him with a haughty air.

A man took a robber in the very act, and
brought him to the police office. " Oh, that
is an old acquaintance," said the commissary, and let him go.

A certain physician had attended the
family of the commissary of the first district of St. Petersburg. The latter, on
asking him how he could recompense him
for his attendance, the physician replied,
" If you would do me a great pleasure, give
me the watch that is hanging up against
the wall." It was, in fact, the very watch
which had been stolen from him some time
previous, and had since remained in the
hands of the police.

Prince M * * * gave notice to the
police that he had been robbed of his cloak.
Some days afterwards an officer came to
inform him that all his endeavours to find
his cloak had been fruitless. The prince
went out with him into the antechamber,
and actually saw the man put on his
own cloak. He was amazed, but did not

make any remark to the obliging police officer, for it is this name by which the catchpoles are designated in Russia. General Kakoschkin, in particular, takes pleasure in so designating them even in the Russian language. He was desirous of obtaining for them the right of wearing epaulettes, but the Emperor has had the good sense to refuse it.

Count Benkendorf once lost 1000 rubles in bank assignats, and immediately acquainted the police of it. General Kakoschkin instantly had them recovered; but, lo and behold, the count's valet de chambre, on brushing his clothes, found the sum in the lining of his great coat! The money was restored to General Kakoschkin, but he was not removed from his office; on the contrary, he had reason to be grateful to the minister, who rendered him an important service on the following occasion:—

M. Perowsky, Minister of the Interior, being desirous to regulate the sale of provisions, caused the journal of a butcher at St. Petersburg to be seized; in this ledger there was a daily entry of the quantities of meat which he delivered gratis to the police officers. The minister denounced this abuse to the Emperor, who instructed Count Benkendorf to institute an inquiry, but recommended him at the same time to screen his favourite aid-de-camp, Kakoschkin, in case he should be found to be too deeply implicated. The fatal book was soon brought to M. Perowsky, with the request that he would put his seal upon it, a formality which he had omitted. This being done, it was found that the butcher had not given anything to the police, for, of course, the book in question had been exchanged for another, perfectly similar, with the omission of the items to the police, and thus the affair dropped.

A person who was travelling in one of the carriages on the Paulowsky Railway, had his pocket picked. On arriving at Petersburg he lodged his complaint in the faithful hands of a police officer; I say faithful, because they never give up what they have once taken. The officer required witnesses, asking whether any one had seen the thief in the act of stealing. " I did," replied an old man. " And who are you?" demanded the officer. " M. ——, Privy Councillor of State." "I beg your Excellency's pardon." " What is there to pardon? insolence is your trade."

M. Roidofnikin, head of the Asiatic department, was put into the guard-house for having crossed a parade; when the police were about to enter his name in in the book, he mentioned his titles. "Why did you not speak before?" said the Commissary. " You did not ask me anything," he replied; and was immediately dismissed with all the respect due to his rank.

A veteran officer one day mentioned in company at St. Petersburg, that it was

an error to suppose that duelling was prohibited in Russia; for that he once had
the misfortune to kill an officer in his
regiment without having been called to
account for it. Walls have ears in this
country, and his words were soon reported
to the police, than they secured him who had
uttered them, and then commenced a search
for the person whom he affirmed that he
had killed. They soon discovered an individual of the same name who had served
in the army, but had afterwards entered
a civil employment. A colonel of gens-
d'armes waited on him.

"Your name is ——?" said he.

"At your service."

"You were acquainted with, or are acquainted with M. ——?"

"We were of the same regiment, but as
I was an officer and he an ensign, we were
but slightly acquainted with each other."

"Can you tell me, Sir, how you pass your
day?"

"Nothing is more easy. I pass my days as I pass the weeks, months, and years. I go daily to my desk at the post-office, every Saturday to the baths, and every Sunday to mass."

"Would you be so obliging as to undress before me?"

"Why so, if you please?"

"I cannot tell you, but I must positively see you undressed."

"I am a particularly modest man, Sir, and you will really oblige me by not insisting upon so extraordinary a demand."

"I am extremely sorry, Sir, but it must be; I dare not take a refusal."

"Well, if it must be, it must; but I can only think of one expedient: you must come on Saturday to the bath, and then your curiosity may be satisfied, whatever strange motive gives rise to it."

The Colonel was punctual to the rendezvous, and after having examined the body of the ex-officer, he told him that his ancient comrade had boasted of having killed him, and the police thought that he might at least have wounded him, and had directed him to ascertain the truth. He was delighted at being able to report to his superiors, that there was no foundation for the assertion.

General D. formed a *liaison* with a French actress, who had previously been acquainted with a young man, who owed her three thousand rubles. She requested the General to obtain this sum for her. Her former lover was in fact arrested at the fair of Nischneinovogrod, without in the least suspecting the cause, and was brought by gens-d'arms in a post carriage to St. Petersburg, where General D. ordered him to pay the debt in twenty-four hours, which he was obliged to do with the best grace he could.

M. Michalowsky, an advocate at the tribunal of Warsaw, had been implicated in the Polish revolution, and the third section of the chancery of the Emperor—such is

the official name of the secret police in
Russia—gave orders to arrest him and convey him to Viatka, where he was to pass
two years in exile. In his stead, another
M. Michalowsky, a notary of Wilna, was
arrested and sent to Viatka. When he
arrived there, he protested, and the error
was acknowledged, but he was nevertheless
compelled to atone for the fault of another,
and to suffer the penalty incurred by his
namesake for the whole term, because
Count Benkendorf would never confess his
mistake to the Emperor, and preferred to
let an innocent man bear the punishment.

This is by no means an isolated fact of
the kind, and puts me in mind of another
which happened during the reign of Paul I.
That emperor was absolutely resolved that
a certain criminal should be brought before
him, whom the Governor-General of St.
Petersburg could not possibly discover.
Being unable to make his master forget the
matter, and dreading his anger, Count

Pahlen caused a poor German to be arrested, just as he was coming from his own country, and utterly unsuspicious of evil, appeared at the barrier of the capital. His nostrils were slit, he received the knout, and was sent to Siberia.

The Emperor Alexander caused justice to be done him, and indemnified him, at his request, by granting him liberty to import German files, duty free, into Russia.

The expulsion of M. Kalergi likewise does little honour to the Russian Government. It is this Government which, by its agents, has sowed discords in Greece, in the hope that that kingdom would thereby fall into its hands; it alone excited the late revolution, thinking that, after the expulsion of the reigning family, Greece would be obliged to place herself under the protection of Russia; and when the movement produced a totally different effect from that which it expected, and gave a constitution

to Greece, the Russian Government wished
to clear itself of the part which it had
taken, by ordering the brother of the Greek
General to quit the empire. "If you insist
that I should tell you wherefore you are
sent away," said Count Benkendorf, "it is
because the Emperor thinks the conduct of
your brother unworthy towards himself and
unworthy towards his king."

"Your Excellency," replied M. Kalergi,
"I do not allow anybody the right to call
my brother's conduct unworthy. A man
who has served his country twenty years,
who was covered with wounds, who has
been a prisoner among the Turks, where his
ears were cut off, cannot be other than an
honourable man."

"Sir," replied Count Benkendorf, "after
using such language, you have only to pack
up your things, and set out at once."

King Otho on being informed of the manœuvre, cried, "I do not comprehend why
the Emperor interferes in my affairs; M.

Kalergi is my Adjutant-General, and besides this, my best friend."

M. J * * *, at a supper in Florence, on Easter eve, was so imprudent as to take out his watch and say, "At this hour"—it was midnight—" the tricoloured flag floats on the walls of the Kremlin, and a new conspiracy has triumphed!" His own uncle informed against him to Count Benkendorf. On reaching Vienna, M. J * * * was sent to St. Petersburg, and there gave the names of innocent persons, as having taken a part in the plot, which had no existence, save in his own imagination. The Government became convinced that all his depositions were fictions, yet, nevertheless, summoned the persons whom he had designated. One of them, M. R * *, was torn by gensd'armes from his quiet retreat on his estate; another, M. F * *, was summoned from Naples, and having proved that he had never known M. J * *, was told that he might go back again. M. J * * himself, after having passed six months in the dungeons of Schlusselburg, was sent in the garb of a felon to Viatka. His uncle had been ordered to make a domiciliary visit to the residence of his own sister, the mother of the young man, and while he was conversing with her in the drawing-room, his agents forced open the bureau in the adjoining apartment; but they found only papers which were perfectly harmless. This *excellent* relative then presented himself at Court, to receive the reward of all his villanies; but not content with the remuneration given him for having *unmasked his monster of a nephew,* he quitted the service, and having returned to his native country published a book against Russia, which caused some sensation at the time. This is what may be expected from those zealous servants who regard neither good faith, family ties, nor country, and in whom, nevertheless, the Russian Government is so infatuated as to place its confidence. The

family of M. J * *, indignant at the treatment which they had received, and fearful
of further persecution, sold their estates in
Russia, and quitted the country.

A Russian nobleman, Count K * *, who
was living in retirement on his estate at
Pskow, having gone to St. Petersburg to
present himself at Court, was overwhelmed
with astonishment at being reprimanded by
the Czar, for some words which he had spoken
when no person except his son was present.
After his return home one of his friends was
entering on a political conversation, when
he instantly imposed silence upon him,
telling him to distrust his son who was
in the room.

The secret police of Russia has its ramifi-
cations both among the upper and the lower
classes of society. Nay, many ladies notoriously act as spies, and are yet received
in society and have company at home;
even men who are stigmatized with the
same reputation, are not the worse treated

on that account, and bear their disgrace with a kind of haughty dignity. There is not a single regiment of the guard which has not several spies; in the theatres, and especially in the French theatre, there are often a larger number of spies than of mere spectators. In short, there are so many spies that people imagine they see them everywhere, an apprehension which admirably serves the turn of the Government.

As it is impossible to be on one's guard against everybody, those persons who are not inclined to be suspicious, soon lose all their terror, and confounding spies with men of honour, suffer themselves to be drawn into confidential conversations, which often prove very dangerous to them; the majority, on the contrary, distrusting everybody, feel themselves shackled, and are so reserved in their intercourse, that it is impossible to conceive any conversation more insipid than that which is carried on in the drawing-rooms of St. Petersburg.

Private correspondence bears the same stamp, in consequence of the precaution taken by the Goverment. The post-office has a secret department, whose special business it is to open letters; those of suspected persons are always opened, as well as the greater part of those coming from abroad. Of the remainder about a tenth part are opened.

Spies are divided into several classes. Some receive salaries, others act in consequence of agreements, or in expectation of the liberality of the Government. Some, again, are mere complaisant parasites, or gossips, of whose services the Government is glad to avail itself; while others are inflammatory agents, who fill a more or less distinguished position in society. The following is the portrait of one of them. He is a councillor of state, the father of a family, and a man of large fortune. At the time when the Polish revolution had just broken out, he had an evening party, to which he invited several inexperienced young men. As it was his trade to sound public opinion, he of course turned the conversation into this channel; greatly blamed the Russian Government, saying that its conduct to the Poles could not be characterized, and uttered these words in a manner which was calculated to catch somebody in his net. M. B * * *, Secretary of State, indignant at such conduct, went boldly up to him, and, addressing him in a loud voice, said, "Pray, Sir, will you, who are an authority in the Russian language, be so good as to tell me how to translate the French words, '*Agent provacateur ?*' "

There are spies in uniform; these are the gens-d'armes: spies in disguise; these are the police officers: fashionable spies; travelling spies, who reside abroad, or are sent on special missions: certain functionaries are spies ex-officio. For instance; the governors of provinces are bound to make periodical reports respecting those persons

who are under surveillance, or who deserve
to be so; and ambassadors have the superintendence over their countrymen. The
following fact will fully explain this truth:

In the year 1826, after the revolt at St.
Petersburg, orders were sent to the ministers residing at foreign courts to watch the
conduct and political opinions of their countrymen, and to send reports for the information of the Government. Count St.
* * *, the Russian Ambassador at Naples,
immediately wrote that one of the persons
attached to his legation kept company with
the most violent carbonari in the city.
This same gentleman had just registered
the instructions which his chief had received,
when the latter advised him to depart for
St. Petersburg immediately. It is easy to
conceive the misgivings of the poor secretary; at Vienna, M. Tatistschef consoled
him as well as he could, but his terror
increased when he reached the Russian
frontier. It was night; tremblingly he

awoke the officer, who instantly began to turn over the leaves of a large book, constantly repeating his name, which he had just asked, and every repetition of which made the secretary tremble. At last he ventured to say, "What book is that which you are examining so carefully?" "Sir," replied the officer, "it is such a book that whoever is inscribed in it is not permitted either to go out or come in. I do not find your name in it." He was thankful enough to be delivered from this first danger, but his mind was not completely relieved till he saw Count Nesselrode, who allowed that his superior had been too suspicious, and gave him a post at Constantinople.

That part of the Russian legislation, the execution of which is especially intrusted to the police, contains regulations too curious not to be reported. Here we may dispense with all comments, and confine ourselves to copying a few extracts at random from Vol. XIV. of the Swod. The sixteenth article is as follows:—

"Drunkenness is prohibited to each and to all." Art. 219 directs that, "Whoever passes more time in the course of a year in a state of drunkenness than in a state of sobriety, shall be confined in a house of correction till he amends." Art. 227 prescribes a fine equivalent to half a day's support in the house of correction on any man who shall enter a public bath for the women, and on any woman who shall enter a public bath for the men. Those who may be unable to pay the fine are obliged to heat the stoves in the house of correction.

Women who have contracted diseases by a dissolute course of life are taken into the hospital, and when cured, are sent back to their homes. The wives of soldiers are delivered to their husbands, who are obliged sign a written engagement to restrain them in future ; and the wives of serfs are sent to their lords, who are called upon to pay the expenses of cure, and in case they refuse to do so, the women are sent to Siberia.

The 3rd Article is in the following terms :—" All ought to be respectful at church, and enter with devotion and without constraint."

The 7th Article orders people to stop before the holy images, as decorum and the sanctity of the place require.

The 8th Article commands the " worshippers not to talk during divine service, nor to change their seats, or disturb the attention of the faithful by any word, action, or gesture, but to deport themselves with humility, silence, and respect."

Article 13 directs that " even those shall be sent before the tribunal, who merely go to church by constraint, whatever may be their rank."

Article 24 says " Every orthodox person

is to confess and to receive the Sacrament at least once a year, after the age of seven years."

Articles 33 and 34 are intended to efface the remains of idolatry and of Pagan traditions.

Articles 35 and 36 prohibit false predictions and necromancy.

Article 46 is of the following tenor:— "Persons born in the orthodox religion, and those who are converted to it, are prohibited from embracing another religion, even though it be Christian." Those who commit this crime are brought to trial: their orthodox serfs are placed under guardianship, and they cannot reside on their own estates.

Chapter IX.

NICHOLAS I.

When we visit the gallery of the portraits of the Romanoffs, the eye dwells with pleasure on the manly and national features of Peter I., whose defects were those of his country and his age, and whose intellectual qualities were those of genius. Further on we rejoice to trace them in Anna I., whose vices we pardon for the sake of her uncle, even if we do not attribute them to her unworthy courtier, the Kourlander Biren; but all resemblance to the Great Czar is lost in Peter III., and the Russian asks, " Whence did he come?" He gazes upon these fea-

R 2

tures, and this air, and they appear to him to be those of a German, and he mutters the name of Holstein Gottolf! His mouth will never accommodate itself to this dissonance; the Russian will never familiarize himself with the idea that he is governed by Germans. Great care is taken not to disclose to him that his Sovereigns are of foreign origin, and every thing is done to preserve the beloved and revered name of the Romanoffs. The word *nemetz*, German, is odious to the Russian; its signification is *dumb*, and it was formerly the general appellation which designated all foreigners, even him who called himself the Sclavonian, or *l'homme de la parole**.

But to return to our gallery; after all, Peter III. is the grandson of Peter I., and the Russian bears an affection without limit

---

* This antipathy of the Russians to the Germans, is participated by the Poles, who have a proverb, "As long as light shall be light, the Pole will not be the brother of the German."

and without end to his Czars, their grandsons, and their great grandsons.   But since
what time does a mother transmit the name
of her ancestors to her children, and why
are the Holstein Gottolfs, Romanoffs ?

Let us pass over Peter III.; after him
comes his wife Catherine II., and the Russian, remembering that he owes to her the
Crimea and Lithuania, conceives a friendship
for this powerful woman, whom he endows
with his favorite name of *matuschka,*
mother.   But at the sight of Paul I. he is
petrified.   These features do not touch his
heart, they are not those of Catherine, nor
of Peter III., still less are they those of the
Romanoffs.   The infirmity of the chief of
the Holstein branch is well known, and the
order given by the Senate to Catherine, to
admit Soltikow to the Imperial bed, was a
cruel order, if that nobleman resembled her
son.   How could the Senate commit such a
blunder as to make an offer like this to a
woman who was so good a judge as Cathe-

rine! What a singular sport of nature! Paul exactly resembled a Finnlander of Strelna, and his red hair, his pug nose, and his proverbial obstinacy gave rise to more than a suspicion of some strange substitution. The Senate ordered that Catherine should have a son, but what, if she had only a daughter, and that daughter still-born? The need which the country had of an heir to the throne, the ambition of Catherine to retain power, the proximity of the orphan house, where there are so many children of Finnland, give ground for suppositions which may be realities, and we are tempted to believe that the child of some honest Finn was substituted for a still-born daughter of the Empress; for, once more, why this pug nose and this red hair, and above all, whence the invincible hatred of Catherine to her son Paul?

Puschkin delighted to represent the nationality of the reigning family in a very eccentric manner; he took a goblet and

poured into it a glass of pure red wine in
honour of Peter I., whose Russian origin
could not be disputed, and added a glass of
water for the father of Peter III.; here he
ought to have stopped, and to have turned
the goblet upside down, but, faithful to the
principles of the Russian Government,
which makes the Gottolfs pass for Romanoffs, he poured out another glass of water
in honour of Catherine II., a Princess of
Anhalt.   This time he should, perhaps,
have added a glass of wine, but fearing
to compromise himself, he proceeded and
poured a fourth glass of water for Maria
Feodorovna, the mother of Nicholas I.;
then a fifth for the reigning Empress, by
which time the liquor was so faintly tinged
with red, that he raised a general laugh by
asking the company to decide whether it
was wine or water, and whether, by comparison, the present Czars were Russians or
Germans?

Maria Feodorovna, the wife of Paul, a

Princess of Wurtemburg, was as much distinguished for her personal beauty and mental qualifications, as Paul was for his deficiency in both these respects. The children of this marriage were Alexander, who inherited the personal beauty as well as the mind of his mother; Constantine, who was an exact counterpart of his father, ugly in person and wayward in disposition; Nicholas, who can boast only of personal beauty; and lastly, Michael, who is neither very good nor very handsome.

Next to her usurpation, which was a crime, according the words of Nicholas himself, who was astonished that she should be called Great, after her licentiousness, history must reproach Catherine II. with the bad education which she gave her children. She detested Paul, as a son unworthy of her, and could not reconcile herself to the idea that he was to succeed her on the throne ; she consequently neglected his education, which, added to his extravagant character, was the cause of his violent death. Catherine devoted all her care to her grandson Alexander; but his education was too alien to the manners of his country and to the genius of his nation. He always wanted courage to carry into effect what his mind had recognized to be just and useful. Equally weak and good, equally crafty and liberal, he could only scatter among the people germs of liberty which his successor has delighted in destroying or eradicating.

Struck with the troubles which his brother had bequeathed to him, Nicholas imagined that, in order to reign well, it would suffice to act in every case the opposite part which Alexander would have taken; to persecute liberty to the utmost, to endeavour to be as national as his predecessor had been foreign, as orthodox as the other had been catholic. Thus he disappointed the hopes and the expectations which he had given on his accession to the throne, in his

several manifestoes, wherein he proclaimed
that his reign should be in all respects the
continuation and counterpart of his la-
mented brother's.

The education of Nicholas was as deficient as that of his other brothers, who
were not destined to the throne*.

During the whole of Alexander's reign,
he did not rise above the rank of General
of Division, and he contracted in that post
a narrowness of mind, and a predilection for
the military service which he has since carried to a ridiculous excess. He is so ignorant that he writes *mné* (to me) without an

---

* The Grand Duke Constantine could not write two
words in Russian, although he wrote French tolerably
well. I have heard that a student of Moscow was sent
into banishment because, in a collection of autographs
which he had formed, there was one of the Grand Duke
Michael, which was signed " Benevolent Michael,"
Benevolent, in Russia, with an accent. It is notorious
that most of the Russian ministers cannot write their
language correctly, and they have not all the excuse of
knowing too many foreign languages, which is the case
of the Princes of the Imperial family.

accent, which is equivalent to writing Nicholas in French without an *s*; and his despotism is such, that no statesman has hitherto dared to tell him of this fault in spelling which he so frequently commits. It is astonishing that no Russian author has yet taken it into his head to abolish that unhappy letter, were it only to pay his court to the Sovereign.

The favourite and daily reading of Nicholas is the *Abeille du Nord,* the most insignificant journal that ever was published in the two hemispheres. His Majesty, nevertheless, takes pleasure in it, and writes remarks in pencil on the margin. On one of these papers, which are all carefully deposited in the Hermitage, we read that the names of the tribunals of the governments of districts, &c., ought to be printed in large capitals!

The ship of the line called " Russia," is an overwhelming proof of the despotism of Nicholas. On visiting the vessel while on the

stocks, he thought that there was not sufficient room to walk about, and accordingly
commanded the space to be enlarged; even
enforcing his opinion against that of competent judges. By consequence, this vessel
is the very worst sailer in the whole Russian
navy, and is very seldom employed.

When he takes it into his head to command the movement of a ship, which
he does almost every time he goes to
sea, the captain of the vessel takes care
always to keep behind him, in order, by
counter signals, to prevent the strict execution of his Majesty's orders, which would
inevitably lead to the loss of the ship and
its august passenger.

His cannon shot at Shumla is the parody
of Napoleon at Montereau. An artillery
officer thought that the mark was too distant—but Nicholas ordered him to fire,
and the ball fell short.

The campaign in Turkey has imposed
silence on the courtiers, who had always made

it a point to endeavour to extol the military talents of Nicholas. We must do him the justice to say, that he has since had the good sense to relinquish making war, and to confine himself to presiding at reviews. It is impossible for any man to command with more grace and elegance of manner; his voice rises above every other; and it would be difficult to exercise the troops better than he does. He is admired for his quick-sightedness—for the facility with which he distinguishes, even in the most distant ranks, the slightest defect in the dress of a soldier or an officer; not a button or a buckle escapes his vigilance. This is a talent possessed by all the Imperial Family; and, on observing his penetrating look, philanthropists have often said with a sigh, that if this capacity had been applied to objects more important, more worthy of the attention of a Sovereign, the country would have derived valuable advantages from it.

"Stand firmly," said Nicholas, one day, to General Muravief, before the whole diplomatic body, who were present at the review at Schlusselburg, "I am going to beat you."

"Sire," replied the intrepid warrior, "I have never been beaten in war."

The general in fact beat his Majesty completely, and Nicholas never forgave him.

"What do you think of my disbanded men?" asked he, when he came to review his corps.

"Sire," replied Muravief, with too much frankness, "you should have seen them a fortnight ago, when they arrived from their homes; they then looked like a troop of beggars."

The Emperor revenged himself cruelly. On the following day, when he saw the corps commanded by Muravief approach, he said to him, "Your corps has the appearance of a troop of beggars." The brave general

quitted the service, and the country suffered doubly by not having in Nicholas I.
a Frederick II.

What, in fact, are these soldiers (*Licen-
cies*) but one of the most unhappy concep-
tions that can be imagined; the truth may
not be spoken at all times, and every
fact must not be revealed; but when the
country suffers in consequence, it cannot be
proclaimed too loudly.

The Emperor has reduced the active
service of the soldier from twenty-five to
twenty-two years in the regiments of the
Line; and from twenty-two to fifteen years
in the Guards; and during the remainder
of the time, the soldiers are liable to be
called out, are obliged to attend the reviews
every year, and, in case of war, to return to
their standards; but the principal thing
has been overlooked, namely, to provide
for their support. Having ceased to be
good villagers when they entered the service, they cease to be good soldiers when

they quit it: useless to the army, they become a burden to their districts; and finding it difficult to procure a livelihood, they excite trouble and discontent in the rural population. The landowners fear them, the peasants reject them, and the Government has thus created a class of dangerous and warlike petty landholders, instead of well-disciplined soldiers.

A quality which is most generally allowed to Nicholas, is that strength of character which it is affirmed he manifested in a high degree on the very day of his accession to the throne. But it appears, nevertheless, that he with difficulty could be persuaded to shew himself to the insurgents, and it is certain that before leaving the palace he prayed to God with fervour. Was this piety, or was it fear? He is deemed quite enough of a dissembler to display the one and to conceal the other. In the square itself he was observed to be pale and trembling, while his satellites cried

"All is lost," at the moment when all was going on as well as possible. The insurgents having no military chief, remained inactive the whole day, and Nicholas did not take courage till the evening, when twelve pieces of cannon were brought against 1300 men; whereas, there were more than 13,000 faithful troops!! The insurgents were fired upon at a distance of a hundred paces. The guns were then turned upon the people along the street of the galleys and the quays. A woman who was at this moment looking out of her window, had her head carried off by a cannon-ball. "What a melancholy commencement of a reign," exclaimed Nicholas, on his return to the palace. His former tutor, Baron D——, one day asked him how he had acquired so much firmness, as he had always known him to be so weak. "My crown was at stake," he answered, "and it was well worth while for me to appear courageous." "I only did my duty," said he to the Marquis Custine, in a strange fit of modesty.

An official journal has related, that meeting in the palace a company of the insurgent grenadiers, who did not return his salutation, Nicholas told them that they had mistaken their way, and that they had better go and join the mutineers in Isaac-square. The courtiers go further, and say that he had commanded the service of the guards in the palace, had made them point their muskets at him, had confronted their looks, and had made them lay down their arms.

When the rebellion was at length quashed, and the soldiers of the regiment of Moscow led the prisoners away, bound and handcuffed, the Grand Duke Michael appeared for the first time on that day, and reproached them in the coarsest terms; one of them having kept on his cap, received a blow in his face by the fist of his Imperial Highness*.

---

* The soldier who was an eye-witness of this scene

After the victory, Nicholas exercised clemency; the penal commission had condemned the principal conspirators to be quartered : the Czar commuted their punishment for that of the gallows. The gallows was then unknown in Russia, and the honour of introducing it was reserved to Nicholas. No hangman was to be found in the empire, and one was accordingly obtained from Sweden. In the course of the executions the ropes broke, and three of the sufferers fell to the ground, still alive. A messenger was instantly despatched to Nicholas to inquire what steps were to be taken. "Hang them again*!"

related it to me on his death-bed, manifesting the indignation of a true soldier, not to say of a real gentleman.

* The King of Denmark displayed more humanity on a somewhat similar occasion, having stopped the punishment of a criminal just as he had laid his head on the scaffold; he afterwards found that he had well deserved death, but he nevertheless pardoned him, in consideration of the terrors which he had already endured.

was his laconic answer. Muravief re-
mounted his horse, saying in French, "*Dans
se f—— pays on ne sais seulement pas
pendre un homme!*" Ryléiéf said that,
having been an officer, he ought to have
been shot.

After all these executions, a poet wrote
an immortal stanza: "He had scarcely
mounted the throne when he showed his
character; he erected five gallows, and sent
an hundred people into exile!"

Ryléiéf, the Russian Chénier, was among
those who were hanged; the flower of the
Russian nobility was cut down without
mercy; and what did the conspirators aim
at? A constitution; which Alexander
himself had ardently desired, and when
giving one to Poland, had expressed his
deep regret at not being able to do the
same for his own country. Who knows,
perhaps there were among the conspirators
men who engaged in the plot only to pay
their court to their Sovereign?

The ex-Ambassador Markopff was on his death-bed when his nephew came to relate the details of the revolt, and ended his recital by saying, "At length it is just as in France!" "You mistake," replied his uncle; "*there* cobblers would fain be princes: *here* princes would be cobblers!" If this were not a reproach, it might be a commendation.

One day the Emperor sent for one of his generals; he was quite beside himself. "Have you any knowledge of this pamphlet?" inquired he eagerly, giving him the draught of a constitution for Russia, which had just been discovered among the papers of Constantine.

"No, Sire," replied the general; "and your Majesty, can you have yourself been ignorant of it?"

"Could I otherwise have judged the conspirators of the 14th, as I did," cried the Emperor, quite bewildered; "tell me, who drew it up?"

The general could only give him the name of the person who copied it,—Prince B* * *.

The fate of the victims of a noble illusion, of those whom the Russians themselves designate only by the name of *unfortunate,* was not alleviated in consequence of this discovery. The happy events which took place in the circle of the Imperial family, and enterprises which had need of divine aid, led, however, to some amelioration of their condition. Thus, on the delaration of war against Turkey, Nicholas, as he came out of the church of Casen, ordered Count Benkendorf to release from their chains the persons condemned for the part they had acted in 1826. But at the expiration of the time for which they were condemed to hard labour, the Count wished to assign them the principal towns of Siberia for their residence, "in order," he said, "that they might be the more easily watched." "What!" cried Nicholas, "would you let them enjoy their lives, in the great centre of the population?" and, taking a map of Siberia, he marked with his own hand the most desert and the most remote part of that dreary country, as the places where they should reside. Accordingly all those unfortunate men suffered even more by the treatment in the colonies than by their hard labour, which in itself was not severe, and moreover, at least afforded them the comfort of living together.

It is true, that on the first complaint against the person who had the care of the prisoners at Nertschink, and who had received them in his dressing-gown, and said, "What have you been plotting? you will soon be cured of your turbulent humours here;" Nicholas cashiered him, and put in his place General Leparsky, a good and enlightened man, formerly colonel of the regiment of chasseurs on horseback, which bore his name, and with whom the exiles had every reason to be satisfied.

We will here mention another fact, which does honour to Nicholas. Prince Obolensky, one of the conspirators, was his personal enemy; he had answered every question in French, and even went so far as to address him by no other title than that of *Monsieur*. The Commission, to please the Emperor, condemned the Prince to death; Nicholas struck out his name, saying, "It is a meanness!"

But the colonel of a regiment of Moscow, with whom Nicholas had had some differences in the service, was worse treated than the others, and had the smallest share of the rare and restricted favours of his former colonel.

"What has your Emperor done to you?" said Nicholas, to one of the conspirators, when he did them the honour to examine them himself; "We had not an Emperor," they replied; "we have had two, one was your brother, and the other Arakhtschcief;" and as he continued in this strain, the Grand

Duke Michael, who was present, exclaimed, "That man should have his mouth stopped with a bayonet." "You inquired just now," said the accused, "why we wanted a constitution; it is that such things may not be said."

His first success emboldened Nicholas, and rendered him still more intractable. He also proceeded with more resolution on less important occasions.

At the time of the revolt, during the cholera, he drove in an open carriage to the Haymarket, in St. Petersburg. When he arrived there, he told an assemblage of the populace to pray to God; and they took off their caps. He told them to fall upon their knees; and they did so. Accordingly the Emperor has been represented on this memorable occasion in water colours and in oil; but it is forgotten that he addressed the assemblage in these words: "Are you Frenchmen?" Neither is it said that the avenues were guarded by the military.

At Novgorod he appeared accompanied only by Orloff, and armed merely with a sword among the revolted colonists, and made them return to order by an energetic oath. "An oath," says the Russian, "is butter to the gruel, salt to the sauce, and on that day the Holstein was equal to a Romanoff." But the executions which followed this insurrection, equalled in cruelty the excesses which had been committed by the insurgents. If the colonists flayed some of their officers alive, there were some among them who received as many as 12,000 stripes with the rod.

One day, as Nicholas was exercising the troops, a storm arose; the Emperor turned pale, drew his hat over his eyes, and raised his voice:—*Ne svoï brat ne schoutit*, said the soldiers maliciously, which may be translated by these words: "He who is on high is not one of us, there is no joking with Him."

Obstinacy and cruelty cannot be called

strength of character: a man of a really strong mind, and who is conscious of his strength, is naturally mild; Nicholas was as weak as he was cruel before he became Emperor. He tore off the mustachios and whiskers of the soldiers of his brigade, and trembled in the ante-chamber of Alexander, not daring either to go forward or to enter; he and Michael pushed each other, each attempting to make the other go first into the Emperor's cabinet.

A soldier of the engineers was condemned to run the gauntlet. Nicholas, who was then a colonel of engineers, wrote down a greater number of blows than the man was sentenced to receive, upon which M. P * * * *, his aid-de-camp, observed that it was useless to make any alteration in the sentence, for it was very uncertain whether the unfortunate culprit would not die under the infliction, without any addition. Nicholas yielded to this argument, but what most astonished his aid-de-camp was, that he spoke of the matter as something totally indifferent. Nero wept when signing a sentence of death.

We must attribute to a want of knowledge, as much as to a want of energy, the failure of the laudable plans which Nicholas has conceived since his accession to the throne. He was anxious to abolish the *tschinns,* to give publicity to the proceedings of the tribunals, and he recoiled at the bare word advocates, whom it would have been necessary to appoint. It is more through ignorance than through fear of the nobility that he suffers the project for the emancipation of the serfs to remain a dead letter.

Nicholas, annoyed at his German origin, does his best to pass for a Russian; thus he often calls the Empress by the name of Baba (a peasant's wife). One day, as she was going with him to the barracks of the Prosbrajensky regiment, he said to the soldiers, "I think this is the first time since

Elizabeth, that a *Baba* Czarine visits the barracks."

He has the pretension not only to equal, but to surpass Peter the Great. He would appear more national than Peter, and retain the usages which he had violently proscribed. "I have seen you with a beard," he observed to a merchant, "why have you shaved it? we ought not to abandon the customs of our forefathers." Then, by a strange contradiction he issued a ukase in 1837, forbidding the civil officers to wear mustachios, or beards, in the *Jewish or French fashion*. He aimed at wit, and forgot that, while Peter shaved the beard of barbarism, Nicholas shaves that of civilization. On the other hand, the mustachio was ordered for the whole army*.

The Emperor returning from a journey, came home with a slight mustachio. The Empress complimented him on this innova-

* Till that time it had been worn only by the Light Cavalry.

tion, and expressed a wish that he would retain it; to please her, he caused it to be adopted in the army. "I have opposed it," said the Grand Duke Michael, "but since the the Emperor positively wishes it, I will let my mustachios grow an ell in length;" and he kept his word, and set the example to the courtiers.

What can be more national than the head dress *à la jeune France,* which was likewise called *à la Moujik;* but it was sufficient that it was adopted at Paris and the Court, for Nicholas to turn it to ridicule. One day, meeting with M. Jakovlef wearing his hair and dress in the French fashion, the Emperor signed him to approach; ordered him to get into his carriage, and drove him to the palace, where he presented him to the Empress. "I present to you," said he, "the most elegant man in my empire!" Then turning to the young man, he cried: "You may go!" and, after having scratched his face, he ordered him to go and be shaved. This anecdote was circulated a long time by the courtiers, as an instance of the Emperor's humour, but when they saw that their hearers shrugged their shoulders, they attempted to deny it, when it was too late.

In imitation of the Czar, a lady of rank one day sent for a French hairdresser at St. Petersburg. He was introduced into the drawing-room, and the mistress of the house presenting him to the company, said, "See, ladies and gentlemen, this is a *coiffeur à la moujik.*" The hairdresser who related this circumstance to me, added, that he was tempted to show them something else, but that he had been deterred by the example of his comrade at Moscow, who was mercilessly flogged by the servants of a Russian prince, before whom he had ventured to appear without a great-coat at the moment when his Excellency and his lady had entered the shop.

Nicholas was less fortunate with Count

Samoilof; his wig, which had lately arrived from Paris, greatly displeased him, and he caused him to be represented on the stage of Moscow. The Count requested the actor to call upon him, complimented him on his talent, and presented him with three diamond buttons, with the proceeds of which he purchased a house in the suburbs of the city.

Next to Peter the Great, Napoleon is the hero whom Nicholas wishes to resemble, and if he does not succeed, it is assuredly not for want of good will. In default of great victories, he imitates him in certain peculiarities of manner. A soldier in the Caucasus having blown up a fort which was on the point of being taken by the Circassians, the Emperor ordered that the name of the brave man should be called over in his regiment, and that a grenadier should answer in his stead, "Dead for the glory of the Russian arms!" We will not here institute any parallel, out of respect for the great man; we will select one fact from the life of Buonaparte. An author wrote a virulent pamphlet against him; Napoleon gave him epaulettes, saying, " Use your sword for me, as you have used your pen against me." Compared with this, behold Nicholas going about at twilight to examine the booksellers' stalls, to see whether he can find the *Memoires d'un Maître d'Armes,* by Alexander Dumas; and when he sees them in the hands of the Prince of Darmstadt, who had lately arrived at St. Petersburg, exclaiming, "Know, that prohibited books are not to be read in my dominions!"

Another time he saw *Paroles d'un Croyant,* in the hands of the heir to the crown, and finding that it came from Bellizard's library, he caused him to be prosecuted. The man escaped by paying a heavy fine, but the words, "Bookseller to the Court" disappeared from his shop.

Civilisation is the mortal enemy of Ni-

cholas, and liberty is the bugbear; hence,
France, which represents both, is the un-
varying object of his animosity. The relations of that country with Russia, which
were so friendly during the restoration,
have become much estranged since the revolution. On the accession of Louis-Philippe,
Nicholas exclaimed, that "he would rather
have one of Napoleon's soldiers on the
throne." When the news of the July revolution reached St. Petersburg, Nicholas
addressed the French Ambassador in these
words, "Your Bourbons are ninnies: they
have got themselves driven from France for
the third time." Then, shutting himself up
with Prince Lieven, he dictated to him an
order to all Russians to quit Paris in
twenty-four hours; and another, forbidding
vessels bearing the tri-coloured flag to enter
the Russian ports. A fortnight after, the
Minister of Finance represented to him
that commerce was impeded in consequence
of this prohibition; "Well, then, let it be

withdrawn," said he, with perfect coolness. His conduct towards Louis-Philippe has always been brutal: that of Louis-Philippe on the other hand has been distinguished by courtesy, and has invariably been delicate and obliging. Everybody knows the haughty reply of the Czar to the affectionate letter in which Louis-Philippe informed him of his accession to the throne. Subsequently he withdrew his Ambassador, and sent a mere Chargé d'Affaires in his stead. It has been said that this was only a measure of economy, and that the same had been done with respect to England and Austria. But Messieurs Brunow and Medem are Ministers Plenipotentiary, and Mr. Kisselef is merely a Chargé d'Affaires. "France," said the Emperor, "is not a Power worthy to have one of my Ambassadors."

Who has suffered by this measure? In the first place, the Russians, who are now no longer represented in France as they ought to be; and whence does such presumption arise? " I am able," said Nicholas to Pahlen, when he appointed him to the post of Ambassador to Paris, " I am able to support you by 100,000, or if necessary, by 200,000 bayonets." Now, these two numbers are too small to give so much title to arrogance. " Louis-Philippe," said Nicholas one day, "cannot do without Guizot and Thiers." " What would you have, Sire?" replied the Minister; " one is his right hand, and the other his left." " Judging by the way in which matters go on in France," replied the Emperor, " it would appear that the King of the French has two left hands."

" We are indebted for the July revolution to civilization," said Count Benkendorf to the Emperor, during their tour in Finnland. " I begin to perceive," replied the Emperor, " that we must oppose barriers to civilization; a well-informed man will not like to obey an ignorant chief." Instead of civilizing the chiefs, he would brutalize everybody! God will not permit such a crime.

"Liberty is a very fine thing," said Nicholas, one day after dinner, in the Anitschkin palace, where he had withdrawn into his Cabinet with some of his select friends, "but I ask you what have those gentlemen beyond the Rhine done with it?" And you yourself, Sire, what have you done for it?

He would have given anything to have broken off all connexion with France. Twenty times he resolved to make the Russians quit Paris. It is said that Count Pahlen, on receiving such an order, answered, "I am your ambassador, and not your police magistrate." If these were not the very words of the ambassador, they are such as he might have used on that occasion.

Admiral Tschitschagof having replied to an injunction to depart, that he had received permission from the Emperor Alexander to reside in France, Nicholas struck his name from the list of the members of

the Council of the Empire, on which the
Admiral sent him back his diplomas, which
secured him a pension of 50,000 rubles.
The noble Voyard preferred living in want
to obeying absurd orders.

No passports are delivered for Paris, and
all the Russians who are there come clandestinely; but as forbidden fruit is always
the sweetest, they resort thither in greater
numbers than if the prohibition did not
exist.

Persons high in office, who visit Paris,
take care not to be presented at Court,
and the most distinguished do not even set
their foot in this city of perdition. Thus
Count Woronzow, Governor-General of
Odessa, on his last visit to France, did not
go beyond Rouen, whither the authorities
and eminent Russians repaired to pay their
respects to him.

The Treaty of the 15th of July was
made, according to the expression of a
Russian diplomatist, only to annoy the

French Government. This whim has cost Russia much, and has availed her nothing. France has had the good sense not to be too much hurt by the ill conduct of its inimical friends, and Russia has been frustrated in her expectations of a general war against France.

Whence comes this animosity of Nicholas to the dynasty now reigning in France? The July revolution, a necessary consequence of the violation of the constitution which the allies themselves had guaranteed, and which has done great service to the cause of monarchy by maintaining the throne; and the blame of the Polish revolution lies in the Russian Government, and certainly not in France.

The cruelties of Nicholas towards the Poles make all hearts bleed. The Russians cannot desire this conquest at the price of the dishonour which these persecutions cast upon them. The Russian poet Pouschkine exclaims, in the ardour of his patriotism, "He who falls in the struggle is sacred; we never trample under foot the enemies whom we have thrown down." If Alexander knew how to respect the rights of conquered nations, why cannot Nicholas do so? If he is not able to sway the sceptre of Poland with humanity, to organize a free and enlightened government, let him renounce it. The *order* which prevails at Warsaw is worse than the most complete anarchy. We no longer live in the age of barbarous invasion, and the *væ victis* should be erased from the law of nations. Why should brethren be made to tear their fellows to pieces? Why treat the friends of their country and of independence worse than prisoners of war,— more harshly than criminals? The Kremlin has been avenged at Prague: to go beyond is proceeding to the *auto da fé*. If the Gallic cock can do nothing for Poland but

crow, if the French eagle has only crushed
her in its protecting talons, why should not
Russia raise her again, after having had the
glory to conquer her?

The recent persecutions of the Roman
Catholics and the Jews have destroyed the
only liberty which has hitherto done honour
to the Russian Government—the liberty of
religion. The united Greeks, (Catholics
whose service is performed in Sclavonian),
have been incorporated by force with the
Greek Church. Mixed marriages have been
subject to the obligation to bring up the
children in the Greek religion, contrary to
the old law, by which the sons were to be
brought up in the religion of their father,
and the daughters in that of their mother.
Intimidation, cupidity, violence, irony, stratagem, have been employed to increase the
number of proselytes to the prevailing religion in Russia. The Polish priests have
not had the energy of martyrs, and those
among them who are more attached to

their faith than their Government have
been dismissed, and their place is filled by
ecclesiastics, who were, or pretended to be,
devoted to the Emperor. Is it hatred of
the Roman Catholic religion, or hatred of
Poland, which impels Nicholas to these
atrocities? He is considered, if anything,
to be indifferent to religion; in this respect
he depends wholly on the Procuration of
the Synod, who places all his confidence in
a M. Skriptzyn, head of the department of
foreign religion, and in M. Engelhart,
civil governor of Mohilew, whose bitter
animosity to the Roman Catholic religion
is carried even to fanaticism, and has been
equalled only by the hatred of Prince
Khavonsky, the former governor-general to
the landowners of White Russia.

The poor Jews have been subject to
every kind of vexation. At Mstislavl
contraband goods having been seized in
their houses, the Jews committed some
excesses, repulsed a company of Invalids,

wounded several of them, and recovered
their goods. The Emperor ordered a
tenth-part of the inhabitants to be taken
for soldiers. The Jews rose, intrigued, and
sacrificed considerable sums, which disposed
the authorities to represent the fact as of
less importance, and to screen the guilty.
In order to put an end to smuggling at one
blow, Nicholas caused the country to be
razed to the extent of sixty wersts from
the frontier, thus reducing the land to a
desert, and the poor Jews were banished
from their El Dorado.

Not content with this atrocious measure,
and adding ridicule to cruelty, he has just
commanded the Jews to assume the national
costume.

Who can retrace all the persecutions to
which the innocent have been exposed
under this unhappy reign? Who can count
all the cruel acts of Nicholas?

M. H., in a private letter which he put
into the post-office, related a fact which

was current all over Petersburg, namely, that a *boutoschnik* had assassinated a merchant. He was taken at night from his bed by the side of his pregnant wife, who had a miscarriage, and he himself passed three years in banishment.

M. Jakoolef, one of the richest men in Russia, lost 100,000 rubles at *kigles*, in the English club in St. Petersburg. Orders were immediately given to transport him to Viatka, and were revoked only because his father presented 100,000 rubles to the charitable institutions, the head of which is, at the same time, by a strange inconsistency, also the head of the secret police; a police which is not equalled in China or Japan, and is the most pernicious of all institutions.

M. Kologrivof was driven away from Paris by an unworthy subterfuge, and made a private soldier in the Caucasus, for having taken part in the July revolution. " You have a taste for the army," said the Em-

peror, " go and serve me in the Caucasus."
In order to draw him away from Paris, his
mother had solicited his pardon ; the Emperor replied that he should return on the
condition only of entering the service, and
this service was that of a private.

M. D. shared a similar fate, for having
engaged in the Foreign Legion in Algeria,
which he was impelled to do by a want of
money.

A fashionable spy denounced a noble
Courlander who had attended political so-
cieties at Paris, and gave him up to the
Russian authorities, who banished him to
Vladimir.

Bestuchef, who had rendered the name
of Marlinsky famous in literature, a name
which he assumed on his exile to Siberia,
was sent as a private to the Caucasus, and
on the day when, after having gained his
epaulettes at the point of his sword, he
returned to society, on that very day he
was sent with some men against a corps

of Circassians ten times as numerous, who
cut them all to pieces.

M. Madvinof was deprived of his office
for having authorized the publication of the
portrait of Bestuchef; not of Bestuchef who
had been degraded for his participation in
the revolt of 1825, but of Marlinsky who had
regained the rank of nobility by his sword.

M. Tschedaeff was declared mad by order
of his Imperial Majesty, for having ventured to write in a Moscow Review that "it
was not possible to pass four-and-twenty
hours in a reasonable manner in Russia,
because the Russians are not Europeans;
because one Czar has opened for them a
frozen window towards Europe; because
another has led them about at beat of
drum;" and, lastly, for having added that
" Russia has retarded her advance in civilization by preferring the Greek to the Roman Catholic religion."   Boldoref, the
censor, who had suffered this article to
pass, was banished to the Monastery of

Vassilewsk, and M. Tschedaeff was subject
to a daily visit from a physician, who
poured a glass of cold water upon his
head.

Angel, a subaltern officer, was condemned
by a court-martial for some act of insubordination, and the Emperor enhanced the
punishment.

A grenadier, who seemed disposed to kill
his captain, who frequently struck him
without reason, was condemned to run the
gauntlet. The Emperor wrote with his
own hand, *that the first* 1000 *blows should
be given him on the head.*

Prince Sanguschko was condemned to be
transported to Siberia, for having taken
a part in the Polish Revolution. The Emperor added to the sentence, "*that he
should perform the journey on foot.*"

Madame Gracholska went with her son
to visit her husband, who had emigrated to
Switzerland, and the child begged that he
might stay with his father. The Emperor

caused the mother to be brought to trial on
her return to Russia. The nobles of the
government of Podolia made a subscription
to furnish her with means to perform the
journey to Siberia, whither she was sentenced. The subscription amounted to
14,000 rubles. Nicholas ordered 13,000
rubles to be kept back for the benefit of
the invalids, saying that 1000 rubles was
ample for the journey in the Polish campaign !

The dilatoriness of Diebitsch obtained
for him, from the Prussians, the nick-name
of " *I cannot so soon*," which is a parody of
his title Zabalkanski (the Transbalcanian).
It appears that the cause of his indecision
was his mistress, a Polish lady, who paralyzed his movements and prevented his taking
advantage of his victories; unless, indeed,
we regard him as the instrument of an
intrigue in a high quarter. Nicholas had
not the courage to dismiss him, and Diebitsch died of the cholera, or of poison,

taken either by choice or compulsion, a point which history has not yet been able to clear up. The death of Constantine followed soon after, at the very moment when he was about to become an object of constraint to his brother. His physician was not present at his death, and his place was supplied by the physician of the city, who received an order of knighthood; the governor of the province was also recompensed.

It suffices for the death of an individual to be advantageous to the Sovereign. He is immediately accused, if circumstances afford the slightest pretext for it. Princess Lovitz died just at the moment when some embarrassment arose respecting the etiquette with which she was to be received at the court of St. Petersburg. I am aware that there are obsequious servants who go beyond the will of their masters, but in truth deaths frequently happen here quite *à propos,* especially if we add that of Elizabeth.

The Emperor, as we before observed, has a predilection for the military which exceeds all bounds. He imagines that a military man is fit for everything, and far better calculated than a citizen to fill a civil office. Most of his ministers have been or are still in the army. Count Cancrim himself has not escaped the folly of desiring military rank, and was made a general at his own request. By making his aid-de-camp, Count Strogonof, Minister of the Interior, the Emperor has rendered ill service to the country as well as to the count himself, who is an honest man, rather than a skilful minister. Count Pahlen was another general whom Nicholas gave a civil appointment. "Sire," said the count, "I have all my life followed the profession of arms, you call me to a difficult post." "Look at me," replied the Emperor; "had I ever anything to do with politics before I ascended the throne, yet I have

acquitted myself pretty well, as you know."
In Poland, the post of Minister of Public
Instruction was at first filled by General
Golovine, and then by General Chipof,
both of whom acquitted themselves very
indifferently. The Principal of most of the
universities are military men; and General
Krafostrom, the Principal of Dorpat, passed
at once from the command of a brigade to
that of a university, thus realizing the
saying of Griboiédof, "I will give you a
serjeant for Voltaire." The students relate
anecdotes of him, some of which are too
singular to be passed over in silence here.

In the Latin examinations, whenever he
caught the word *curator*, he immediately
rose from his seat, thinking that he himself must be the person spoken of, and of
necessity in very flattering terms, he gra-
ciously saluted the individual who had
uttered the word.

"How many years have you been in the
service?" said he one day to a Professor of

Gymnastics. "Two-and-twenty years," replied the other. "And have not yet obtained a professorship in the university!"
exclaimed the head of that learned body,
indirectly holding out a flattering prospect
to the teacher of gymnastics; perfectly
ignorant that a man does not become a
priest by having spent his life in ringing
church bells.

"All these flower-pots ought to be of
equal size," said he to the celebrated Professor Ledebuhr, as they were walking together in the Botanic Garden. "How can
that be," said the Professor, "without
cutting the plants?" "Very well, then,
have them cut."

"Let that student be struck off the list,"
cried he, on seeing a young man in the
dress of a citizen, and wearing the university cap. "He has been already struck
off," returned the beadle. "Let him be
struck off a second time, then!" said the
sage Principal.

"The laws have no retro-active force," objected a student, in the hope of maintaining his right. "You affirm that the laws of his Majesty have no active force? You are a rebel," cried the General, and drove the young man from his presence.

The chiefs of the police are military men, and it is notorious how rudely these gentlemen act.

"Great complaints are made of the police," said Nicholas one day to Kakoschkin, the Grand Master of the Police at Petersburg. "They are said to be too uncivil." "Sire," replied the Adjutant-General, "if they were otherwise, they would not be so vigilant." The Emperor said nothing in reply, nor did it occur to him to say that the police ought to be civil, and at the same time vigilant

As a consummation of the ridiculous, the tiara has been placed under the hussar's cap. Protassof has been created Chief Procurator to the Synod; albeit, there is

perhaps no reason to be surprised at this,
since the Czar himself is the Patriarch.
He makes and unmakes saints at pleasure.
He has canonized Mitrophanes, to divert the
people and to enrich the province of Voro-
nesch. He added Stanislaus to the saints of
the Greek church; because when it was proposed to introduce the Polish order of St.
Stanislaus, the clergy observed that there
was no such saint in the Russian calendar.
"Very well," replied the Emperor, "then
the order need not be given to the priests;"
and so the affair was settled.

While speaking of Russian orders, we will
say a word on that of *the Buckle,* instituted
by Nicholas. It is intended as a mark of
distinction for those who have served irreproachably for the period of fifteen years or
more. Are the instances of serving *irre-*
proachably so rare in Russia, that it is necessary to distinguish an individual whose
conduct has merited it?

It happened one day, in the capital of a

small German state, that the Chargé d'Affaires of France was playing at whist with
the Russian Chargé d'Affaires, who wore
this mark of distinction. The Frenchman
begged to be informed of the meaning of
this badge; and when he learnt•that the
number on the breast of his partner indicated the number of years he had been in
the service, replied, "Well, then, you are
marked like cattle." This nearly led to a
duel, and the Russian was recalled for having brought contempt upon the Imperial
badge.

A man who was waiting at table with the
buckle attached to his button-hole, indi-
cating twenty years' service; "This man
will certainly not upset a dish upon us,"
said a wit, who was immediately summoned
to St. Petersburg, where Count Benkendorf gave him a severe reprimand.

One thing was wanting to complete this
ridiculous affair—namely, to confer this
distinction upon women; and accordingly

Nicholas has not failed to do so: he has instituted the *Mark of Mary*.

The Emperor carefully conceals from his wife his little and great infidelities. The Empress has the more merit not to observe that she is deceived, or at least not to show that she sees it; although the lady in waiting, who for the moment is honoured with the good graces of the Autocrat, is frequently in attendance upon the Empress, and has not always sufficient tact to hide the preference of which she is the object.

We must do Nicholas the justice to say, that he is nevertheless pretty constant in his illicit connexion, and keeps his mistresses a long time, though he indulges in some caprices. His present favourite charms him by her wit and amiability, rather than by her beauty. These things are natural enough, and perhaps excusable, if we consider that the Emperor is still in the prime of life, and that the health of the Empress is completely shattered, so that her physi-

cians have enjoined her to keep quite apart
from her husband, and this not for the purpose of pleasing the Czar*.

Nicholas is less indulgent to others than
to himself; and has often proceeded with
great rigour against irregularities of this
kind. He compelled the General-in-Chief
R * * * to marry his mistress, whom he had
seen riding in a carriage bearing the General's arms; and constrained Prince S. T. to
marry a young lady in waiting, whom he
abandoned almost immediately.

A colonel, who was both ugly and unamiable, married a beautiful and impassioned Italian lady. The result of this ill-
assorted union was such as invariably happens in like cases. This fascinating wife
formed an intimacy with a young man

---

* "Does he who is blameless in the sight of the
Czar commit a sin in the sight of God?" said M. ——
to his wife, after having ascertained the fact that she
was unfaithful to him, and favoured the Czar. Such
laxity of morals in subjects accounts for many faults in
princes.

named Souch * * *, by whom she had a son,
for whom his legal father conceived a strong
affection, from a strong resemblance to
himself. " Heaven knows what the women
of our days are made of!" said a lady of
the old school, in reference to this subject, "they know not only how to deceive
their husbands, but they know a vast deal
more besides." The charming Italian was
soon offended at the caresses which the
colonel bestowed upon her son, and told
him the plain truth. The colonel was
beside himself, and immediately reported
the case to the Emperor, who in Russia
does every thing alone. A divorce was
ordered; the Italian expelled from the
country with her mother, and her lover
thrown into prison, and excluded from the
service : for the service in Russia, it must
be observed, is of a mixed nature; sometimes it is inflicted as a punishment, and
sometimes it is taken away from those
whom it is intended to punish.

Nicholas is a good father; but is that a virtue which merits to be so lauded? Do not the most ferocious animals love their young? If the ladies consider the Emperor Nicholas a handsome man, the phrenologists, on the other hand, have no very exalted idea of his cranium, and say that it has little of the organ of causality; the physicians affirm that his skull contains water; while historians pretend that the members of the family of Holstein Gottolf lose their senses after the age of forty. But on this point, perhaps, as on many others, the fair sex alone are in the right: this much is certain, that the Emperor is a tall man, but there are hundreds of grenadiers, cuirassiers, and even cadets, who have the great honour to equal him in stature.

His eye is that of a despot, and nothing delights him more than to see people stand in awe of him. The man who looks at him with a steady eye will never be one of his

favourites: as a proof of this I will mention
the following anecdote. A young *fiancé*
was walking in the gardens of Alexan-
drovka, the Trianon of Peterhof, which is
the Russian Versailles, dreaming of love
and of his future bliss; he unconsciously
entered into the avenues reserved to the
Imperial family. Two grenadiers addressed
him rudely, and desired him to retire ; but
the young man pointed to his uniform,
which was that of the Imperial Chancery,
and the soldiers, whose orders, or whose
understanding, were not up to this stratagem, suffered him to pass on. Emboldened by this unexpected success, he
ventured yet further. On a sudden the
Emperor stood before him, and, looking at
him with an air of dignity and menace,
fixed his eagle eye upon him. The young
man was confounded, turned pale and
speechless, and his knees gave way under
him. His sudden and great fear calmed
the Emperor, and prevented the explosion

of his wrath; but the young man was so seriously affected by the rencontre that he became extremely ill. His affianced bride was annoyed at the consequent delay of the marriage, and as she had no inclination to wait for his recovery she actually espoused another. Her faithlessness affected the patient so deeply that he grew worse, was obliged to quit the service, and to seek in foreign countries means for the restora-of his health, and escape from the effects of his despair.

Repnin, the governor-general of Little Russia, committed great embezzlements during his administration. The remonstrance of Count Benkendorf produced such an effect on him, that decorum forbids me to speak more plainly. The news of it satisfied the Emperor, and gratified him so much, that he ordered all proceedings against the culprit to be suspended.

One of the Emperor's aides-de-camp was

dismissed for having gesticulated when speaking to him. Another was transferred from the cavalry to the infantry, from the regiment of horse-guards to that of Preobrajenski for a miserable pun, as some say, or as others have it, for having allowed himself an air of too great familiarity.

Two students who omitted to salute the Emperor were confined in the guard-house, and summoned to appear before his Majesty, to whom they declared that they had only just arrived from their Province, and had not recognized the Sovereign. The explanation appeared to him so satisfactory, that Nicholas made them dine in his palace, and the sensation throughout the city was great, that all were loud in their praises of the Emperor's conduct.

As I am above all things desirous to be impartial, and even lenient, I have often applied to the best informed persons, and to the most devoted courtiers, and requested them, as a favour, to point out to me at

least one laudable action of Nicholas, and
I was ready to feel for him all the enthusiasm which noble actions can inspire.
Some stammered out a few monosyllables
and stopped short; and others directed my
attention to the dignity of his foreign
policy, and uttered some vague expressions
about the elevation of his sentiments. I
however met with some individuals who
quoted several traits which they called
cheveleresque. The following are among
the numbers of those which I have collected.

A colonel boxed the ears of his ensign,
upon which the latter drew his pistol and
shot him dead on the spot. The Emperor
asked whether the pistol was loaded at the
moment when the insult was offered, and
being answered in the affirmative, pardoned
the murderer.

An officer did the same to his colonel,
who had only insulted him by words. Ni-

cholas exclaimed, that his death would lie heavy on his conscience.

Another officer who had permitted a serious offence which he had received from one of his comrades to go unpunished, was excluded from the regiment by supreme authority.

These are trifling facts,' and have been collected with much difficulty, while numerous others present themselves to my mind and pen, which prove that these laudable traits were only the offspring of caprice, and not founded on fixed principles.

Captains Issakof and Likatschef, of the artillery of the guards, had an altercation with a captain who had passed from the Polish into the Russian service, and one of them told him "He was a traitor." They were brought to trial, and the tribunal decided that their previous imprisonment should be accounted a sufficient punishment. The Emperor caused the tribunal to be reprimanded, appointed a commission, and had the accused officers sent to distant fortresses as officers of the line.

A degraded nobleman in the Caucasus, while in the ranks received a blow with the fist from his serjeant, upon which he immediately thrust him through with his bayonet. He was condemned to run the gauntlet, and General Laventzof ordered all the degraded nobles, who are very numerous in the Caucasus, to be present and take a share in inflicting the punishment, thus making them act the part of executioners.

Notwithstanding all that I have said, I do not think that Nicholas is a tyrant by nature but only from conviction. He is persuaded that if he acted otherwise, public affairs could not succeed, and he is very well satisfied with the manner in which they have gone on during his reign. The habit of governing upon this principle has given him a taste for cruelty, for the habit of

tyrannizing makes man a tyrant. The
Russians say that it requires an iron hand to
govern Russia, but that his hand should be
gloved. Nicholas has the iron hand but he
has forgotten the glove.

———————————

CHAPTER X.

THE FAMILY AND COURT OF THE CZAR.

THE EMPRESS has always exercised a beneficial influence over her husband, by tempering his passion and his excesses, and there is, consequently, a great apprehension of the results, if she should die before him, which appears but too probable. It is presumed that her death will produce the same effect upon Nicholas, as the loss of his first wife did upon Ivan IV. Though she does not possess any superior qualities, the atmosphere in which she lives has not been able to efface the good principles which she imbibed at the Court of Prussia.

The GRAND DUKE, HEIR TO THE THRONE,
is not a very promising character, if we may
take the word of those who are the most
about him; but those who promise the
most do not always perform most; and his
father, by the manner in which he governs,
will have greatly facilitated his task; and it
will be comparatively easy for him to content a people who have been subject to so
rigorous a reign. It is certain that he is of
an amiable disposition, and this is much to
go upon. While still a child, his father
asked him how he would have treated
the conspirators of the 26th of December.
" I would have pardoned them," he replied. The young Czarwitsch is thought to
be a great deal like his uncle Alexander,
and this too is in his favour. His education has not been so brilliant as his
father imagines, who, in fact, has under-
taken to finish it himself, but it is to be
hoped that he will not succeed in modelling
him according to his own likeness.

The young GRAND DUKE CONSTANTINE NICHOLOWITSCH is the phœnix of the family, for he is said to be possessed of great intellectual powers. At the conclusion of the first lesson in the Russian language which he received from M. Pletnef, the latter was about to withdraw, when the Grand Duke stopped him, saying, that he wished to go on a little longer. One day he addressed an officer of the Horse Guards, and said, "How is it that there is not a day but what I see you in a green dress, that yesterday evening you wore a red one, and now a white coat?" The officer set about explaining this transformation; to which Constantine replied, " Oh, I see! you do exactly like the clown on the stage." In his character of Admiral, he took pleasure in arresting his elder brother, who was on board his ship, for which he was himself put under arrest for a considerable time by order of his father.

The GRAND DUKE MICHAEL, the Emperor's brother, has a kind disposition, but a rough exterior, and has a propensity to make puns. It is affirmed that he has been seen to weep at seeing Russian soldiers slain in Poland, while his brother Constantine rubbed his hands, saying, " What do you think of my Poles ?" It is not said whether Michael shed tears for the soldiers whom he sacrificed at Brailow, but it is pretended that he would not wear the order of St. George, conferred upon him for the deplorable siege of that place. He is, however, the greatest courtier in Russia; in public he is always seen bent double while speaking, with manifest veneration, to his brother. He is the first servant of the Czar. I once heard him say, with regret, at a ball, " All my colleagues have preceded me in the service." At one time, however, there was a coolness between the two brothers, after which, Michael went to Moscow or abroad, where he pretended to amuse himself excessively, and sought popularity, not only among the nobles, but likewise among the officers. The Emperor reprimanded him severely for fraternizing with his inferiors, to which he answered, that he had not expected to be so treated by his brother and his Sovereign.

His wife, the GRAND DUCHESS HELEN, is a woman of superior understanding, which often exposes her to a degree of jealousy on the part of the Empress, which is betrayed in frequent petty domestic quarrels. On one occasion, when the Grand Duchess returned from abroad, her trunks were strictly examined at the custom-house, and although her new dresses lost something of their freshness, they, nevertheless, eclipsed all others at Court by their novelty. Let us proceed to the Ministers.

Seven cities in Greece contended for the honour of having given birth to Homer; so, four European Powers might claim the glory of having COUNT NESSELRODE for their subject. He was born in sight of Lisbon, on

board an English ship, of German parents,
in the service of Russia. As there was no
Lutheran clergyman on board the vessel,
the infant diplomatist was baptized according to the rites of the Church of England.
He might, therefore, be claimed by Great
Britain, since he was born under her flag,
since the vessel of a Power is always considered as part of its territory; England,
however, is rich enough in statesmen to
give up one to Russia without much detri-
ment.

His family is of Westphalian origin; the
Nesselrodes are counts of the Empire, and
therefore the Chancellor has always positively refused the title of Russian Count,
which the Emperor has repeatedly offered
him. It is not thus that Russians acted,
who, like him, and long before him, were
Counts of the Holy Roman Empire; the
Golovines, and the Menschikofs, have never
hesitated for an instant to accept the titles
of their country, but Count Nesselrode is

not enough of a courtier to be national,
and thinks that a title of the Holy Empire
is highly preferable to an equivalent Russian
title. Nevertheless, he would doubtless do
violence to his feelings and accept the title
of *Prince* if it were offered to him. Meantime he is waiting patiently, obtaining vast
estates in the south and east of Russia,
where he pays a great deal of attention to
the breeding of sheep.

Count Nesselrode was first a seaman, and
then a cuirassier, and an officer in the
Horse Guard, but the Emperor Paul thought
that he looked like a diplomatist, and accordingly transferred the count to the
department of Foreign Affairs. It is well
known that Paul was no physiognomist; he
several times made his subjects interchange
parts, transforming masters into servants,
and servants into masters, from mere caprice. Having become a Diplomatist by
order of the Czar, Nesselrode, like so many

others, made his fortune through the fair
sex, though the woman to whom he paid his
addresses, or who addressed him, was not
distinguished by her beauty. For a first
essay, this was a master-stroke; it was
playing with the certainty of winning, and
the conditions of the bargain were fixed
beforehand. Countess Gurief, daughter of
the Minister of Finance, after having in
vain intrigued for several good matches,
where her riches were not considered a
compensation for her ugliness, turned her
attention, for want of doing better, to Nesselrode, who brought, by way of portion,
the powers with which she undertook to
invest him. His wife has ever since exercised unlimited influence over him; and
no person, unless sure of her assent, can
rely upon any favour from him. To please
the countess, it is necessary to flatter her
taste in the fine arts; she is a great admirer
of pictures and busts, and does not disdain

either copies or originals. The count is short and restless, and generally wears the cross of St. Andrew on his coat, with the medal of the Turkish campaign, a very adroit mode of paying his court to the hero of Varna. He is passionately fond of cards, and people say that he has lost his heart to them, but he has lost nothing else, for his Merinos thrive admirably.

Count Nesselrode is the chief of the German party; two-thirds of the officers in the Foreign Department are Germans, Lippmann, Ostensacken, Beck, Molcke, and Fuhrmann; and Russia is represented in England by Brunnow, in France by Pahlen, in Prussia by Meyendorf, in Austria by Medem, at Stockholm by Krüdner, at Berne by another Krüdner, at Hamburgh by Struve, at Copenhagen by Nicholai, at Dresden by Schröder, and at Teheran by a second Medem. Somebody once advised Count Nesselrode to endeavour to place Russians in official stations abroad, to which he coolly replied, " The Russians have never done any thing but make blunders." He alluded to M. Kakoschkin, who, in fact, seems to have made some gross mistakes at Turin; but what, it may be asked, has Count Nesselrode himself done? The treaty of the 15th of July,—a bravado which has become ridiculous,—and, the abandonment of our constant policy towards Turkey. " We have too much to do with Poland to attend to Turkey," say the Russian diplomatists. Our relations with France are endangered. " Such is the good pleasure of the Emperor," they reply. " The Chancellor can do nothing—our interests are often sacrificed to England—we make advances by it —Russia complains of our conduct towards her—the country above all things," say the creatures of the count. We shall see !

COUNT BENKENDORF was a good man in the full sense of the expression, for he was as good as he was incapable. In order to advance his own fortune, he made drawings of frigates in the Emperor Paul's album, which obtained for him the epaulettes of the aid-de-camp to the Czar. He was General of Division at the accession of Nicholas, who placed him at the head of the Secret Police, that infernal machine, the offspring of fear and insanity. Every body agrees in saying, that Count Benkendorf, in this melancholy post, did as little evil as possible, which is a pretty considerable negative merit. But an unskilful friend is worse than an intelligent enemy, and the incapacity of the count has undone many persons, whom more clear-sighted men might have saved and even made useful.

The official title of the office which Count Benkendorf held, is that of chief of the corps of gens-d'armes, which means that of chief of the spies. The Emperor has placed a superior officer of the gens-d'armes in every provincial city, to watch over the magistrates and people. "I have thus found some valuable men," said he one day to Prince Vassiltschikof. "Why don't you make them governors?" replied the President of the Council. He might as well have said, "Why don't you place them in the Council of the Empire?" If you set a rogue to watch a rogue, they combine, and in order to render their gains sufficient, they double their extortions. This is what happened on the present occasion. The superintendents placed themselves on a footing with the superintended, and were soon in connivance with all these officers, who grew rich at the expense of the public. The following is an instance which happened at Novgorod. M. Sukovkin, the Governor of that Province, had committed great embezzlements, which came to the knowledge of the Emperor, without any notice having been given to the competent authorities; thanks to the relationship of M. S. with

Kleinmichel, who was already in great
favour with Nicholas; his Majesty informed
M. Bludorf, who acquainted Count Benkendorf with the matter. The Minister of
Police immediately sent a severe reprimand
to the colonel of gens-d'armes at Novgorod, who had not made any report to him
on the abuses which were committed in the
circle under his inspection. The colonel
was a German; and "a German," as the
Russians say, "is never burnt nor drowned."
He went and threw himself at the feet of
Countess Orloff, who was then performing
her devotions in a convent at Novgorod,
and whose piety disposed her to clemency.
The artful colonel vowed to her that it was
his amiable disposition which ruined him,
and that it was from pure good nature that
he had winked at all the abuses which were
committed in the Province. The countess
wrote to her husband, and the colonel's
pardon was secure.

Latterly, Count Benkendorf lost both his

memory and inclination to work. He did not even read the letters which were addressed to him, and overlooked the most important matters. He has forgotten many in exile, and others in prison. General Douvelt was his factotum, who took with both hands, and it was therefore more than once in contemplation to dismiss him; but Count Benkendorf having declared that in that case he would immediately quit the service, the Court shut their eyes, waiting for the time when the count should do the same; but after his death they forgot to open them.

It is well known that Count Benkendorf was the director of several steam navigation and other companies, which was a source of revenue to him, and a more or less illicit protection to the parties interested. He did not disdain the most trifling presents, if they were adroitly made, and we know of a certain emerald necklace which obtained for M. L. the order of St.

Stanislaus. We could also name some diamonds which were offered on the occasion
of a marriage, and to which Count B. is
indebted for retaining his title, which was
strongly disputed. "His family being
equally rich and powerful, it would not have
been advisable to deprive him of it," was
the plea urged by Count Benkendorf to the
Emperor, and there the matter dropped.
But I will not dwell on these petty matters,
which are so common in Russia, where it is
considered a merit to take but little and to
receive indirectly.

Count Benkendorf died in the bosom of
the Catholic church, through the influence
of Madame Krudner, to whom he latterly
devoted his fortune, his time, and his
repose. He had conceived for her that
affection of an old man, which ends only
with life, a platonic and unhappy affection
which hastened his end. His conversion
was not made known till after his death,
and greatly scandalized the Emperor and

Court, but his having become a Roman
Catholic is said to have saved a great number of innocent persons, who professed the
same religion.

Madame Krudner designated him the best
man in the world; and her opinion has
become that of the whole country; and for
my own part I take pleasure in not contra-
dicting it, especially considering the wrongs
which the Count may have done me.

COUNT ORLOFF, who has just succeeded
Count Benkendorf, is one of the confidants
of his Majesty. He owes his rise to the
events of the 26th of December, 1825.
Being at that time colonel of the regiment
of horse guards, the barracks of which are
nearest to the palace, he was the first to
place himself at the head of his men, and
march to Isaac Square. He has since been
loaded with favours and kindnesses. One
day, however, the Emperor struck him on
the chest, upon which the favourite thought
fit to be offended, and to say that he was

old, and had need of repose. "Never mind that," answered the Czar, "go where-ever you please." Orloff was confounded, he immediately redoubled his assiduity and attention to the Autocrat, who soon forgot this incident, but said on another occasion, "Nobody is so indispensable to me, Tscher-nyschef." Count Orloff, when he was made Minister of Police, made a profound obser-vation: "I do not comprehend the utility of all this institution." May the Count one day see its total inutility, and contribute to abolish it.

TSCHERNYSCHEF, Minister of War, owes his rise to the skill with which he searched the archives of France, in 1811, and pro-cured the plans and the projects of the campaign of 1812. Being raised to the rank of General, he entered Cassel, and since that time, the expression, "When I took Cassel!" is always in his mouth.

At the accession of the Emperor Ni-cholas, he manifested cruel energy in the persecution of the conspirators. An officer who had been unjustly accused, and was bold in the consciousness of his innocence, was provoked to an expression of anger towards him, and on that account was worse dealt with than the guilty. He himself superintended the condemnation of Count Tschernyschef, in order to get possession of his property. The Emperor went and presented him to the mother of the accused, and endeavoured to persuade her to adopt him, but this worthy lady answered that, though she gladly received his Majesty's Adjutant-General, yet she could never look upon him as a relative. The affair was then brought before the Council of the Empire, and when the reporting secretary stated that he could not find a law in support of the demand which was made for the transfer of the estates of Count Tschernyschef to the General, a noble and clever member of the council said, "Search diligently, it must be found!"

The secretary persisting in his assertion, Count M—— added, "There is a law, which enacts that the property of the person executed belongs to the executioner!" Thus alluding to an English law, which gives to the executioner the boots of the person whom he has executed.

Being disappointed in his hopes, Tscher-nyschef turned his thoughts to marriage. Three ladies, whom he espoused successively contributed to make his fortune. Instead of the title Count he has obtained that of Prince.

Count Cancrin was the only statesman in Russia who possessed considerable knowledge, though he was rather deficient in the very branch which was under his administration. He was a very good bookkeeper; but chemistry, mechanics, and technology, were wholly unknown to him. The sense of duty predominated over all his German nationality; he really aimed at the good of Russia; but at the same time he did not neglect his own affairs, which his post peculiarly enabled him to attend to. Colbert has been reproached for his fortune; but we may be permitted to reproach Count Cancrin with his, even though he leaves the trouble of spending it to his children. He has amassed an amount of 400,000 rubles. "All this will pass over," says he, "my children will take care of it."

He was the most ardent partisan of the prohibitive system, as well as that of manufactures; but the favouring impulse which he gave to the latter does not compensate for the sufferings of agriculture, to which he refused to pay attention. A truly Russian heart would not have fallen into this error, and would have known that the Empire is, in an especial manner, an agricultural country.

The question of the slavery of the vassals was above the sphere of this minister; and his regulations respecting the coinage were a mere groping in the dark, where, by dint of feeling at random, he sometimes hit the right mark. He, however, opposed the dissipation of the Emperor with a perseverance which the Czar called obstinacy, without venturing to cross him too much. The merit of Mazarin is that of having given Colbert to Louis XIV. Count Cancrin, by leaving M. Vrontschenko as his successor, has rendered a very ill service to Russia.

COUNT KLEINMICHEL, a count by the favour of Nicholas, like almost all the counts and princes who serve him, is a creature of Count Arakhtschéief, and a most ungrateful man to his former master, for he was the first to turn his back upon him when the Emperor abandoned him; and hence it is not surprising that Arakhtschéief, when he was asked for information respecting his former aid-de-camp, should have replied that "he did not know him." However, when the complaints which his administration excited reached his ears, he exclaimed, "Do not complain too much, I will give you my Petrouscha;" and in fact the latter is already following him with gigantic strides, both in the favour of his master and in the hatred of the people. It is affirmed that the Grand Duke Michael said to the chief of the department of Public Works, after he had caused some cadets to be flogged and sent as private soldiers to the Caucasus, "You have cast a stain on the reign of my brother!" The nobility, for the first time, murmured loudly; the mothers complained, and took their children out of the hands of the executioner.

The secret of the ties which unite this man to Nicholas, is not so much the conformity of their tastes and character, as reciprocal forbearance. The Sovereign must doubtless take care of him who takes care of his mistresses.

Count Kleinmichel is the most brutal

functionary in the Russian empire; and this is saying a great deal, where so many people glory in being such.

The Winter Palace, so tyrannically rebuilt, has raised the fortune of the count; nor has the falling of St. George's Hall injured his prospects. "Make yourself easy," said the Emperor, "the fault is all my own, I was in too great a hurry;" and, as a colonel who was present, and looking up at the ill-fated ceiling, thus suffered the semblance of a beard to be visible above his cravat, the Emperor vented his spleen upon him.

The predecessors of Count Kleinmichel, in his post of head of the department of Public Works, were MM. Toll and Betancourt, men of probity and talent, who enjoyed a high degree of public esteem, but could not succeed in persuading the Government to adopt their plans,—a government which is so lavish for itself, and so niggardly for objects of public utility. Seeing

that with eight millions it was not possible
to give good roads to Russia, M. Betancourt
turned all his solicitude to the corps of
cadets, which was confided to his care, and
organized it on the model of the Poly-
technic School; but here too the German
spirit did not fail to attain the ascendant
over the French, and the Prince of Wurtemburg, who took the direction of that
department after M. Betancourt, replaced
the whole on the ancient footing. Count
Toll was a distinguished chief of the Staff
under Diebitsch, in the campaigns both
of Turkey and Poland.

COUNT KISSELEF, Minister of the Domains, is one of the leaders of the Russian
opposition, of the liberal party, and a reformer; an opposition which cannot be
called one: a liberalism which is so only in
name; reforms, which are destitute of
plan. He is considered as the most dangerous enemy of the Emperor, for the
inevitable effects of his measures are to

raise discontent, and seem calculated to excite revolutions.

Being a moderate liberal, and not daring on open opposition; a moderate statesman, and under the influence of such opposing principle, he cannot pursue a steady course. Instead of seeing in his injudicious measures a tendency to revolution, it would be better to ascribe them only to the bad faith of his agents. What does him most honour is that of being an advocate for the emancipation of the serfs; but the old Russian party stops his mouth, whenever he reproaches them with not having a peasantry. The considerable possessions of his adversaries should, however, impose on them more disinterested language.

M. OUWAROF, Minister of Public Instruction, who is not yet a count, but must, doubtless, ere long acquire that title, is a man of knowledge and understanding, but deficient in the qualities of right feeling.

His self-love and his vanity are equalled only by the envy which he cherishes towards all those who advance more rapidly than himself.

"I and the Emperor have decided," he repeats at the end of every sentence; and then, correcting himself, begins again: "The Emperor and I have, &c., &c." *Nationality* and *Autocracy* are the motto of his administration; he is now as devoted to absolutism as he was formerly liberal: nay, he is even more so. M. Ouwarof is too good a philosopher to be deeply versed in other branches of learning, which however does not restrain him from dictating his ordinances like a sovereign lord, in medicine as well as in jurisprudence.

"You are wrong to think of professing political economy," observed he to M. Dsch * * *; "political economy is not a science; you ought rather to take up history." It is but justice to say, in spite of every defect, that the administration of M. Ouwarof has been favourable to education, especially to the higher branches.

It is, besides, an easy task for one who succeeds to the ministry after such a man as Schichkof. We find the following anecdote in the memoirs which he left behind him. He was on his way to Moscow with the Emperor Alexander, and his Majesty having gone to some distance from his equipage, the minister who was left alone began to contemplate the heavens. He there distinguished, as he says, two clouds, one of which resembled in shape a dragon, such as it is represented on paper, and the other a lobster. The two images advanced against each other, and commenced a desperate conflict, and the dragon was destroyed. The minister considered this as an emblem of the war of 1812 which had just broken out, but which of the two belligerent parties was represented by the lobster? "Evidently Russia! because in that language the two words begin with the letter R !"

PRINCE VOLKONSKY, Minister of the Court, was the friend and the drudge of the Emperor Alexander, who often carried his familiarity so far as to treat him extremely ill. One day, when bad tea had been set before him, he compelled the prince to swallow the whole pot full. Another time, when Prince Volkonsky spoke contemptuously of the Polish ladies, the chivalrous Alexander, who was just then in love with Madame Naryshkin (a Princess Czetwertinski) gave him a box on the ear ; and, in 1814, when he was about to set out from Paris, a carriage with indifferent horses was brought him, upon which the Czar scolded the prince as if he had been a groom.

The following anecdote will convey an idea of the administration of the prince in particular, and of that of the Russian Government in general. A ring had disappeared from a casket of jewels; the sentinel was asked if he had seen any person enter the room where the theft had been committed, and in this case whether he could recognize the individual. On his answering in the affirmative he was taken to the office of the ministry, and had no difficulty in pointing out the clerk whom he had seen enter. Volskonsky struck this unlucky man, and expelled him from the service, with a certificate, in these terms, "Dismissed on suspicion of theft." The prospects of the young man were inevitably ruined, and his family and himself dishonoured for ever. Fortunately, his father was a retired general, a man of honour and high principle. He immediately addressed a letter to the Emperor, in which he said that, "having no proofs of the crime of his son, he knew not whether he ought to drive him from his presence, or to press him to his bosom. He therefore begged the Sovereign, not as Czar, but as a father, to cause

inquiry to be made into the affair." He
put on his uniform, and went to present his
letter to Nicholas, just when the guard was
being mounted. It was then discovered
that the person who had stolen the ring
was a porter of the hotel. The Emperor
took the young man into his chancery, but
Prince Volkonsky retained his post.

The following fact will furnish another
proof of how far the Russian Ministers are
from being disinterested.

A dealer in Persian shawls, at Moscow,
was ordered to wait upon the Empress, as
she passed through that city. She selected
two shawls, inquired the price, and ordered
them to be paid for. The shawls were
taken, but the dealer with difficulty obtained
a part of his money, and was compelled to
submit to a reduction. M. R., a jeweller,
had to complain of a similar proceeding on
the part of the Minister of the Court.

M. PEROVSKY will be honourably distinguished in the annals of the Russian admi-

nistration: he is far superior to all his predecessors, by his activity and his zeal in promoting what is good. His entrance into the Department of the Interior has been signalized by laudable regulations and measures. He has made a useful *razzia* against the governors, and has been very fortunate in the appointment of successors to many of them. He vigorously attacked the unworthy police of St. Petersburg, and desisted only in consequence of the Imperial protection, which has obtained for M. Kakoschkin the nickname of "*Cache Coquin.*" The agent of the ministerial department had discovered at St. Petersburg the existence of a band of robbers, amounting to several hundred men. M. Perovsky demanded the dismissal of M. Kakoschkin, but his Majesty contented himself with reprimanding him, and told the minister, "that it was thanks to the grand master of police that he had slept in tranquillity for twenty years!" The malefactors were punished, but some intriguers contrived to persuade the Emperor that he had punished innocent men; and the credit and the zeal of M. Perovsky hereby sustained a great shock.

No choice which Nicholas has made for the Department of the Interior appears to have been so happy as that of Perovsky. Lanskor was a cypher, and Zagreosky a narrow-minded man, who, during the cholera at Moscow, caused the chests of tea to be fumigated! and awakened his clerks in consequence of *important* ordinances which prescribed a new mode of *wiping pens!* His successor Bludof, was an intelligent and upright minister, but devoid both of system and energy, though he is accused of cruelty in drawing up the reports of the committee which was appointed to investigate the affair of the conspirators of 1825; a task which has insured him a brilliant career. He has since succeeded Count Speranski in the office of drawing up the laws, without however filling up the vacuum which has been left by the death of that excellent man, the only learned lawyer in Russia. Count Strogonof, who was called to succeed Bludof, and who was thought to be a man of strong mind, proved to be worse than weak. At the time when he was Governor-General of Charkof, he had already given many proofs of inability, but which, thanks to the favour of Bludof, passed unperceived. One day the Emperor pointed out to him a street in Charkof, which he wished out of the way. Count Strogonof immediately had bills posted on every house, which stated the time when it would be pulled down, and replaced by another. He listened neither to remonstrances nor entreaties, and caused his orders to be executed to the letter.

The circumstance which led to his dismissal, deserves to be related. An ex-officer of the guards asked the protection of the Grand Duke Michael to obtain the

office of a *gorodnitschi*. His Imperial
Highness gave him a letter of recommen-
dation to Count Strogonof, who having consulted his lists, declared that he had not a
place vacant. But the officer was not discouraged, and had recourse to the chief of
the Chancery of the Minister, who was of
opinion that for 5000 rubles, a vacant place
might be found. The officer went and informed the Grand Duke of the result of his
application, upon which his Highness gave
him the 5000 rubles from his privy purse.
The same evening he met Count Strogonof
at the palace, and told him that he had
become his creditor; and then informed the
Emperor of the whole proceeding. His
Majesty exclaimed, that he would rather
have in his service "able men who stole,
than men who suffered others to steal without perceiving it." He immediately became cool towards his minister, who asked
leave of absence for four months. "Four
years, if you please," replied the Emperor.

Count Strogonof then solicited the post of Ambassador at Vienna; Nicholas answered that he alone had the appointment of persons to those offices. The minister asked no explanation of this evasive refusal, and retired to Paris, where he is seen assiduously attending public lectures; better late than never; it is true that these are medical lectures.

PRINCE MENTSCHIKOF, the Minister of Marine, is rather witty and rich, than profound and independent. He is seen to wait for hours together for Count Kleinmichel to consult him respecting the daily dress of the seamen. The count is considered as an authority on this subject, which is the Emperor's weak side; and the wit of Mentschikof makes him so many enemies, that he is obliged to seek the support of the strong. Count Nesselrode is his greatest enemy.

COUNT PANIN has been too good a diplo

matist to be a good minister of justice; but as General Protassof presides in the synod, it is the more easy for Count Panin to take his seat in the senate, where his ability and assiduity are not disputed; this was not the forte of his predecessor M. Daschkof, who considered it his duty not to importune the Emperor.

PRINCE VASSILITSCHIKOF, who received his title from the Emperor, President of the Council of the Empire, and General-in-Chief, is a well meaning man, but has little influence over the Emperor, who in truth will not be advised by any body. "I have reigned these fifteen years; it is too late to teach me how to govern," replied Nicholas, one day when the Prince requested him to modify a severe and unjust measure. His predecessor, Count Novosiltzof, formerly curator of the University of Wilna, has left a painful remembrance behind. He did not hesitate, while at Wilna, to bring innocent persons into trouble, in order to his own aggrandizement, and to excite plots, for the bare honour of defeating them.

Field-Marshal PASKEWITSCH, Count of Erivan, Prince of Warsaw, has obtained European celebrity, and enjoys an indisputable military reputation. His campaign in Persia was admirable, and that in Asiatic Turkey is a severe criticism on the war carried on upon this side of the Bosphorus. It is true that in these two countries he was opposed by troops but little inured to war. Good fortune has certainly had a great share in his exploits; but, as Suwarrow, who was also reproached with being only fortunate, used to say, "Merit ought surely to be reckoned for something in a succession of victories!" It was necessary to have recourse to Paskewitch to conclude the war in Poland; and his arrival alone raised the spirits of the army. The faults committed by the Poles are evident; but they take little from the merit of Paskewitsch, who turned them to advantage as he repaired his own. Having been appointed Governor of Poland, he has been so happy in this post as to moderate the cruelties of his master.

YERMOLOF has been one of the best generals of Russia. It was he who drew up the plans of Borodino and of Kulm, the two battles which have done the most honour to the arms of his country. Yet this brave general has fallen into disgrace; whether it be owing to some dispute with Nicholas at Paris, in 1814, where it is affirmed that he reproved the Grand Duke, who interfered in a review at which he commanded in chief, addressed him in these energetic words : " You are young enough to learn, but not old enough to teach!" or whether he had not shewn much zeal in making his corps take the oath to Nicholas; or, lastly, whether in consequence of the triumph of the German party, which, after the revolt of 1825, gained the ascendancy over the Russian party, which reckoned Yermolof amongst the most eminent of its leaders, it is difficult to divine. Paskewitsch was sent to watch over his conduct with equal rights. Yermolof planned his ruin, and sent him with a division against the whole corps of Abbas Mirza, following him with the main body to repair the check which the others might suffer. But the result was far otherwise. Paskewitsch defeated the Persians, and Yermolof was recalled. He was received with enthusiasm at Moscow, but he was so impolitic as to resume his uniform, and his popularity died away. Brave, skilful, national—as liberal from discontent as he had been despotic while in power, he remained a living reproach to the Emperor. A fit of remorse caused the order of St. Andrew to be sent to him on the erection of the monument of Kulm.

END OF VOL. I.

RUSSIA

UNDER

THE AUTOCRAT,

NICHOLAS THE FIRST.

BY

IVAN GOLOVINE,

A RUSSIAN SUBJECT.

———

IN TWO VOLUMES.

VOL. II.

LONDON:

HENRY COLBURN, PUBLISHER,

GREAT MARLBOROUGH STREET,

1846.

LONDON :
HARRISON AND CO., PRINTERS,
ST. MARTIN'S LANE.

RUSSIA

UNDER

NICHOLAS THE FIRST.

CHAPTER I.

OF THE CLASSES OF THE PEOPLE.

OF THE NOBILITY.

THERE are two kinds of nobility in Russia—hereditary nobility and personal nobility. The first is acquired by the rank of officer in the army; in the civil service, down to the eighth class, which is equivalent to the rank of major. It may be conferred by the Emperor, and is also attached to certain orders that are bestowed on personal nobles or members of the clergy. Traders were excluded from this prerogative by the decree of the 30th of October, 1826.

Military officers, on passing into the civil service with a rank inferior to the eighth class, retain their rights of hereditary nobles.

Children born before the promotion of their father to the hereditary nobility are noble whenever the father acquires nobility by a rank or by an order. If he receives it by the favour of the Emperor, it must be specially indicated in the grant whether it is to extend to the children previously born. He whose father and grandfather have served, each for at least twenty years, in ranks which confer personal nobility, has a right to hereditary nobility.

The latter is divided into six degrees; 1stly, the nobles with the title of Prince, Count, and Baron; 2ndly, the ancient noble families; 3rdly, the military nobles; 4thly, the nobles of the eighth class; 5thly, the nobles of imperial creation; 6thly, foreign nobles.

Personal nobility is attached, in the civil service, to the ranks below the eighth class, or it is conferred by a nomination of the Emperor. The order of St. Stanislaus confers it on members of the Catholic clergy and on Baschkirs.

Of late years, the Emperor Nicholas, with a view to enhance the value of nobility, resolved not to confer it below the fifth class in the civil service; but, by limiting the service of the soldier to fifteen years in the guard, and that of the subaltern to twelve years, he has facilitated the access to the rank of officer, and consequently to hereditary nobility. The examinations of candidates, it is true, are conducted with greater strictness; but the liberty allowed them for a certain time to choose between the epaulette of officer and a pension of from 340 to 500 rubles per annum, has contributed not a little to discredit nobility. The number of those who preferred the money

to being ennobled became so great, that it was
found necessary to suppress.that arrangement.
The access has, moreover, been facilitated to
civil degrees by what has been done to favour
the advancement of the licentiates of the Universities.

The present institution of the Russian nobility is quite revolutionary. Whether Peter
purposed to strengthen his own power, or to
raise the people by weakening the nobility, it
is not the less certain that he revolutionized
the country, and paved the way to the reign
of equality. To this end there were two
means that might be adopted—either to destroy the rights of the nobility, or to generalize
them by rendering them easier of access. He
preferred the second oftener than he employed
the first; and his successors have ever since
adhered to his policy without comprehending
its drift.

Nobility has actually sunk in the public
opinion; and if it no longer serves for a barrier
against power, neither does it furnish a sup-

port to it. Invaded by the people, its foundation has been undermined; and, its wealth melting away from day to day, it is losing the last spell of its power. All its lands are mortgaged to the Crown, and the existence of serfage paralyses the development of wealth. On the day when the people shall have become noble, or when only the number of the nobles has become immense, on that day nobility will have given place to democracy. What will then become of the throne?

The Russian nobility possess the faculty of entering the public service, without being liable to be forced into it, unless by a nominal decree of the Emperor.

The nobles have a right to go abroad with passports, and to enter foreign service with the authorization of the Government; but they are obliged to return home without delay on the first summons.

Every noble retired from the service has a right to wear the uniform of the government in which he is inscribed.

The noble cannot be deprived without trial of life, honour, or property: he must be tried by his *Peers**, and the sentence must be confirmed by the Emperor.

The noble is exempt from all corporal punishment before as well as during the trial, and cannot be subjected to it but for a fact posterior to that which has deprived him of nobility.

The crimes which entail the loss of his rights are treason, robbery, and murder.

The Russian noble is exempt from personal taxes and from the recruiting. His country-houses cannot be occupied by troops.

The hereditary noble has a right to establish on his estates any kind of fabric or manufacture; he may do the same in towns on inscribing himself in a guild. Upon the same condition he is allowed to carry on any sort of commerce.

He may acquire landed property with serfs,

---

* It is a mockery to call ordinary judges, ennobled *employés*, the peers of ancient nobles.

but he cannot possess serfs without having lands.

Emancipated serfs who have become hereditary nobles, cannot, before the third generation, acquire the lands on which they have themselves been inscribed as serfs; and, in case such an estate should devolve to one of them by inheritance, it must be placed immediately under guardianship, or sold within six months.

With the exception of Tartars anciently settled in the country, none but Christians have a right to possess Christian serfs.

The property of slaves devolving to a personal noble passes to the Crown, which pays a fixed price per *soul*. There are paid, besides, 50 silver rubles for every mother of a family*.

It is obvious that all these rights are negative rather than positive, and give nothing more than what belongs to every man in civi-

* In Russia, the women are not included among the *souls* belonging to nobles.

lized countries*. It required nothing short of
the simplicity of Russian legislation to enume-
rate in its codes rights such as those which we
have just specified. Accordingly, they cannot,
with the progress of civilization, continue to be
the exclusive appanage of a class; time will
completely annul them. The distinctions of free
men and serfs once abolished, the privileges of
the nobles will be done away with, and become
the patrimony of the entire nation, as they are
of humanity.

"The rights of the nobility," said one day a
celebrated Russian Professor, who might have
been a distinguished writer, as well as he has
since become a high functionary—"the rights
of the Russian nobility consist in entering the
service, if they are pleased to admit him into
it; in leaving it, if he is allowed to do so; in

* The meanest rag-gatherer in France can take service if he chooses, leave it when he likes, go abroad
with a passport; he may, if he has the means, purchase
negroes in the colonies; he is exempt from corporal
punishments, and he cannot be punished without trial.

going abroad, if he can obtain a passport; in purchasing landed property, if he has the money." And these rights are the same for the descendants of Rurick and of Guidemine, and for the latest upstart.

The nobility of each government forms a separate body, and has the faculty of assembling, to consult upon its common interests. Assemblies of this kind are held by governments or by districts, and they are ordinary or extraordinary.

The ordinary assemblies, for governments, are held every three years, habitually from the month of December to that of January: those of the districts three months before.

The right of sitting in these assemblies, with a deliberative voice, belongs to the hereditary nobles who have at least 100 peasants or 3000 dessiatines of land fit for tillage. Those who have 50 peasants at least may attend them, but not deliberate. Colonels or Councillors of State, and functionaries of superior ranks, need not have more than five

serfs to be electors. In the governments of
the two capitals, of Tauride, and of Astrakan,
the nobles possessing country-houses or lands,
producing them at least 600 silver rubles, take
an active part in the assemblies. Moreover,
no one can be a member of them till he has
attained the full age of twenty-one years, and
unless he has acquired at least the fourteenth
class in active service.

The noble who possesses, at one and the
same time, in several governments and districts, the property requisite to give him a
right to attend the elections, participates in
them in each of those governments or districts.
He who has in different governments or districts small parcels of property, amounting
together to 3000 dessiatines, with 100 peasants, has the choice of the place in which he
may prefer exercising his rights of elector.

Petty proprietors have a right to unite their
possessions into a joint stock till the quantity
of lands and peasants amounts to that which is
required by the law, and then to send a representative to the assembly.

Guardians and life possessors of properties, the importance of which fulfils the conditions fixed by law, can take part in the assemblies, if they answer the other prescribed conditions.

The father can depute a son to represent him, and a woman one of her relations, or even a noble stranger.

Nobles who have been turned out of the service, or brought to justice for some crime, are deprived of the right of sitting in the assembly.

The assembly of the nobles has a right to have a house of its own, a secretary, archives, and a seal.

The duties of the government assemblies are to elect to the different offices which are dependent on them, to discuss the interests of their government, and to present their opinions to the Governor, to the Minister of the Interior, and to the Emperor himself, to whose own hands they can address petitions. They have to make choice of three deputies, in case the supreme power should see fit to summon them before it to confer on the complaints and demands of the nobility. These assemblies can, after receiving permission, send deputies to the Emperor, *to thank him for the rights and privileges which he may have granted to the nobility.*

The assemblies of each government, and the marshal and deputies in particular, are charged to verify the titles of the nobles of the province, and to keep a vigilant eye upon the book of the nobility.

The assembly of the nobility cannot, in any case, appear before the tribunals, and cannot defend itself there but by delegates.

If it issues any decisions contrary to the laws, it incurs a fine of 150 silver rubles; the marshal of the government has to pay in addition 60, and the district marshal 30 silver rubles.

The head of the government cannot form part of it, even though he should possess estates in the same province. The attorney of the government must attend merely to furnish necessary explanations on points of law, but he cannot take any active part in the proceedings.

The duties of the marshals of the governments as well as those of the districts, elected by the assemblies of the nobility in each of these circumscriptions, are to preside at and to close the assemblies from which they emanate, to preserve order in them, to communicate to them the commands and the dispositions of the central power, and to lay out the funds belonging to the nobility according to its directions. They receive the oath of the officers elected by the nobility, and are members of the recruiting board.

The marshals of governments have, moreover, to deliver the necessary certificates to the nobles who wish to enter the service, and to keep in readiness the relay-horses requisite for the use of the Imperial family. They take part in the appointment of guardians to the estates of nobles who maltreat their serfs, who are too prodigal, or who swerve from the orthodox religion.

The nobility of each district nominates a deputy for the *assembly of the deputies*, which is dependent on the senate alone, and over which the marshal of the government presides. This last assembly is charged with the formation of the book of the nobility, to which it adds the persons who have furnished undeniable proofs of their nobility, delivers diplomas, and gives notice of them to the *geroldie* which revises its decisions. It has also a hand in placing the estates of nobles under guardianship.

At the time of the general assembly, the nobility of each district chooses a district marshal, the district judge, an *ispravnik*, the judges of the two tribunals, and the inspectors of the corn magazines. It has also to elect candidates for the offices distributed throughout the whole government. These are, the marshal of the government, the presidents of the civil and criminal courts, the justice of peace, the curator of the gymnasium, who is also curator of the schools, the assistants of the three tribunals, civil, penal, and of peace, the secretary of the nobility, and the members of the commission of public beneficence.

The marshal of the government is elected from among the former marshals, beginning with the actual holder of the office, the district marshals, ancient, or in office, and the presidents of the chambers. If these refuse, the nobility is at liberty to elect a new candidate. The votes for each candidate are given by balls for or against.

The government assemblies may exclude, by a majority of two-thirds of the votes, any noble on whom any judicial sentence whatever has cast a stigma, or who has committed a disgraceful act, even before he has been tried. From such a decision there is no appeal but to the senate, and then only in case of irregularity in the scrutiny.

The members who have obtained the greatest number of votes after the persons elected to the different posts, prefer a natural claim to each of those functions, and are called candidates.

The district marshals may be chosen from among the hereditary nobles who do not combine as proprietors all the conditions of eligibility; and when they have once served that office for three years, they acquire the right of taking part in the assemblies.

The presidents of the two courts may be elected from among the nobles who are unconnected with the government. They ought to have filled the posts of assessors, an office equivalent to the sixth class, or else to have belonged to the seventh.

The personal nobles may be elected to the offices of assistants, and, for want of other candidates, to those of *ispravniks*.

The elections for the judicial posts take place only every six years, the others at each assembly of the nobility.

The marshal of the government, and the curator of the schools must be confirmed by the Emperor.

Every noble has a right to declare beforehand that he will not accept such or such an office. He who has occupied a superior post cannot, without his consent, be appointed to an inferior employment.

In the governments of Archangel, Olonetzk, Wiatka, Perm, and in all those of Siberia, there are no elections, on account of the small number of nobles residing in those countries.

Limited as are the rights of the assemblies of the nobility, the sphere of activity allotted to certain posts which are in their nomination is so extensive that this institution might be beneficial, if it were duly exercised; but such is the disfavour attached to the public service in Russia, and so deeply have sordid principles penetrated there, that the inferior posts are considered as a disgrace. To no purpose have generous patriots devoted themselves with a view to raise them in the public opinion; they have failed in their attempts, and have been obliged to relinquish them to men who have no other means of subsistence but the

extortions inseparable in Russia from every
public office.

The posts of presidents of the two courts
are rarely occupied by persons elected from
among the nobility, in which are found few
who combine the conditions required for those
offices; and most commonly the Government
itself fills them with functionaries of its own
choosing. Peculations having been discovered
in the government of Novgorod, Nicholas last
year issued a decree insulting to the whole
body of the nobility: he said that, if it knew
not how to make a better use of the rights
which he had granted to it, he should take
them away. The daw tricked himself out in
peacock's feathers. It was not Nicholas but
Catherine who conferred the right of election on
the nobility. What would be the consequence
if the nobles, who occupy certain posts of
internal administration, were removed to make
room for agents of the Government? The
good which the former still do would be destroyed; venality and partiality would exceed

all bounds, and the little probity, which is owing to the presence of the nobles in public employments, would disappear. While the Government shall not become moral and its agents shall not be independent, every effort ought to be made to extend the share of the nobles in the administration, and to gain respect for the functions which are allotted to them.

In order to form a just idea of the Russian nobility, we must not blend it together into one mass, but divide it into several classes. The courtiers and the functionaries have nothing in common with the nobility properly so called. Their life is regulated from above; their minds are contracted by the etiquette of the court, or the routine of their office; their hearts do not beat at ease in their tight uniform, or under the weight of decorations. In the country you meet with men, who, having all served for a longer or shorter time, and occupied posts more or less important, have abandoned that career, either from necessity

or from a fondness for rural life, or perhaps
merely from aversion to the public service.
Some occupy themselves successfully with their
lands rather than with their serfs; others have
gone into voluntary exile, and retired from the
world in the pleasing hope of better times.
Beside them you find a host of gentry who
have never been out of their province, or who
have served either in the interior or in regiments of the line, but have never emancipated
themselves from the deep-rooted prejudices of
their caste. In them the grossest ignorance is
frequently united with the principles of a more
than equivocal morality. Exceptions are,
however, to be found in both classes; and at
times you meet with warm hearts among the
functionaries, and enlightened minds among
the landed proprietors.

The Russian nobility is the head and the
heart of the nation, nay, it is the entire nation; for, unhappily, it alone possesses rights,
though illusory, while the rest of the people
have nothing but obligations. It is in its

ranks that the most civilized and the most distinguished men in every respect are to be found. Hitherto its only virtue was a patriotism which displayed itself as much in great sacrifices in the time of national wars, as by a blind devotedness to the throne, which it considers as the only guarantee of the public and private welfare. For it, liberty will necessarily be the first consequence and the immediate effect of the law of progression. So long ago as 1825, more than one hundred nobles sacrificed themselves for this sacred cause. Literature and the army are indebted to the nobility for their most illustrious characters. The Puschkins and the Karamsins, the Suworofs and the Kutusofs, were nobles before they became great authors and great captains. Upon the nobility then must rest the hope of the reforms necessary for Russia, for it is far less from it than from the Government that every obstacle to the development of the nation proceeds.

The nobility ought further to be distin-

guished according to the different provinces.
The Germans have nothing in common with
the Russians: the Little Russians have scarcely
any more resemblance to them. The nobility
of the Baltic provinces, (I speak of those who
like better to attend to their own interests
and those of the country, than to scramble at
court for distinctions which excite the jealousy
of the native Russians,) the German nobility,
I say, has a sense of its dignity, a truly European civilization, honourable manners, and
usages. The Emperor Alexander, who was
often disgusted with the meannesses of his
courtiers, being one day at a ball at Reval,
said aloud to his generals, "Take notice, they
do not salute here as with us."

In Little Russia, the Tartars have not left
such profound traces of their domination as
have thoroughly demoralized Russia, properly
so called. Serfage was not even introduced
there before the time of Elisabeth, who took
it into her head one day to make a present of
50,000 free men to her paramour Rasou-

movsky; and the inhabitants of that country, who were till then attached to their military chiefs and not to the soil, have since been forcibly inscribed as serfs.

OF THE SERFS.

No free man can be reduced to the state of serf. Since the year 1801, the emperors have renounced the custom of making presents of serfs, though there have been exceptions to this rule for Poland, where several entire villages have been arbitrarily deprived of their liberty. Voluntary enslavement is not valid, and none but orphans, picked up before the age of eight years, brought up and instructed by a noble, can now be inscribed in the number of his serfs.

Children are of the same condition as their father; they are free if born after his emancipation, his entrance into the military service, or his being sent to Siberia. Free women who marry serfs retain their liberty, but yet owe obedience to their new master. Marriage with a free man emancipates the female serf.

Proprietors are forbidden to force their serfs to contract marriages contrary to their inclinations; on the other hand, the clergy are prohibited to marry serfs without the authorization of their masters. As the serfs belonging to one master can in general marry only among themselves, they soon become united together by such ties of relationship as scarcely allow them to seek new alliances. Petty proprietors, in particular, deprived of the right to purchase girls among their neighbours, see their serfs doomed to perpetual celibacy, and their substance gradually wasting away.

Runaway serfs must be restored to their masters, even though it may be more than ten years since they absconded. If, during this interval, they contract marriages with serfs belonging to other masters, the latter, husband or wife, and their children, go to the proprietors of the fugitives. In case they should have married other runaways, such families go back entire to the master of the husband, and that of the wife receives an indemnity fixed by law.

If a fugitive female marries a free man, she continues free; but her husband is obliged to indemnify the proprietor.

If a serf has been killed without premeditation, the murderer pays the proprietor 600 silver rubles; but if there has been premeditation, no indemnity can be made, the criminal being liable to the punishment prescribed by the law.

The master of a vessel, on board which a serf dies in consequence of his service, is obliged to pay the master of the serf three years' wages and the tax upon the deceased*.

The serfs are bound to work for their master three days in the week, but not on Sundays or holidays.

Masters are forbidden to make their serfs

---

* Proprietors pay a personal tax of about eight francs per annum for their serfs.

work in the mines on conditions which the latter would not have accepted of their own accord.

The master decides without appeal all quarrels between the serfs on his estate, and inflicts on them such punishments as he pleases, though he has no right to mutilate them, or to endanger their lives. His power does not extend to the punishment of crimes, which must always be submitted to the cognizance of the tribunals. He may also leave to them the punishment of his people for disobedience or ordinary misdemeanours; and he can also make a soldier of a serf who misconducts himself, or give him up to the discretion of the Government.

The proprietor may remove his serfs from one estate to another, be the distance and situation what they will; but, in case his estates are mortgaged, he cannot do so without the consent of his creditors.

Whoever is not an hereditary noble cannot possess serfs. The noble who has no lands cannot possess men. Neither the emancipated serf who may have become noble, nor his son, nor his grandson, can possess the lands on which they have been serfs.

It is forbidden to announce in the public papers any sale of serfs without lands, or to proceed publicly to such sales at fairs or markets. Proprietors cannot divide families and sell separately the husband, the wife, or the unmarried children, whether orphans or not.

The proprietors must secure his serfs from want. He pays a fine of one silver ruble fifty copecks for every serf taken in the fact of begging.

Serfs ruined or maltreated by their master are placed under guardianship, and certain cruelties of masters towards their serfs may be carried before the tribunals*. Proprietors

---

* An extraordinary trait of the justice of Nicholas is related. M. S * * * a landed proprietor in the government of Witebsk, having been murdered by his serfs for attempting to violate one of their daughters, an investigation was ordered. Twenty nobles, neigh-

placed under guardianship cannot reside on their estates, but are at liberty to sell them or to dispose of their revenues. In case of their acquiring new serfs, these would fare the same as the others. Estates on which arrears of imposts are suffered to accumulate are placed under guardianship till the debts are entirely cleared off.

Serfs cannot possess any immoveable property. Their lands and their houses belong to their masters. Inheritances which devolve to them are sold for their benefit. With the permission of their masters, they may establish manufactories, engage in commerce, and temporarily inscribe themselves in the trades.

The master may give freedom to his serfs, either collectively or individually, with or without land. The freedman is required to make choice of a condition before the next census; otherwise he becomes a soldier or

bours of the deceased, bore testimony in favour of his morality. The Emperor ordered the estates of all these false witnesses to be sequestrated.

colonist, and his young children are placed in
the military schools. The children who have
thus lost their parents continue free, on condition of their choosing a profession when they
shall be of age. If the act of enfranchisement
is found to be not valid, the emancipated person returns to servitude, unless he has meanwhile made choice of a condition; but, once
inscribed in a liberal profession, he retains his
independence, and his master receives from the
Government 114 rubles $28\frac{4}{7}$ cop. for a man,
and 57 silver rubles $14\frac{2}{7}$ cop. for a woman.

Serfs falling into the possession of persons
who are not Christians become free on paying
4 silver rubles 50 cop. per head, for the benefit of the master.

The serf who denounces, with proofs, his
master for treason or intended violence against
the Emperor, obtains his liberty and that of
his whole family.

The serfs made prisoners in war do not
return to their masters on recovering their
liberty.

Sentence of transportion or forced labour gives liberty to serfs, and their wives can accompany them to the place of their exile.

In another place*, I have declared myself in favour of the Decree of the 2nd of April, 1842, which empowers nobles to emancipate their serfs by making with them agreements that are freely assented to. I still maintain my opinion in its full extent. I have hailed this decree as a forerunner of the emancipation of the serfs; in fact, trifling as it may be, still a great deal has been done in broaching the question; and already the fear of seeing the Government one day cut this knot urges the nobles to prevent its direct interposition, and to remedy the present state of things in one way or other. By the method which the Government has adopted, it has declined the initiative, and thrown the responsibility on the nobles, by opening a clear field for their philanthropy. This was a politic proceeding on its part, and has singularly lightened its task.

* *Esprit de l'Economie Politique.*

Having once got so far, no matter whether willingly or unwillingly, it would be pusillanimous to recede; and I seize its decree as a plank of safety. I call upon it in the name of humanity to fulfil the engagements which morally it has contracted before the face of the whole world. I think the decree good, because to me it appears moderate, and it respects the pretensions of each, leaving to the nobles as to the serfs full latitude to make such agreements as they shall deem advantageous. This law is the more wise, inasmuch as it reserves to the Government the faculty of selecting, after some time, from among all these conventions which shall have been framed, and adopting as a model, that which shall be judged to be the best, and which will probably be rendered obligatory. I did certainly think, and I still believe, that the force of circumstances will imperatively command the adoption of conditions, differing according to the difference of localities*.

* I am met with the objection, I am told, that the serf being a thing, one cannot treat with him; that,

Thus far the results have not corresponded with the hopes entertained. The nobility has not shown that eagerness to enter the track opened for it which one had a right to expect; power has not brought the necessary perseverance to bear on this point, and has incurred the suspicion of timidity or duplicity. The serfs have not sufficient intelligence to frame the conditions of their enfranchisement, and would be afraid of compromising their future welfare. They distrust the Government more than their masters, and would rather remain serfs, than place themselves in greater dependence on authority. "Whenever," say they, "we should have differences with our masters, the judges would be sure to decide in their favour." They are afraid that then they should not be able to satisfy the rapacity of those magistrates, whereas at present they have

---

being a property himself, he cannot have wherewith to answer his engagements. The objection is subtle. The serf is a serf only because the law wills it, and it is to give him a property that he is emancipated.

scarcely any reason to complain of the cruelty of their masters. The nobility, on its part, has no wish to cause the Government to interfere in its relations with its peasants; and the latter, groping its way, dares neither come to the succour of the serfs, nor take any definitive resolution. The question thus finds itself indefinitely adjourned, thanks to the wretched state of the Russian administration, and to the bad faith of the officers charged by the law of 1842 to settle the differences between the freedmen and the nobles. But, with the deplorable situation of the Russian tribunals, not only is it impossible to think of any emancipation whatever, but existence itself becomes a burden. 'Tis there that the knife must first be applied: the administration must be improved, either by encouraging the most intelligent and the most upright nobles to take part in it, or by calling to it well-informed young men of good families. But the evil lies deeper than it is imagined; it arises from the very organization of the Russian government, and it is in the upper regions that it must be attacked. The edifice is faulty at the foundation; it is impossible to make a real improvement in any part without rebuilding the whole. You cannot emancipate the serfs without emancipating the nobles, moralize the subjects without moralizing the government. You must at one and the same time give dignity to the law, purify the legislation, amend the judicial proceedings, inculcate upon each and all a sense of duty: civilize the people, in short. But this is not a reason for neglecting the details, for renouncing partial ameliorations, because one cannot modify the whole: it is necessary to labour at both at once, and to begin somewhere.

It is not means that are wanting to accomplish a work which God himself would be pleased to protect: and it is much more difficult to subsist with the serfs than to extricate one's-self from the embarrassments which their emancipation is liable to produce.

If you would not decree liberty unless upon

the basis of the relations at present subsisting between masters and serfs, beware of attempting more than it is possible to do. The *barstschina* serf, that is to say, one who works for the account of his master, has three days in the week for himself, and the use of three dessiatines of land, one for each kind of crop, according to the system of fallows which generally prevails in Russia. In certain provinces he has even six—two for each crop*. He has, moreover, a hut, implements of labour, and the requisite animals. The most rapacious master respects the moveable property of the serf, and the levy of sheep, poultry, eggs, and cloth begins to be relinquished. At times, it is true, he does put him out of his hut and his field, but he cannot help giving him others in their stead, being obliged to provide for his subsistence, and finding that the usual mode is after all the easiest. The farming peasants enjoy the whole of the lord's lands for a very

---

* A dessiatine is rather more than a French hectare.

moderate rent, which is fixed by mutual agreement.

If the law were to declare this state of things fixed and obligatory, by ensuring to the serfs the property of their land in exchange for the labour or the rent which they pay, the nobles would raise the outcry of spoliation and those who cultivate their lands themselves would consider their rights as invaded. The most enlightened, who might be disposed to renounce their rights to men, would not consent to give up for ever the smallest corner of their lands. If then the present state of things evidently protects the serfs, how is it that arrangements satisfactory to both parties cannot be devised? The nobles, having no rights over their serfs, have none over their labour, any more than the serfs have any right over their lands. The compact is easy to break, and the Government can, with perfect justice, prescribe a new order of things. Leaving to the two parties the faculty of discussing and settling their relations, it can, and ought to urge them to it, by declaring itself in favour of a rule of some sort, which should be imposed by force, if, within a certain time, they had not come to an amicable arrangement.

" It is not yet time," say these nobles. This is the cry set up by the patient at sight of the surgeon's instrument—a cry which changes into a sigh of relief when the operator has taken off the gangrened limb. The serfs, they further say, are not capable of making a proper use of liberty. If this is not the language of the wolf to the lamb, it is that of prejudiced men. Slavery has never been the education for freedom. The Russian government, by interdicting every kind of instruction to the serfs*, prevents their understanding from conceiving the benefits of a free condition, and dooms them to a brutal ignorance, which makes them pleased with their slavery.

* The serf cannot be admitted into the public schools until after his emancipation, and nothing has yet been done on the score of instruction for this class of the population.

The Russian nobles wish for the emancipation of the serfs, because they are ashamed to pass for slave-traders in the eyes of civilized Europe; because they begin to perceive some profit in emancipation, and to be apprehensive for their own safety, fearing that the serfs may by and by seize that liberty which is now refused them. The Government wishes for it too, in order to *whitewash* itself before foreign nations, and to augment its revenues. At that rate there would be none but the serfs themselves who would not wish to be free; for, to listen to the partisans of the *status quo*, their condition is ensured at present, but would become quite precarious on the day of their emancipation. If, in fact, the nobles are determined not to part with any of their lands, in this case indeed liberty would be a dangerous weapon in the hands of the serfs.

The Government, on the one hand, has not the courage to take a decisive measure, and, on the other, the serfs know not how to stipulate for their interests. The Emperor, yielding to foreign influences, would fain crown himself with an immortal laurel; but he knows not either how to avoid or to meet the dangers which emancipation presents, and he is too well pleased with the darkness which surrounds him to decree the freedom that would dispel it.

Before emancipating the serfs of the nobles, it would be necessary to enfranchise the serfs of the Crown, for it is universally admitted that their state is more wretched than that of the serfs of private persons. They cannot shift from one place to another when they like, nor pursue any trade that suits them, nor establish themselves where they please; and the multiplicity of their chiefs only paralyzes their activity, only ruins their fortune. On the most frivolous pretexts, all the *employés* of the Government and the elected *employés* vie with each other in fleecing them, alleging, as a reason for their extortions, high motives of State which they are not capable of comprehending; and the uniform ridicule with which

peasant functionaries are overwhelmed increases their rapacity as much as their
influence.

The half measures which Nicholas has
hitherto taken, are deficient in energy; and,
but recently, the Government, coming forward
as guarantee of the engagements which the
serfs attached to the personal service of their
masters had contracted for their liberation,
neglected to fix a maximum which should be
obligatory for the lords. It is, therefore, said
that nothing great will be accomplished under
this wretched system, and that the heir to the
crown will inherit with it all the difficultie
which his father was incapable of resolving.

OF THE REGULAR CLERGY.

A MAN cannot enter a convent before he is
thirty years old, a woman before forty. They
must be free from all personal engagements
and obligations, such as the public service,
dependence on a master, ties of marriage,

have no debts, and no accounts to settle with
justice. In case a married couple wish to
renounce the world both at once, they must
not have any children of tender age.

The monk who quits his convent does not
recover either the ranks or orders which he
may have acquired by service, and merely
returns to the class to which he belonged in
right of birth. He cannot be admitted again
into the service, nor dwell, before the expiration of seven years, in one of the capitals,
or in the government in which the monastery
that he has left is situated.

Monks expelled from the convent for misconduct are at the disposal of the Government.

Monks are exempt from taxes, from the
recruiting, and from corporal punishments.

No member of the regular clergy can
acquire or possess immoveable property; he is
obliged to dispose of it on taking the tonsure,
and has no right to redeem it on his return
into the world; but he may build or buy cells
in the interior of his monastery. He is prohi-

bited from all commerce, excepting in the articles which he makes himself, and which, with the permission of the superior, may be sold by aged monks. He is forbidden to contract any engagement, to receive in deposit any thing besides books, and to place any capital in the institutions of credit.

The monastic authorities alone have a right to make wills. The property of the mere monks belongs after their death to the monastery.

OF THE ECCLESIASTICAL PROFESSION.

EVERY man, who is not a serf, is at liberty to embrace the ecclesiastical profession, when there are vacant places in the clergy, and when the conduct and education of the applicant are conformable to the duties of that ministry.

The deacons who renounce their functions cannot be admitted into the public service till six years, and priests not till ten years afterwards: they cannot recover the rights which they may have previously acquired. If they have been excluded from the clergy for misconduct, the term before which they cannot be admitted into the civil service is doubled; it is then twelve years for deacons, and twenty for priests. As for the military service, they may be admitted into that immediately, but as common soldiers.

Mere clerks, excluded for misconduct and deprived of the free choice of a profession, are made soldiers, or in case of incapacity, colonists in the least populated governments.

The members of the clergy are exempt from taxes, from corporal punishments, and from the recruiting. Those who are noble by birth, or by the collation of an order, are authorized to possess serfs.

The houses belonging to ecclesiastics, whether in office or retired from the service, are exempt from all contribution excepting that for lighting the streets and keeping them in repair. They are forbidden to turn them

into cook-shops or public-houses. No member
of the clergy can give valid security, or legally
manage the business of private persons. They
are prohibited from engaging in any kind of
trade that requires an admission or reception
of those who devote themselves to it.

OF THE INHABITANTS OF THE TOWNS.

By the term middle class, Russian legislation understands all the inhabitants of the
towns without distinction, merchants as well
as artisans. Properly speaking, there is no
middle class, unless we include in it the
inferior nobility and clergy, the *employés*, and
the merchants.

The merchants inscribed in a guild* are
exempt from military service and from personal imposts.

---

* There are three guilds of merchants in Russia,
differing according to the contributions which they pay
to the government, and the nature and importance of
the commercial affairs to which inscription in each of
these guilds gives them a right.

In the capital towns, the citizens cannot possess houses of the value of more than 7,500 silver rubles, if they are not inscribed in a guild. Neither can they possess lands with serfs, and these must, when the case does happen, be removed elsewhere or sold in the course of a year, to some one who has a right to possess them.

By virtue of ancient privileges, the city of Smolensk retains in full property lands with serfs, under the dependence of its hôtel de ville. The Tartars of the Tauride and the Polovniks of the government of Wologda are likewise beyond the operation of the law just adverted to.

The peasants have no right to possess houses in the capitals.

The inhabitants of each town have the faculty of meeting to consult upon their common interests. These meetings are general, or partial and special, either for different classes of the inhabitants, such as those of the merchants, artisans, &c., or for different quarters of the towns.

General meetings are usually held every three years, in winter, a fortnight after those of the nobles. They may also be summoned extraordinarily as circumstances may require.

The assembly of each town may have its particular house, archives, a seal, a secretary, and a fund for the general expenses.

Every citizen of the age of twenty-five years, possessing a capital the interest of which amounts to at least fifteen silver rubles, can take an active part in these meetings. Those who are not so old or so rich have a right only to be present. Peasants dwelling in the town, and possessing a house there, are not admitted to the assemblies.

The attributions of these assemblies are to deliberate on the propositions of the head of the government, to address to him presentations to certain places, and to submit to him reflections upon the interests of the community.

In cases where the rights and advantages of commerce are grievously violated or compromised, the assembly may refer the matter directly to the Minister of the Finances.

The commune pays a fine of sixty rubles for every decision contrary to the laws. It does not appear before the tribunals, but defends itself by means of an advocate.

The communes have a right to possess meadow-lands granted to them by the Government. They have the faculty of erecting mills, constructing canals, and establishing banks.

The elections are general for the whole town, or special for each quarter, or each body of the State. The general assembly elects the Mayor of the town, the Burgomasters, and the Town Council. It elects, by districts, the Verbal Judges, the Deputies of the Assembly, the Members of the Commission for billeting and for the assessment of contributions. The elections attributed to particular bodies are those of the brokers and the notaries, of the members of the Commercial Schools, of the inspectors of the Primary Schools, of the valuers of goods destined for exportation, of the comptrollers of the precious metals, of the commissioners of the Beneficent Society of Moscow, of the members of the River Navigation to Twer and Orel.

Each body of the State that has a voice in the commune sends a delegate to the Municipal Council, which in its turn composes a committee of six members. The merchants, the citizens, and the artisans, form particular corporations, and elect chiefs: each guild has its Mayor, each trade has its Elder, and all the trades united make choice of a Syndic. Elections of this kind take place every year. Each town has moreover to elect twenty-four jurors for the recruiting.

The deputies of the districts form, with the Starosts and the Mayor, the Assembly of the Deputies, charged to keep the book of the commune, in which are inscribed all the citizens of the town, and to furnish them with extracts from it and attestations.

Bankrupts, and persons who have suffered judicial condemnation cannot be admitted to vote at elections; nay, even such as are in bad repute, or whose characters excite distrust, may be excluded from them.

Those who have introduced a new branch of industry, the masters of cloth manufactories which supply the crown, and apothecaries, are not obliged to serve.

The merchants of the first guild are not bound to accept any posts but those of mayor of the town and adjuncts of the tribunals of peace. Those of the second guild are besides obliged to perform the offices of burgomasters and councillors (rathmann). The members of the third guild cannot refuse the places of deputy. The other posts fall only to the citizens properly so called.

The persons elected must be confirmed by the authorities to whose jurisdiction their functions belong.

All these agents have uniforms, according to their offices, and those who perform the duties of them for three sessions keep these uniforms for ever. They are exempt from the recruiting while they are in place, and become so for ever when they have remained in it for three sessions. The merchants of the third guild, who hold posts equivalent to rank in the public service, are exempt while in office from corporal punishments.

The elections are for three years, excepting those of the verbal judges, and the deputies and commissioners of quarters, who serve for one year only.

These persons receive no salary from the Crown, but they are paid by the town, agreeably to arrangements prescribed by the Minister of the Interior.

On the 10th of April, 1832, there was instituted a particular class of citizens, called *honorary* citizens. This quality is hereditary or personal. Under the first head are included the children of personal nobles, the merchants having decorations, the merchants who have remained ten years in the first or twenty years in the second guild, without having ever failed or been sued at law, those who have been councillors of commerce or manufactures, the doctors and masters of arts of the universities, if they do not prefer to enter the service, the artists of the Academy of Arts, and those of the Imperial theatres of the first class, after fifteen years' service.

Personal honorary citizens are the candidates and graduated students of the universities, the pupils of the schools of commerce of St. Petersburg and Moscow, who have completed their courses, and the actors of the first class, after ten years' service.

Either of these distinctions may be granted by the Government to persons of eminence in commerce, manufactures, sciences, and arts.

The rights of honorary citizenship cease on account of fraudulent bankruptcy, and for any crime entailing the privation of civil rights. They are suspended in regard to those who pass into a servile or menial condition, without prejudice to their children, if in them the quality was hereditary.

OF ELECTIONS IN THE COUNTRY.

THE peasants of the Crown alone have a right to hold public elections.   They send two delegates to the court of conscience, one of whom is a member of the college of public beneficence.   They elect a *zemski* for the local police, *sotskis* and *dessiatskis*, or superintendents of a hundred and of ten houses.

These elections likewise take place every three years in each district, and by delegates, to the number of one for five hundred house or land holders.   The elector must be at least thirty years of age, father of a family, and of irreproachable conduct.   The candidate ought to possess the same qualifications; he may moreover be a noble or public functionary, provided that he consents to serve the office. The elections are held in the town specified by authority, and must be confirmed by the chief of the province. The persons elected cannot be punished without trial, nor enrolled as soldiers; and those who have performed the duties for nine years, by virtue of three successive elections, are exempted for life from the recruiting. The assessors have uniforms, and a salary from Government. The election of the *sotskis* and *dessiatskis* is decided by universal suffrage. The villages which have fewer than ten or one hundred houses are joined to others, with which they take turns for the election of the *dessiatskis* and the *sotskis.* The *sotskis* are elected for three years, and the *dessiatskis* for one month only. There are officers of this kind among all the peasants without distinction, and it is their duty to execute the orders of the police, and to preserve the public tranquillity. Proprietors nominate them at pleasure for their serfs.

The elections are local or general; particular for each village, (selo,) or general for the district, (voloste). The first are limited to the choice of the electors for the general elections, in the proportion of two for every ten houses. The electors form the general election of the commune, and have to appoint the elder of the village, the mayors, the collectors of the taxes, the inspector of the magazines of corn, the keepers of the forests, the judges of the court of conscience, the *starosts* for fires, the sotskis, and three candidates for the office of volostes. These elections take place by ballot, the candidates being taken from among the electors, in the ratio of two in ten. Each district electoral college chooses a mayor from among the adjuncts and the judges, out of whom the chamber of the domains selects one for each office. The various persons elected must be twenty-five years of age. Disbanded soldiers are eligible to these employments.

In Siberia, the elections of the peasants take place annually by means of delegates, in the ratio of one for every hundred inhabitants. The elective offices are confined in the volostes to those of mayor, starost, and clerk, and in

the villages, to those of the elders and the
dessiatskis. In Siberia, as in the Caucasus,
the peasants send no delegates to the tribunals,
and these offices are conferred by the Government. In the western provinces, all the inhabitants of the villages and the volostes vote
in common at elections.

Chapter II.

OF THE PUBLIC SERVICE.

The right to serve his country is not granted to every Russian. The tributary classes, the serfs, emancipated persons, the citizens (bourgeois) properly so called, the traders of the second and third guild, are deprived of the right to enter the civil service. This interdict does not extend to public instruction; but serfs cannot study.

The nobility, on the contrary, are obliged to serve, for such is the will of the Sovereign, and consequently of public opinion, its faithful companion; there is, moreover, a law which deprives of nobility every man whose father

and grandfather have not served   The consequence of this fact is, that the civil functions
are encumbered with nobles, while there is a
want of capable officers in the ranks of the
army.

Active service is reckoned to begin at the
age of sixteen years. Young men, who have
been educated abroad, from the age of ten to
eighteen years, are deprived of the right to
enter the service.

If a merchant of the first guild has not
remained in it twenty years, or has been
bankrupt, neither he nor his children have the
right to be admitted into the civil service.

Deacons, who voluntarily quit the church,
cannot be taken into the service till six years
and priests till ten years afterwards. Those
who have been excluded from the church for
misconduct must wait double that time.

There are fourteen classes of *tschinns*, viz.,

CIVIL RANKS.	MILITARY RANKS
1. Chancellor	Field-Marshal.
2. Actual Privy Councillor	General-in-Chief.

CIVIL RANKS.	MILITARY RANKS.
3. Privy Councillor	Lieutenant-General.
4. Actual Councillor of State	Major-General.
5. Councillor of State	Brigadier (abolished.)
6. Councillor of College	Colonel.
7. Court Councillor	Lieutenant-Colonel.
8. Assessor of College	Major.
9. Titular Councillor	Captain.
10. Secretary of College	Second Captain.
11. ——	——
12. Secretary of Government	Lieutenant.
13. ——	Sub-Lieutenant.
14. Registrator of College	Officer.

These military ranks are those of the regiments of the line: in the guard, the same titles represent a rank two degrees higher, the artillery excepted, where the advantage is of but one degree. The ordinary members of the Academy of Sciences are of the sixth, the extraordinary members of the seventh, and the adjuncts of the eighth class.

The professors of the Academies of Arts and of Medicine are, if they belong to the first degree, of the sixth class, those of the second are of the seventh, and those of the third degree are of the eighth.

The *ordinary* professors of the universities
are of the seventh, the *extraordinary* professors
of the eighth, and the *lecturers* of the tenth
class.   The Pedagogic Institution, the School
of Law, and the Lyceums of Odessa and
Tzarskoie-Selo follow the same classification.
The professors of the Besborodko and Demidof Lyceums are of the eighth class.   The
directors of the gymnasiums are of the seventh,
the inspectors of the eighth; the masters of
science of the first degree are of the ninth,
those of the second of the tenth, and the
drawing and writing masters of the 12th class.

The inspector of the Lyceum of Tzarskoie-
Selo is of the sixth class.

The director of the School of St. Peter and
St. Paul is of the eighth class, which he
retains after six years' service.   The inspector
is of the ninth, the masters are of the tenth,
and they retain their rights after four years'
service.

All the professors, masters, and teachers,
are reckoned as being in active service, and

advance according to the general rules. Private tutors are likewise considered as being in the service, and they have the rights of personal nobility, even when they have no rank.

The masters of the parish schools (écoles communales) are included in the fourteenth class, but are not actually admitted into it till they have served twelve years.

At the Don, the teachers of the Cossacks have military rank; their promotion, nevertheless, takes place not according to military order but to the regulations of the public instruction.

Masters who have no certificate of study acquire the rank of the fourteenth class at the expiration of three years, if they are noble; at the end of five, if they are sons of personal nobles; at the end of seven, if their fathers were not invested with any rank; and at the end of ten, if their parents had no right to the service. Those, on the contrary, who have gone through their courses at the gymnasium, without acquiring rank, attain to the fourteenth class at the end of two years if they come under the first head; of three if they are under the second; of five if under the third; and of eight years in the fourth. Those who have obtained ranks are confirmed in them after a year's service.

Doctors of medicine and surgery are of the seventh, ordinary medical men of the eighth, apothecaries of the ninth, veterinary surgeons of the tenth, candidates of medicine of the twelfth, assistants of the fourteenth class. The first are confirmed in their tschinn after ten years' service, the second after eight years*. Physicians of the first degree are admitted into the ninth class after three years' service, those of the second after four years, and those of the third after six years. The veterinary surgeons and apothecaries employed are subject to the same rule. Dentists attached to the public service are admitted into the fourteenth class after they have served twelve years. Doctors

* Decree of May 24, 1834.

are promoted from the eighth to the seventh
in five years, to the sixth after eleven years,
and to the fifth after fifteen years' service.
Surgeons, veterinary surgeons and apothecaries
of the first degree are promoted to the eighth
class after eight years, those of the second
after nine years, and those of the third after
ten years' service. These last cannot rise
above the eighth class.

The chamberlain is considered as being
councillor of state, and the gentleman of the
chamber as titular councillor. A man cannot
be invested with these offices at court, unless
he has acquired corresponding ranks in the
active service.

The valets-de-chambre of the court are promoted to the twelfth class after ten years' service; but, while in that situation, they cannot
rise above the eighth. The grooms of the
chamber are admitted into the sixth at the
same time that they are invested with their
office. The great singers of the court are
made of the twelfth class after ten years' ser-

vice; when they have attained the ninth, they are obliged to pass into some other service.

The master workmen of manufactories may, at the end of twelve years, obtain the rank of the fourteenth class, on condition of continuing in their profession for eight years.

The actors and artists of the Imperial theatrical companies are reckoned as belonging to the public service. They are divided into three classes: the first-rate characters, the solo performers, the machinists, the managers, the leaders of the band, form the first; the performers of secondary parts, prompters, and masters of the wardrobe, belong to the second; and the chorus-singers to the third.

The artists of the first class who have been ten years at the theatre may enter the service of the State, and have a right to be admitted into the fourteenth class at the end of six years. Those who have been educated at the institutions of the Crown do not acquire the same rights till they have been fifteen years at the theatre.

The directors of the relays are reckoned to belong to the fourteenth class.

Promotion in the service depends on two conditions: birth and a good education. To each of these two heads there are three subdivisions.

As to birth, a distinction is made between hereditary nobility, personal nobility, and individuals foreign to the nobility. In regard to education, there are in the first place persons who have completed their courses at the universities and obtained degrees, those who have been educated in the gymnasiums, and lastly, those who have received only a private education.

Whoever has not gone through a regular course of study, classes himself in the service in virtue of the rights of birth. In this case, he enters without distinction, without any rank, and as a mere clerk of chancellery. But hereditary nobles arrive at the fourteenth class at the expiration of two years, the children of former *employés*, of merchants of the first guild, and of ecclesiastics, in four years; and the children of those who never had any rank in six years.

Between the fourteenth and the ninth class, every *employé* included in this category is obliged to continue four years in each rank, and at least three years in case of eminent services; but, from the ninth class to the eighth, hereditary nobles must be promoted in five years, and the others in ten only. It takes six years to ascend from the eighth to the seventh, and the same number of years to pass from the sixth to the fifth class. Hereditary nobles, when they have distinguished themselves, may acquire the eighth class in three years; but for those who are not so eight years are required. In all the superior classes the same cause may obtain for all, without distinction of birth, a diminution of two years.

Young men who have obtained degrees at the universities enter the service with the *tschinns* which are attributed to them. The doctor is admitted as being of the eighth, the master of arts of the ninth, the candidate of the tenth, and the graduated student of the twelfth class.

The theological academies confer licences of the first and second degree, which correspond with the titles of masters of arts or candidates; and the licentiates who relinquish the ecclesiastical career enter the civil service with rank in the ninth or the tenth class.

The seminaries confer on their pupils licences to two degrees, the first of which only gives a right to the fourteenth class.

The Lyceum of Tzarskoie-Selo and the School of Law are authorized to confer on their pupils ranks up to the ninth inclusively; the Lyceum of Odessa and that of Prince Besborodko cannot go beyond the twelfth, and that of Demidof, is limited to the fourteenth class.

Educated persons of the first category rise from the fourteenth class to the twelfth, and from the twelfth to the tenth, in three years;

from the tenth to the ninth, and from the ninth to the eighth, in four years, if they are of noble birth, and in six years if they are not; from the eighth to the seventh, and from the seventh to the sixth, in three years; and from the sixth to the fifth, in four years. Eminent services may produce an abatement of two years for each rank, to the eighth inclusively, and of one year for the superior ranks.

Persons who have not followed the courses of the public institutions, may undergo examinations at the universities, which give them the rights of literate men.

The students who have been instructed at the expense of the State are required to serve for six years.

In the second class of literate men are included the pupils of the secondary schools, the gymnasiums, &c. They acquire the fourteenth class at the end of one year's service if they are noble; of two years if their fathers were but personal nobles; and of four years if they had no title of nobility.

Up to the ninth class, they pass four years in each rank; then, to gain the eighth the noble takes but four years, and the others, ten. Afterwards, four years are required from all to obtain the superior classes, excepting the fifth, which demands six years' service. Whoever distinguishes himself, may obtain a diminution of one year for each rank, of four years even for admission into the eighth class, if he is not noble, and of two years for the fifth.

The corps of pages, of seamen, and of ensigns, can place their pupils in the civil service, in case of unfitness for the military service, by causing them to be included among the literate persons of the first or second class, according to the examination which they have to undergo on the sciences that form the object of their studies. The pupils destined for the guard have a right to the tenth, and the others to the twelfth class.

Military men pass into the civil service with the ranks which they have in the army; but they do not obtain advancement till after

the promotion of their comrades who remained
in the regiment. In the civil service, they are
included in the first class of literate persons, if
they have been in the artillery, sappers of the
guard, or officers of the staff; the others are
comprised in the second.

Beyond the fifth class, there is no rule for
promotion, which then depends solely on the
pleasure of the Emperor.

Up to the seventh class, inclusively, ordinary
promotion, or by seniority, depends on the
directing senate, and is effected by diplomas
given by that assembly. Above the sixth
class, promotions are submitted to the Emperor, and the diplomas are countersigned by
him. Promotion for eminent services must be
submitted by each minister to the committee of
ministers, and by that committee to the Emperor.

Young men are obliged to set out in the
service by an employment in a province, and
to pass three years there. They are under
the express superintendence of the governors,

who address reports of their conduct to the Emperor himself. The ministry of Foreign Affairs is the only one which takes beginners at their first starting.

The different employments in the administration correspond with the classes, so that each *tschinn* has a right to certain functions, and to the person who is invested with it no employment inferior by more than a single degree can be assigned, unless he prefers a more subordinate place; but he may occupy a place two degrees superior to his *tschinn*.

On quitting the service, if a man has performed his duty in an irreproachable manner, he is dismissed with the next superior *tschinn*, provided that he has been at least a year in his rank. The eighth class, which confers the rights of hereditary nobility, is not granted to persons who are not noble, unless they have served in the ninth class for the number of years required for them. Those who wish to return to the service are received only with the rank which they have actually occupied.

Service in Siberia, or the Caucasus, and in
certain districts of the governments of Wiatka,
Astrakhan, Archangel, Olonetsk, and Wologda,
entitles to particular privileges, in consideration of the disagreeableness of residence in
those countries.

Persons belonging to the tributary classes,
but free, are admitted into the service in
those provinces, and obtain the fourteenth
class at the expiration of eight years. Those
who have a right to public service there enjoy
a diminution of half the time otherwise required for their admission into the fourteenth
class. The allowance for travelling expenses
is double for the whole distance between the
place of abode and the place of destination.
The *employé* receives moreover a sum varying
from 100 to 150 silver rubles towards his
expenses of removing, and every five years a
gratuity equal to one-third of his annual
salary. Persons who have accepted the
indemnification for removing are bound to
pass three years in the service, or in the

contrary case, to repay to the Crown all the money received on this account. In the thirty-five years' service necessary to obtain the order of St. Wladimir, three years are reckoned as four; in Astrakhan, four years count as five. The sick are admitted into the hospitals, and the children of the *employés* into the schools at the expense of the Crown.

Every *employé* who has completed an irreproachable service of twenty years, receives a pension equal to one-third of his appointments. For thirty years he has two-thirds; and, after thirty-five years' service, he retains, by the title of pension, the whole of his salary. On the two latter terms, it is possible to obtain a benefit of six months. In case of ruined health, by means of the service, the *employé* has a right to the above-mentioned pensions, with a benefit of ten years,—that is to say, he receives one-third of the appointments after ten years', two-thirds after twenty years', and the whole after thirty years' service. In case of severe and incurable disease, such as paralysis, mental derangement, blindness, he retains one-third of his appointments after five years', two-thirds after ten years', and the whole after twenty years' service. As for the agents who have had no fixed salary, their pensions are calculated at the rate of a total of 28 silver rubles 50 cop. per annum.

The *employés* in the department of public instruction receive as pension one-third of their salaries after fifteen years', two-thirds after twenty years', and the whole after twenty-five years' service. For every five years beyond this they receive in addition a sum equal to a fifth of their salary, which is paid them at the same time as the pension so long as they continue in the same service.

The *employés* of the court retain, after fifteen years' service, one-third of their appointments, by the title of pension, half after twenty years, and the whole after thirty. If they complete fifty years' service they receive, moreover, the whole of their expenses for board, that is, for table and other things; for thirty-five years they have a right to one-third, for forty years to half, and for forty-five years to two-thirds.

After twenty years' service the artists of the Imperial theatres keep the whole of their appointments, if they do not exceed 1142 silver rubles 80 cop., and half, after ten years.

The time passed in leave of absence or vacation beyond four months for the ordinary *employés*, and two months for the actors, is deducted from the effective time of service, and is not included for pensions any more than for salaries and ranks.

The widow, without children, of an *employé* who has died in the service, receives half the pension to which her husband would have been entitled. If she has children, she is paid moreover, for each child one-third of the pension, so that with three children she receives the entire pension. No distinction is made between the children of the *employé* and those of a former husband.

The right of widows and orphans does not extend to the pensions which their husbands and fathers would have received, had they lived, for some act of particular distinction.

Children who have lost their mother receive each one-fourth of their father's pension; four children receive the whole of it; and, if there are more, they divide it equally among them. The children who are of age, that is to say, boys at seventeen, and girls at twenty-one, when provided with an establishment, the daughters by marrying, the sons by admission into a public institution at the expense of the Crown, lose their rights to their father's pension.

Saving some exceptions, nobody can enjoy a pension and his appointments at once. In the military service, the years passed in the field are counted double for the pension.

The uniforms of the civil functionaries are green, excepting those of the ministry of public instruction, which are blue, and the state dress of th senators, which is red.

There is the great and the little uniform: for the first, the coat has one row of buttons, with standing collar, of cloth or velvet, embroidered with gold or silver, according to the different ministries. There are generally twenty-five buttons, nine before, three to each sleeve, three on each hip, and two on each skirt. The first five classes have white pantaloons with lace; the cravats must be white. The waistcoats are of white cloth, with uniform buttons.. Coloured cravats, waistcoats, and pantaloons, are strictly prohibited, as are also beards and moustaches. No person is allowed to wear plain clothes in the public offices. There are uniform great coats for travelling. The embroidery of the dresses has ten varieties, according to the ranks. The *employés* who have swords of honour, acquired in the military service, retain them with the civil uniform.

Need we insist on the extreme absurdity of

this organization? Why not forty-one classes as well as fourteen? Fourteen, when in reality there are but twelve? What similarity is there between the civil and military ranks, from which the former have been copied? The relation between the rank and the functions is quite arbitrary; hence it is found necessary to deviate every moment from the rule, and to admit exceptions which tend to become rules. Would the titles of chief of section, office, or department sound worse or inspire less respect than those of honorary councillor, councillor of college, or actual councillor? Are not the Russian *tschinovniks* downright Chinese mandarins? They are, it is true, exempt from the discipline of the cane; but then, as a wag once observed, why not promote the whole nation to at least the fourteenth class?

From the fourteenth *tschinn* to the eighth, from the rank of officer to that of major, persons are called *your nobleness;* from the eighth to the fifth class, *your high nobleness;* for the fifth, or the rank of councillor of state,

there is a special denomination, that of *your
high birth;* from the fourth to the second, the
style is *your excellency,* and in the second and
first, *your high excellency.* The addresses of
letters bear these titles; soldiers, servants, and
coachmen have them incessantly in their
mouths. What an honour! Women also
enjoy the like designations, and are called
madame la conseillère titulaire or *intèrne,* as it
may happen to be, and *madame la generale.*
On the door of one of them, I saw one day the
inscription, *Conseillère de college,* Poulette
(Kourotschkine);" and another, being accosted
in the street by a stranger, haughtily replied,
" What do you take me for? I am *conseillère
d'état!*"

The highest Russian functionary pays no
attention but to his own interest, and performs
his duties only in proportion to the material
advantages which he derives from his service.
Honour and glory are nothing to him, beside
crosses, *tschinns,* rubles, and dessiatines of
land.

The ranks, even the very lowest, are but
stepping-stones to arrive at fortune.   The
aiguillette of the Emperor's *aid-de-camp*, and
the ribbon of St. Andrew, at the top of this
may-pole, are the only prizes considered
worthy of the trouble which the Russians
take to climb up it.   The over-excitement of
vanity is in proportion to the multiplicity of
distinctions.   Where blind obedience is the
only virtue, individual merit is of no value.
Not a creature studies the interests of the
country: the country of the Russian is the
Emperor, and the people serve him only
according as he pays them: hence the avi-
dity of the functionaries is equalled only by
the prodigality of the Tzar, who has ruined
Russia by the presents of all kinds made to
his confidants.   Poland, Bessarabia, the Caucasus have been thus given away: and who
can count the millions which Nicholas has
lavished upon his courtiers?   Knowing that he
has many enemies, he conceives that he cannot
attach his creatures to him strongly enough,

and the sweat of the people pays for their incapacity and their carelessness. Casual and
incessantly-repeated donations, annuities for
life, grants of the whole of their appointments
to those who retire from the service—all these
absorb the greater part of the revenue, and
make Russia the most wretched of countries.

Chapter III.

OF THE RUSSIAN ORDERS.

THERE are eight orders in Russia: 1. the order of St. Andrew; 2. that of St. Catherine; 3. of St. Alexander Newsky; 4. of the White Eagle; 5. of St. George; 6. of St. Wladimir; 7. of St. Anne; 8. of St. Stanislaus.

The White Eagle and St. Stanislaus are of Polish origin: the order of St. Anne is from Holstein: the order of St. Catherine is that of the ladies; the Empress, who is grand-mistress, retains that dignity as long as she lives. The grand-master of all the others is the Emperor alone. All the grand-dukes of Russia become at their baptism knights of St. Andrew, St.

Alexander, the White Eagle, and St. Anne;
the princes of the blood when they attain the
age of majority. The grand-duchesses are
invested at their baptism with the order of St.
Catherine, and princesses of the blood on their
majority.

In Russia, an order confers the rights of hereditary nobility. The Baschkirs are exempted
from this prerogative; they acquire thereby no
more than personal nobility. Since the 10th
of April, 1832, orders confer on Russian merchants the hereditary rights of *honorary citizens* only. The nobility inherent in the order
is transmitted to the children born before the
elevation of the father, excepting, however,
such as may have come into the world in the
condition of serfs or tributaries.

Knights of an order are deprived of it for
crimes and offences contrary to dignity and
honour, after judgment, confirmed by the Emperor. Degraded officers are deprived of the
right of wearing their orders, till they are re-
instated; the same course is pursued with

ecclesiastics excluded from the service. In general, the number of the knights of any order is not determined; but that of the salaried members of each is fixed. On their admission, all pay a fee, according to the decoration and the class which they receive. Foreigners are exempted from this tax, as are also the Circassians, and such persons as receive decorations adorned with diamonds. Foreigners out of the service have no right to the revenues attached to the order with which they may be invested.

The administration of all the orders belongs to the chancellor, who is elected from among the knights of St. Andrew. He has for assistants the treasurer of the orders, and the grand-master of the ceremonies, who holds the same office in the Imperial court. Both wear the order of St. Andrew about the neck. The other orders have each a master of the ceremonies, who wears his insignia in the same manner. Each order has, moreover, a secretary and two heralds, wearing the cross at the

button-hole. All the knights and the officers
have robes, the colour of which is specified in
the statutes.

Each order has its festival-day, and the 8th
of November, St. Michael's day in Russia,
is the festival of all. The knights resident
at St. Petersburg and Moscow then elect six
members of each order, who are charged with
the superintendence and direction of the charitable institutions situated in each capital.

The Academy of Sciences is commissioned
to publish, every five years, a complete list of
the knights of all the orders, with their titles,
and another of the new creations and ex-
tinctions.

A person cannot obtain a decoration till he
has served fifteen years, excepting for particular
merits, or for having served either in Siberia or
in the Caucasus; in these cases, he may be
allowed a benefit of five years. Moreover, to be
qualified to receive an order, he must be of at
least the ninth class, or occupy a post equivalent
to that rank. Besides, there are particular con-

ditions of time and position in the service for the different degrees of each order. Thus, neither the order of St. Anne of the first class, nor that of St. Wladimir of the second, can be given to any person whatever, whose rank or function is below the fourth class; the order of St. Stanislaus of the first class cannot be conferred on any one whose function is below the fifth, and his *tschinn* below the fourth; no more can the St. Wladimir of the third be given to those whose rank or post is below the sixth class.

Moreover, the Russian decorations are classed according to their respective importance; and their hierarchy must not be infringed, that is to say, a superior order must not be given to one who has not the inferior orders. Nevertheless, exceptions to all these rules are met with, and, indeed, are of daily occurrence.

The order of St. Andrew has but a single class; the decoration consists of a sky-blue ribbon, worn over the right shoulder, the star on the left side; the cross, suspended from a ribbon, is blue, and stands upon an eagle surmounted by three crowns. It displays the image of the crucifixion of St. Andrew, with the four Roman letters, S. A. P. R. (Sanctus Andreas, Patronus Russiæ). The reverse represents a scroll, with the inscription in Russian, *For Faith and Fidelity.* The star is of silver in a field or, where is seen the Russian eagle with the cross of St. Andrew, surrounded with the motto of the order, in gold letters on a field azure.

The costume is composed of a long robe of green velvet, lined with white taffeta, with collar, strings, and shoulder-band in silver. The star of the order is sewed on the left side. The upper vest is white, and the hat of black velvet, with a red feather and a St. Andrew's cross on the ribbon.

This order is not to be acquired by any right whatever, and can only be conferred at the pleasure of the sovereign.

The knights of this order must hold offices

of the third class, and by their promotion they acquire, at the same time, the orders of St. Alexander, St. Anne, and the White Eagle. But, in general, this order is conferred only on functionaries of the first or second class, and after they have all the inferior orders.

Each kinght pays on his nomination a fee of 240 silver rubles *. Twelve knights, comprehending three ecclesiastics, receive among them 6092 silver rubles, 507 rubles 66 cop. each, per annum.

The order of St. Andrew, the first in point of creation as in importance, was instituted by Peter the Great, on his return from his travels abroad. The first knight was Count Feodor Alexcïvitsch Golovine, chancellor, field-marshal, and high-admiral of Russia, who, in his turn, invested Peter I. with it, as a reward for his memorable naval victory over the Swedes.

The order of St. Catherine was instituted in commemoration of the deliverance of Peter I.

* The silver ruble is equivalent to 4 francs, or thereabouts; the assignat ruble to 1 fr. 11 c.

at the battle of Pruth by the Empress Catherine I. This order has two classes, those
of the great and the little cross. The ribbon is
red, with a silver border, and is worn over the
right shoulder. The cross is white, placed
upon the hand of St. Catherine, and in the
centre is another small cross, with rays and
the four Roman letters, D. S. F. R. (Domine,
salvum fac Regem). On the cross is inscribed
in Russian the motto of the order, *For Love
and Country*. The star is of silver, with a
cross of the same metal in a field gules, surrounded by the motto. The dress is silver
stuff, embroidered with gold; the sash and hat
are of black velvet.

The office of deaconess of the order belongs
to the next highest personage to the Imperial
family. It devolves by right to the reigning
Empress, when that of mistress of the order is
held by the dowager Empress.

There are twelve members of the great
cross, exclusively of the ladies of the Imperial
family, and ninety-four of the little. The

order cannot be conferred on any but noble
ladies.

It is allowed 1278 silver rubles per annum
for six ladies of the great cross, and 2428
rubles for twelve of the little, including five
members of the clergy.

The obligations of the lady-knights of this
order consist in thanking God every day for
the deliverance of Peter I.; in praying for the
health of the Emperor and his family; in
reading the Pater Noster thrice every Sunday;
in striving to convert infidels to the Greek
religion; and in delivering, at their expense, a
Christian out of the hands of barbarians.
These ladies are, moreover, charged with the
superintendence of the institution of St. Catherine; and those who are decorated with
the great cross have a right to place in it one
pupil each.

The order of St. Alexander Newsky has
but a single class. The ribbon is red, and is
worn on the left shoulder, with a cross of gold
in red enamel, adorned with four eagles with

two heads crowned. On one side is represented Alexander on horseback, and on the
other his cipher in Roman letters under a
princely crown. The robe is of red velvet,
lined with white, the upper vest embroidered
with silver; and the hat is black, with a white
feather.

Twelve knights, including five ecclesiastics,
receive 7014 rubles, 28 cop., per annum.
Each knight pays 180 rubles at his admission.

The order of the White Eagle has also but
a single class. The decorations consist of a
dark blue ribbon, worn over the left shoulder,
with a two-headed black eagle of gold and
crowned, in which is seen a red cross with
a white one-headed eagle. The star is of
gold, and is worn on the left side. The motto
is, *Pro fide, rege, et lege.* The members pay
150 rubles on admission.

The order of St. George was founded by
Catherine II., on the 26th of November, 1769.
It has four degrees: for the first, the ribbon
has three black and two yellow stripes, and

is worn over the right shoulder beneath the uniform. The star is square, of gold, with a field of gold, the cipher of St. George in a black ring, and the motto in Russian, "For service and courage." The star is worn on the right side. The cross is of white enamel, with the arms of Moscow, or the image of St. George piercing the dragon. The second degree is distinguished by the star and cross worn about the neck. The third has the cross only about the neck, and the fourth at the button-hole.

The upper vest is of orange-coloured velvet with black crosses. There is a separate subdivision for soldiers, the decoration of which is a cross of silver.

This order is given gratis. The pensions are of 200 rubles for the knights of the first class, 114 rubles 28 cop. for those of the second, 57 rubles 14 cop. for those of the third, and 28 rubles 57 cop. for the knights of the fourth class. The annual pensions of this order amount to 10971 rubles.

The order of St. George is given for military exploits, such as the taking of an enemy's fortress, or the defence of one of the fortresses of the empire, and the capture of ships, cannon, colours, or generals. It is conferred also on the author of a piece of information which decides the victory, or on one who cuts his way through the enemy's ranks. The marshals and commanders-in-chief may, in time of war, decorate their subordinates with the fourth and fifth class of St. George, with or without the participation of the council of the order, composed of at least seven knights. The first two classes are conferred by the Emperor himself. The order of St. George is also given for twenty-five years' military service, or for twenty campaigns on land or eighteen at sea. In this case the cross must bear an inscription stating the fact.

The order of St. Wladimir was created on the 22nd of September, 1782, in memory of the twenty-first anniversary of the coronation of the Empress Catherine II. It is composed of four classes. The ribbon has a red stripe between two black ones, all three of equal dimensions. It is worn upon the right shoulder, over the coat, if the knight has not superior orders, and under it upon the waistcoat, if he has another more ancient. The star is octagon, with angles of gold and silver alternately, with a circular black field, surrounded with a black ring, and adorned with a gold cross, around which are the Russian initials of the saint, S. R. K. W.

The motto is, *Utility, Honour, and Glory.* The cross is red, with the cipher of St. Wladimir, surmounted by a crown on one side, and on the other by the date of the institution of the order.

The second class wears the great cross about the neck with a star at the left side; the third, the smaller cross about the neck, and the fourth at the button-hole. When the order is a reward for military exploits this latter is accompanied with a cockade.

This decoration is obtained as well for

services known to the Emperor himself, as for
having restored order in some neglected part
of the administration; for having instigated
or prepared others for the service; for having
unravelled, terminated, or prevented law-suits.
It is besides obtained for having saved ten
persons; for having afforded relief to a locality
in famine, or when suffering from any other
public calamity; for having contributed to
give plenty to one's district by agricultural
operations; for every plan which has produced
to the crown at least 30,000 silver rubles;
for an invention which has served to increase
the national wealth; for any work adopted
as classical; for thirty-five years' active,
irreproachable, and zealous civil service, or
twenty-five only in the Trans-Caucasian provinces. Every supreme testimony of satisfaction abridges this term by a year. The
medical man who has vaccinated 3000 persons
in one year enjoys the same prerogative.

Such nobles as have been thrice invested
with the elective functions, and have been

elected a fourth time to the offices of marshals of the nobility, curators of the gymnasium, deputies, or secretaries, and the commoners who have fulfilled the same condition in the quarantines, have also a right to this order. If any of them have during their functions obtained the decoration by way of special distinction, the law would by this very circumstance be accomplished in regard to them.

For payment of the pensions of this order, there is assigned the sum of 1714 silver rubles $28\frac{1}{7}$ cop. The knights of the first class receive 171 rubles $42\frac{6}{7}$ cop.; those of the second 85 rubles $71\frac{3}{7}$ cop.; those of the third 57 rubles $14\frac{2}{7}$ cop.; and those of the fourth 28 rubles $57\frac{1}{7}$ cop.

On the death of a knight, his wife enjoys the pension for one year only. The knights of the first two degrees have the entry at court on an equality with functionaries of the fourth class, and those of the two others with the *employé*s of the sixth class.

The knights of the first degree pay at their

reception 180 silver rubles; those of the second 60, of the third 30, and of the fourth 9. Those on whom the decoration has been conferred for thirty-five years' service pay nothing.

The commander-in-chief of an army is authorized in time of war to create of his own accord knights of the fourth class, with cockade, for brilliant exploits.

The order of St. Anne is likewise composed of four classes. For the first, the ribbon is red, with a yellow stripe, and is worn on the left side. The cross is red, with the image of St. Anne on one side and her cipher on the other. The star, of silver, worn on the right, has the motto, *Amantem justitiam, pietatem, fidem.* The second class wear the cross about the neck; the third at the button-hole, and the fourth on the sword or sabre, without ribbon, just as it appears on the star. This latter is retained with the superior orders. In the first and second class, a crown is added to the cross, which forms a particular distinction;

and in the third class a cockade for military exploits; in the fourth the inscription *For valour*, which is placed on the weapon, adorned with a cross. There is, besides, a fifth subdivision for soldiers, who have served twenty years. This is a gilt medal, with the image of the cross, suspended from a red and yellow ribbon.

This order was added to the Russian orders on the 5th of April, 1797; but the anniversary is held on the 3rd of February, in memory of Anna Petrovna.

It may be conferred on any ecclesiastic who has converted at least one hundred persons not Christians, or one hundred heretics, persuaded rebellious slaves to return to their duty, or set a good example to the soldiers; to him who has distinguished himself in the sciences, erected convents or churches otherwise than at the expense of the Crown, or who has filled with distinction gratuitous offices for at least five years. It is granted to military officers for the command of a detached corps of greater force

than a company or a squadron, upon condition,
however, that, in the first case, this corps shall
have retained a distinguished place among the
troops, and that the number of the sick, and of
those expelled for misconduct shall not have
exceeded one per cent.

In the civil service, this order may be
granted to any one who has in three years
amicably settled ten lawsuits begun about
matters of sufficient importance to authorize
an appeal to the Senate; to him who, in the
office of judge of the peace, shall have con-
ciliated all disputes submitted to him, and not
suffered any of them to take a judicial course.
He has also a right to it who has ensured the
welfare of widows and orphans, and unveiled
the condition of the poor; he who has procured
for the Government a particular and unfore-
seen advantage; who has risked his life or his
fortune for the public weal; or directed, without the aid of authority, a public seminary for
youth for ten years, to the general satisfaction.
The private tutor receives this order, after

fifteen years' labour, if he is an hereditary noble; after twenty years, if he is a personal noble; and after twenty-five years, if he is neither.

The presentations for this order take place through the chapter, and are decided by ballot in the council, which is composed of twelve knights, the oldest of each degree who are at St. Petersburg in the month of December in every year.

In war time, the commander-in-chief of an army may confer the second, third, and fourth degrees of this order.

In the first class, twenty commanders, four of whom are ecclesiastics, receive each a pension of 228 silver rubles $57\frac{1}{7}$ cop. ; twenty others, four of whom are ecclesiastics, are paid 114 silver rubles $28\frac{4}{7}$ cop.

In the second class, twenty commanders, two of whom are ecclesiastics, receive 100 silver rubles; forty-two, eight of whom are priests, 71 rubles $42\frac{6}{7}$ cop. ; and thirty-six pensioners, six of whom are priests, 71 silver rubles $42\frac{6}{7}$ cop*.

In the third class, ninety knights receive 57 rubles $14\frac{2}{7}$ cop.; ninety others 42 rubles $85\frac{5}{4}$ cop.

In the fourth class, ninety knights are paid 34 rubles $28\frac{4}{7}$ cop.; and ninety others 98 rubles $57\frac{1}{7}$ cop.

The knights of the first class pay, at their nomination, 60 rubles, and on every promotion, 75 rubles; those of the second, 30 rubles; those of the third, 18; and those of the fourth, 9 silver rubles.

The order of St. Stanislaus is established to reward those who shall have contributed to the welfare of the Russian empire and of the kingdom of Poland, *which is inseparable from it* (Art. 621), by such services as shall have attracted the notice of the Emperor.

---

* This latter sum is, no doubt, incorrect. The author seems to have repeated the preceding amount by mistake. *Translator.*

There are three degrees: one, the fourth or
the second, was abolished on the 28th of May,
1839. Those who had it previously have retained the right of wearing a star with the
cross about the neck. This order comes after
that of St. Anne. The knights of the first
class of this last order do not wear at the
same time either the ribbon or the star of St.
Stanislaus, but the cross about the neck.

The cross is red, enamelled red, with four
branches, each divided into two, and adorned
with small gold balls. In the middle there is
a circle of white enamel, with a green border,
and a laurel of the same colour, enclosing in
red the Roman letters S.S. In the angles of
the cross on the four sides are Russian two-
headed eagles of gold. The reverse is of gold,
with a white border and the cipher.

The ribbon is red, two inches and a half
broad, with a double white embroidered border,
and is worn on the right shoulder; the star
is placed on the left side. It is of silver,
with eight rays, and the border, similar to

that of the cross, bears the motto, *Præmiando incitat.*

The decoration of the second degree is worn about the neck, and has two sub-divisions, one with, the other without, crown. That of the third is worn at the button-hole.

The festival of the order is held on the 25th of April (7th of May with us). The first and second degree are left at the disposal of the Emperor. The third is conferred, exclusively of services known to his Majesty, for acts of beneficence; on those who have sacrificed their fortune for the public good or for that of the service; on persons who have filled a useful office without pay, or performed a duty beyond the sphere of their ordinary functions for a year. It is likewise granted for inventions and works of incontestable utility, for setting to rights a complicated business, and for the discovery of heinous abuses and crimes. It may be bestowed on a private tutor for fifteen years' service, if he is an hereditary noble; for twenty years' if he is a personal noble; and for twenty-five years' if he is not noble.

Whoever has, agreeably to the statutes, deserved the order, has a right to solicit it through the medium of his superiors, if he is or or has been in the service, or through the head of the government, if he has retired. This third degree can be conferred by a council composed of twelve knights of each degree, under the presidency of a *grand-cordon*, by a nomination by ballot, the result of which is submitted to the decision of the Emperor.

The chief of an active army may confer the St. Stanislaus of the second and third class for brilliant military exploits.

At the time of his promotion, each knight of the first degree pays 90 rubles, of the second, 30, of the third, 15. This money is destined for charitable purposes specified by the Emperor.

Persons who have received this order since the 17th (29th) of November, 1831, the day of its annexation to the Russian orders are thereby hereditary nobles: those who obtained it before are not so, if they are not decorated with the first degree. The Russian ecclesiastics do not receive this order, and the members of the Roman Catholic clergy acquire with this decoration the right of *personal* nobility only*. Merchants are personal nobles if they obtained this decoration before the 10th (22nd) April, 1832, and hereditary honorary citizens if they received it since.

There are thirty pensioners of the first degree, at 142 silver rubles $88\frac{5}{7}$ cop. per annum; sixty of the second, at 114 rubles $28\frac{4}{7}$ cop.; ninety of the third, at 85 rubles $71\frac{3}{7}$ cop. each.

The pensioner who passes to a superior degree loses the pension which he was receiving, and must wait his turn for the pension of the new degree. He has to send back to

---

* The Russian law, though ingenuous enough to say it, is not sufficiently so to add that it is because the Romish ecclesiastics are not susceptible of having children.—(Decree of May 28th, 1839.)

the chapter the insignia which he had previously worn. It is the same when a knight
dies; and, if the insignia are then lost, the
heirs have to make good their value. The
knights who turn monks lose the order and
the pension. On the death of a pensioned
knight, his wife enjoys the pension for one
year.

The heirs of a military knight killed in war
are exempt from the obligation to return his
insignia, or to pay the value of them.

The *decoration of the irreproachable service*
is not an order; it is a mere mark of distinction. It consists of a square gilt brooch, with
a laurel, in the middle of which are Roman
figures, specifying the years of service. It is
placed on a ribbon of the order of St. George
for military men, and of St. Wladimir for civil
functionaries. This decoration was instituted
on the 22nd of August, 1827, in commemoration of the coronation of the Emperor Nicholas,
which took place on that day in the preceding
year. It is conferred on the anniversary of

its institution, and is worn below the real orders as being inferior to them. It is given for fifteen years' service, and is renewed every five years.

Neither knights of St. George, after twenty-five years' service, of St. Wladimir, after thirty-five years, nor those of the most important orders, are dispensed from wearing this brooch, which is prescribed to be placed below the second button-hole.

Artists have no right to this distinction but for the time passed in the service, commencing with their reception into an order of knighthood*. The masters of relays, and persons who have no *tschinn*, have no effective right to it.

No kind of diminution is to be obtained in the terms required for the brooch. Leaves of absence for more than twenty-nine days are deducted from the time of service thus calcu-

---

* A general disposition forbids the grant of an order before a person has received the brooch.

a ted; the service of an *employé*, who, in the
space of fifteen years has thrice changed the
line of service, is declared invalid, whenever he
has remained for less than three years in the
same post.   Any default in a half year may
cause the loss of a year's service, unless sufficient causes can be assigned to satisfy authority; default of four months wholly takes away
the right to the brooch.   Reprimands entered
in the statements of service entail the loss of
a year ; and arrest, accompanied with formality, delays the obtaining of the decoration
for three years.   The institution deprives of
their right to this distinction those who have
been brought before a court of justice, and
have not gone out of it acquitted, whether
they have been left under the reproach of suspicion, or have been pardoned by an Imperial
proclamation, or all proceedings of justice in
regard to them have been suspended; but if
after this they complete fifteen years' irreproachable service, the brooch will be conferred on them.   Those who have been dis-

charged for want of proofs against them are considered as innocent.

The definitive grant of the brooch belongs to a council composed of generals-in-chief, or actual privy councillors chosen by the Emperor, under the presidency of the oldest of them, or of the functionary of the first class, if he is of the number. This council meets every year, on the 20th of July at latest, and sits in the Winter Palace. The sanction of the Emperor is required for its decisions to render them valid.

Three silver rubles are paid for each brooch. Persons invested with it may place it in their coat of arms and on their seals.

The brooch is not taken away from one who has obtained it for misdeeds which would have prevented the grant of it; but it is not replaced by that which he would have received for the five years during which he has been in fault. If he serves irreproachably for the next five years, the brooch is conferred for that period. If the misdeed is committed before the grant of the brooch, but after the time for obtaining it is completed, the case is submitted to the decision of the Emperor.

The *Mary mark* was instituted on the 14th of October, 1828, in memory of the Empress Maria Feodorovna, the mother of Nicholas. It is conferred on ladies for irreproachable service. It is of two degrees; in the first the decoration is worn on the shoulder, in the second on the bosom. For the former the cross is with four branches, and of gold, enamelled with blue; It bears the cipher of Maria Feodorovna; in the centre is a laurel, with the number of years' service in Roman figures. The badge of the second degree is a blue medallion, with the two figures. The ribbon is that of the order of St. Wladimir. This decoration is destined for ladies of the classes, as they are called, mistresses, directresses, and inspectresses of the institutions which were under the immediate superintendence of the Empress-mother. The first degree is given to ladies who have passed twenty-five years and upwards in these functions, aud the second to those who have been from fifteen to twenty-five years. Every five years the figures are renewed. Claims of this decoration are discussed in a council established at the beneficent institutions, and the decisions of which are confirmed by the Emperor. This mark of distinction is never forfeited.

Officers of the army receive sabres and swords adorned with gold, sometimes with stras*, without any expense, having an inscription recording their bravery. Commanders-in-chief of large armies are authorized to grant them for gallant actions and brilliant exploits.

For saving the lives of persons in danger, gold and silver medals with ribbons of St. Wladimir are conferred.

The mayors of parishes who continue with distinction for nine years in their posts, and

---

* False diamonds, so called after the inventor.— *Translator.*

are re-elected for three years longer, receive medals, which they wear about the neck if they are not noble. Vaccinators are likewise rewarded with medals. Distinguished planters in the Caucasus and New Russia, peasants who excel in the cultivation of the potato, the superior workmen in manufactories, Jews settled on the lands of the crown, who distinguish themselves as agriculturists, are entitled to the same rewards. Pilots, quarantine officers, schoolmasters, after ten years' functions, obtain medals with the ribbon of St. Alexander. The chiefs of peasants, for nine years' service, also have them with the ribbons of St. Anne.

Medals obtained for saving a person's life, or for any other act of humanity, are not liable to any impost. The others pay, according to their ribbons, a fee of from 7 to 150 silver rubles. Persons having medals worn about the neck are exempt from the recruiting, and the others from corporal punishments.

There are, moreover, *kaftans* of distinction, of cloth, velvet, or damask, either in uniform fashion or not. These kaftans are destined particularly for peasant functionaries.

————

Chapter IV.

OF THE HIGH COURTS, ADMINISTRATIVE, LEGISLATIVE, AND JUDICIAL.

THE COUNCIL OF THE EMPIRE.

THE attributions of the council of the empire include all matters requiring the promulgation of a new law, or the modification, explanation, or complement of an existing law; every extraordinary measure in the department of internal administration or external policy, as peace or war, when it can be subjected to a previous examination; special questions relating to finances, the fixing of the budget, and

the regulation of the taxes, the expropriation
of individuals for the sake of the public interest,
or the transfer of a property of the Crown into
the possession of private persons, patents for
inventions, &c. This council decides on the
grant and the withdrawing of letters of nobility,
and directs proceedings against accused ministers and governors-general, with the authorization of the Emperor. It takes cognizance
of suits on which the Senate has been divided,
or the conclusion of which has not obtained
the sanction of the Minister of Justice.

The council of the empire is divided into
departments, which we will also call sections,
or meets in general assembly. The members
of the departments are members of the general
assembly, which comprehends others not belonging to them.

There are five departments: 1. that of justice; 2, war; 3, religion and civil affairs; 4,
economy; and 5, affairs of Poland.

The members of the departments are nominated every six months by the Emperor him-

self, and are composed of a president and at least three members for each department. The sections can summon to their assistance and consult persons of whose knowledge they wish to avail themselves. For matters which concern several departments at once, these can meet and deliberate in common.

The members of the council of the empire can at the same time be invested with any other office in the judicial or administrative line. The ministers are by right members of the council of the empire, but they cannot be nominated presidents in the sections. The president of the general assembly is the Emperor himself, and in his absence the person whom he thinks proper to appoint once a year. The vice-president is the one of the presidents of departments who is of the longest standing.

The general assembly sits in the following order:—The president occupies the middle of the hall; on his right are placed the members not belonging to the departments; on his left the ministers, and opposite to him the members of the sections, with their presidents at their head. In the centre, facing the president, is the secretary of the empire, assisted by a secretary of state and two under-secretaries.

The members speak standing. If several rise at once, the preference is given to the oldest in rank. Amendments to projects under discussion must be presented in writing. The votes are entered beside the name of each member, and the decisions are recorded in the minutes. At the conclusion of each sitting, the order of the day for the next is made known. In the departments members take rank according to the *tschinns*.

When any extraordinary measure is in agitation, the affair is sent directly to the general assembly, by command of the Emperor. The departments refer to it those matters on which their members cannot agree, or for which they have come to a decision cancelling a decree of the Senate, or on which they disagree with the Minister from whom the affair in question emanates.

The council of the empire can refer to the Senate affairs in which the latter has not taken into consideration some important document, in order that it may undergo revision.

The secretary of the empire submits the decisions of the council to the confirmation of the Emperor. The affairs of Poland are laid before him in minutes, whenever they have not been debated in the general assembly; and the others in the form of memorials, signed by the president or the vice-president, and by the secretary of the empire. The will of the Emperor decides the affair definitively, even though it should be in favour of the opinion of the minority. In case of lengthened absence of the Emperor, his Majesty himself fixes the extent of the power which the council of the empire is called upon to exercise in the interim.

Attached to the council is a chancellery, under the direction of the secretary of the empire. It is composed of seven sections, each of which has at its head a secretary of state, excepting the last two—that of archives, and that of the affairs of the secretaryship of the empire, which are managed by assistants.

THE COMMITTEE OF THE MINISTERS.

The committee of the ministry is composed of all the ministers and chiefs of separate administrations completing the ministerial organization, such as the chief of the staff of the navy, of ways and communications, of the posts, the comptroller of the empire, &c., likewise of the presidents of the departments in the council of the empire, and of persons specially designated by the Emperor.

The president is chosen by the sovereign; in default of which the presidency, as in cases of the illness of the holder of an office, devolves to the oldest member in rank.

The committee meets twice a week, in winter at eleven o'clock in the forenoon, and once a week in summer at ten. In case of important business, the president can summon an extraordinary meeting. The members sit according to seniority of rank.

The attributions of the committee of the ministers embrace all business which requires the combined action of several ministries, and embarrasses a minister, or exceeds his competence, and renders the supreme resolution necessary. The ministers are bound, moreover, to submit to the committee accounts for each year of their administration, as well as to refer for its decision, in extraordinary cases, matters concerning the public safety, or the subsistence of the people, the causes of heretics, the reprimands to be given to governors, the rewards and pensions to be granted to the civil *employés*.

The Governor-General of Finland is likewise authorised to refer to the committee all affairs that demand the concurrence of two administrations, but without requiring modifications in the legislation of the duchy.

The decisions of the committee do not receive the force of law till they have the sanction of the Emperor. From this rule are exempted only the unanimous decisions of the committee concerning pensions and the momentary aid to be afforded to *employés*, and the affairs of the heretics, excepting extraordinary cases. The changes to be made in the legislation are previously submitted to the second section of the chancellery of the Emperor, specially charged with the framing of the laws.

The committee of the ministers exercises no executive power, and leaves the duty of fulfilling its decisions to the minister to whose department the matter in litigation belongs.

The chancellery of the committee is composed of several sections, an office of general despatch, and a division of archives.

THE SENATE.

The senate is the high judicial court of Russia: the dispenser and director of justice, it attends to the execution of the laws and to regularity in the administration.

Its members are nominated by the Emperor from among the dignitaries of the first three classes, whether civil or military. The president is the Emperor himself; the ministers have seats there, but not their substitutes. The governors-general and the military governors are admitted.

The senate is divided into eleven departments, six of which reside in St. Petersburg, three in Moscow, and two in Warsaw. The presidents are appointed by the Emperor. The number of the senators is unlimited, but the minimum of the members who must be present before deliberations can be held is fixed at three for the departments of St. Petersburg and Moscow, and five for Warsaw. The

Minister of Justice makes up the number, in case of need, by the youngest of the senators of the corresponding departments. In each department sits a grand attorney, who attends to the regularity of business.

The first department is charged with the promulgation of the laws and their despatch to the competent authorities, with the verification of the civic rights of all those who are neither nobles nor serfs, with the naturalization of foreigners, with the superintendence of the elections, with the appointment and dismissal of *employés*. It settles all disputes that arise between the different tribunals, and takes cognizance of suits between the Crown and individuals.

The second, third, and fourth departments at St. Petersburg, the seventh and eighth at Moscow, and the ninth at Warsaw, take cognizance in appeal of civil affairs; the fifth at Petersburg, the sixth at Moscow, and the tenth at Warsaw, are charged with criminal matters. Each of these departments exercises

jurisdiction over a definite number of governments which form its district. The attributions of the surveying department are sufficiently indicated by its name, and extend to
the whole empire.

The departments meet in certain cases and
form general assemblies; there are two in St·
Petersburg, composed, the one of the first
three and the other of the last three departments, under the presidency of the oldest
president, and under the superintendence of
the Minister of Justice. The three departments
of Moscow form a single general assembly, as
do likewise the two at Warsaw, under the
presidency of the lieutenant of the kingdom.
Honorary senators are not admitted into it.

The general assemblies take cognizance of
all matters upon which the members of the
departments could not agree.

The first, at St. Petersburg, besides trying
culpable senators, decides upon the promotion
of *employés* as high as the sixth class, and
confirms the titles of nobles. The oldest

senators in rank supply the places of the presidents in case of their absence, at general assemblies as well as at particular meetings. The ministers have seats in the first department, and the Minister of Justice, with his assistant, attends the general assemblies.

These are held once a week. The Minister of Justice likewise causes the senators to be summoned to an extraordinary sitting, on all business that admits not of delay. The sittings open at ten o'clock. Every week, the Minister of Justice makes his report to the Emperor concerning the members absent, or who came too late. The senators invested with some particular office cannot absent themselves from the general assemblies, and must attend at least twice a week in the departments. The ministers and governors are alone exempt from this obligation. The vacation of the senate takes place in summer; and business is submitted to the assemblies only by extracts. In the departments, matters are decided by unanimity. If a disagreement arises respecting the manner in which questions ought to be put, and it cannot be decided by a simple majority, the youngest member of another department is then called upon to vote. The senator who does not adopt the opinion of the majority is authorized to express his own in writing, but within eight days at furthest for the departments, and in the next sitting for the general assemblies. His colleagues may then recall their vote. Members absent at the time of the meetings of the departments are required to signify their opinion, but that is not the case with the general assemblies, The vote of a minister is not counted on matters which he has himself presented to the senate, or which come within the sphere of his ministry. The grand attorney strives in writing to reconcile opinions ; if he is unsuccessful he refers the matter in dispute to the general assembly. The same course is pursued when the attorney, on his part, does not adopt the decision of the department; but he must first obtain the authorization of the Minister of Justice.

In the general assemblies the majority is two-thirds of the votes. If it cannot be obtained there, the Minister of Justice refers the matter to a consultation of the assembled grand attorneys, assisted by his deputy and a jurist. A fortnight is allowed them to study the question. In case of disagreement, the voice of the minister is preponderant. When such cases come before the senate of Moscow, the consultation takes place at St. Petersburg. The affair is then carried back to the general assembly; and if a majority is not obtained, or rather, if the Minister of Justice continues to be of a different opinion from that which prevails, he then refers to the Emperor through the medium of the council of the empire.

The senate acknowledges no power above it but that of the Emperor. The subordinate authorities cannot defer the execution of its decrees, unless there is contradiction in its prescriptions, and then they are bound to lay the difficulty before the senate itself. The latter may transmit to his Majesty its obser-

vations on the existing laws, through the
medium of the Minister of Justice, in as far as
they require complement, explanation, or
modification, in consequence of other contradictory laws; but it is strictly forbidden to
take advantage of the imperial clemency in
particular cases, for the purpose of authorizing
exceptions to the laws, or to take the liberty
to make any observation on laws recently
promulgated by the Emperor.

If the senate discovers any abuses in the
ministries, it apprizes the ministers; and if it
obtains no satisfactory explanations, it refers
the matter to his Majesty. It sends reprimands to the governors for negligences committed without any ill intention, and, in case
of repetition, it publishes them; but if they
are of such a nature as to draw punishment
upon the parties, it applies for the authorization of the Emperor. The senate cannot of
itself alter *a letter* in the existing laws, or
modify its own dispositions, without the consent of his Majesty. There is no appeal

from the senate unless to the Emperor, who then causes the matter to be reconsidered by the general assembly of the senate, if it has been decided upon in a department, and by the council of the empire if it has been discussed in general assembly. Whoever prefers an unfounded complaint against the senate is brought to trial. Accordingly, the complainant is obliged, in every case, to certify in writing that he is acquainted with the severity of the existing laws on this subject.

"Every senator, as a worthy son of his country, having always in view his duty to God, the State, and the law, ought to be mindful that the obligation which is imposed upon him as judge consists in considering his country as his family, and honour as a friend; in examining with care the applications that are made to him, in amending his errors, in changing and prosecuting suspected judges, and above all in seeking the means of establishing the truth, and not of gaining time.

"Every senator is obliged as a duty of

conscience to make his report on every misdeed that is committed in the country, and on
all the violations of the law that come to his
knowledge*.

Each department has its chancellery. The
first general assembly of St. Petersburg, and
that of Moscow, have, moreover, each of them
a particular chancellery. They are under the
orders of the grand attorneys appointed by
the Minister of Justice, who is the supreme
chief of all the chancelleries of the senate.

The greatest anomaly which exists in the
organization of the senate is the exorbitant
power assigned to the public ministry, which
can suspend or annul by its veto the decisions
of the majority in the departments by the
voice of the Grand Attorney, and of unanimity
in the general assemblies by the voice of the
Minister of Justice. Is the cause of this that
the senators, taken at random from the army
or the civil administration, are ignorant in
matters of law? But if one cannot or knows

* *Swod.*, vol. I., book 3, sec. 1, art. 247 and 248.

not how to remedy this evil, ought one not at least to avoid taking generals or diplomatists for ministers of justice, as has been done hitherto; and, even if men of learning were appointed, their right to paralyze the decisions of the senate ought to be confined to cases of the violation of laws; and, above all, business ought not to be suffered to be protracted by granting delays to attorneys and to the ministers to draw up their opinion in set form. The Russian senators are not proof against offers of money made more or less adroitly; but it is easier to bribe a single individual than an assembly, and the Imperial attorneys are in fact in Russia, both in the senate and in the governments, the only dispensers of justice.

THE SYNOD.

It is at present composed of eight members and four assistants, a chancellery, the administration of ecclesiastical instruction, the ecclesiastical administration, and the chancellery of the grand attorney of the synod.

The eparchies are divided into three classes. The first comprises the four metropolitan sees of Kiev, Novgorod, Moscow, and Petersburg. The second class contains eighteen arch-bishoprics, and the third twenty-six bishoprics and the three eparchies of Georgia.

The ecclesiastical instruction is divided into three districts, those of Kiev, Moscow, and Petersburg, with the same number of academies, and forty-five seminaries.

CHAPTER V.

OF THE MINISTRIES.

There are nine ministries in Russia; 1, the Ministry of the Interior; 2, that of Finances; 3, of Public Instruction; 4, of Justice; 5, of the Domains; 6, of War; 7, of Foreign Affairs; 8, of the Court; 9, of the Marine. There are, besides, three administrations equivalent to ministries, namely, 1, the Control of the Empire; 2, the Department of Ways of Communication and Public Buildings; 3, that of the Posts.

There are in every ministry several directions, which are called in Russia departments, the

council of the minister, and the chancellery of
the ministry. The directions are divided into
sections, and the sections into bureaux. The
council of the minister is composed of all the
directors and of the under-minister, under the
presidency of the minister. To these the
Emperor can add particular members, and the
council itself can desire the attendance of
persons not belonging to the ministry, whose
opinion it may have occasion to ask. Each
direction may also meet in *general assembly*,
composed of all the chiefs of section, under the
presidency of the director, who can, with the
authorization of the minister, summon to the
meeting persons unconnected with the administration, for questions relative to science, art,
and industry. Most of the directions have
particular chancelleries.

The ministers are chosen by the Emperor;
the directors by the minister, with the assent
of the Emperor; the other functionaries are
appointed and removed on the presentation
of the director, by the minister, and the

quite subordinate *employés* by the director alone.

The power of the ministers is exclusively executive. They cannot modify any law, and are obliged to have recourse to the council of the empire about every thing that relates to legislation. When, in the sphere of their duties, they encounter difficulties which it does not belong to them to resolve by themselves; when they feel the necessity of some changes, or that they must take measures which require the concurrence of the other powers; they have to refer to the Senate, or, in important circumstances, to the Emperor, through the medium of the committee of the ministers. In like manner, they have recourse to the Senate on all matters within its competence, such as the moving of *employés* and judicial causes.

Every year, on the 1st of August, all the ministers deliver to the Minister of the Finances an estimate of the expenses necessary for their department. The latter refers it to the council of the empire, and, on its authoriza-

tion, opens the credits demanded. Every
month the ministers give notice to the treasury of the sums which are necessary for
them.

Ministerial responsibility is incurred in two
cases—when the minister deviates arbitrarily
from the laws, or when he occasions abuses, or
does harm by his negligence. He is not an-
swerable for the mischievous effects of the
measures which he has proposed, but which
have been approved by the Senate or the
Emperor. In case of abuses, his Majesty decides whether there is occasion to prosecute;
and the council of the empire takes upon itself
the investigation and the proceedings. If these
prove that the minister has rendered himself
unworthy of the confidence of the Emperor, he
is removed from office; and if they bring to
light serious offences, he has to appear before
the criminal tribunal.

The under-ministers supply the place of the
ministers during their absence or illness, sit in
the council, and can direct such a branch of

the department as their principals choose to commit to their care. In general, it is matters which are not of sufficient importance to require the attention of the ministers themselves that are thus transferred to them. They are thought to acquire in this post the capacity requisite for becoming ministers in their turn; but this plan succeeds very ill with persons who have not previously received a certain education; and, for those who are qualified to manage a ministry, the time passed in this secondary post is absolutely thrown away, while the post itself is but an additional embarrassment for the general administration. If civilized countries can well dispense with these doubles of ministers, why should not Russia be able to do so? And again, since the ministers of foreign affairs, of war, and of the marine, have no need for this kind of assistants, why should not the ministers of the interior and of finances be able to do without them?

The Ministry of the Interior is composed of six directions; a particular section of statistics with its chancellery, a council of medicine, a chancellery, and an ordinary council.

The *Direction of the Executive Police* is charged with internal order, the judicial and penal police, and the collection of the taxes.

The *Economical Direction* attends to matters of subsistence, concurs in the supply of the army, superintends the corn magazines, draws up statements of the crops, and plans of towns and villages, regulates all that concerns fairs and markets. It has likewise under its charge the charitable institutions, the houses of correction, and the insurance companies.

The *Direction of Foreign Religions* has three sections, and a bureau instead of chancellery.

The *Direction of Medicine* is engaged with the placing and superintendence of physicians, apothecaries, veterinary surgeons, and midwives. Its attributions embrace the civil hospitals, mineral waters, vaccination, and the quarantines.

The *Direction of Medical Preparations* is

charged to supply the army, the navy, and some establishments of the civil administration with medicines and surgical instruments ; it has also to keep up the pharmaceutic establishments of the Crown, and the medicinal magazines and gardens. The general assembly of the direction is composed, under the presidency of the director, of three councillors, one of whom is called the elder, and must be a physician or apothecary.

The *Direction of General Affairs* receives the orders of the Sovereign and ensures their execution, makes the necessary arrangements for the journeys of the Emperor, attends to the promotion of the governors : it is charged moreover, with secret and pressing matters, the naturalization of foreigners, the elections, and crimes against the religion of the country.

The *Council of Medicine* is the supreme court in matters of scientific and legal medicine. Its president must be a physician, and chosen by the Emperor, on the presentation of the minister. The directors of the medical

divisions of the Ministries of the Interior and
of War, the physician in chief of the staff of
the navy, and the physician inspector of the
council of guardianship, are members of this
council, as is also a physician of the ministry
of public instruction.   The other members are
elected by the council itself, and confirmed by
the minister.   From among these latter the
council has to choose a secretary.   It meets
twice a week, unless particular circumstances
call it together.   It has a chancellery, the sections of which have physicians for their chiefs.
To the council belongs the censorship of medical works and prospectuses, and that of books
treating of cookery and economical chemistry:
it is charged with the appreciation of disco-
veries in medicine, with the publication of the
instructions necessary in case of contagious
diseases, with the examination of medical men
coming from abroad, with the verification of
the *post-mortem* examinations of persons
struck with sudden death, &c.

The *Section of Statistics* forms part of the

council of the ministry. The under-minister
is president, and the directors form part of it;
the minister adds to them certain members of
his council; strangers may be summoned to it
for the purpose of furnishing information; the
section has correspondents, which it chooses
itself. One of its members, appointed by the
minister, is charged with its administration.
It meets once a week, and has a chancellery,
an architect, a geometrician, and a bureau of
drawing. It is charged with the verification
of the plans of new towns, projects of territorial divisions of the empire, &c.

The Ministry of the Finances is composed
of the direction of internal manufactures and
commerce, that of external commerce, of contributions and rents, of the treasury, of the
administration of the mints, mines, and salt-
works, with the corps of the mines, and the
staff of the engineers of the mines. It has,
moreover, three chancelleries—the general
chancellery, the secret chancellery, and that
of credit.

The *Direction of Internal Manufactures and Commerce* has annexed to it a special council, called council of manufactures, which, under the presidency of the chief of the direction, is composed of persons versed in the subject, selected from the nobility and traders, six from each class, two professors of chemistry and mineralogy, and a technologist. This council has a section at Moscow, and committees and correspondents in the other towns. The section of Moscow is composed of four nobles, four merchants, a chemist, and a mechanician; its president is at the same time president of the committee for the supply of the army with cloth. The director of the council of St. Petersburg is the chief of the first section of the direction; an *employé* of the committee is chief of the section of Moscow. The members have no salaries.

The functions of the council of manufactures consist in completing the statistical information received from the governors respecting manufactures, in promoting their development and improvement, in delivering patents, privileges, &c.

The *Council of Commerce* is composed of four merchants of the first guild engaged in internal trade, four others in external trade, and four foreign traders. The minister can, with the consent of the assembly and the authorization of the Emperor, add to them such persons whose concurrence may be deemed useful.

There are sections of this council at Moscow, Riga, Archangel, Odessa, and Taganrog. They are composed of traders of the first and second guild, and of foreign merchants, two of each class, chosen by the chief of each government out of twelve persons presented to him by the assembly of traders. The members may, upon occasion, amount to six or twelve, but not exceed that number.

The chiefs of the directions of manufactures and external commerce have seats in the council. When questions common to both come before them, the council of commerce may be united with that of manufactures.

The *Scientific Committee of the Corps of Engineers of the Mines* superintends the working of the mines; it corresponds with foreign scientific men, and the *employés* of the ministry residing abroad; it is also charged with the publication of the Journal of Mines. A general of artillery and an admiral belong to the committee, all the members of which must be confirmed by the Emperor. The chiefs of the mines of the Ural and Altai attend the meetings of the committee when they are in St. Petersburg.

The *General Chancellery of the Ministry of the Finances* is composed of two sections, the first of which has as many bureaux as there are directions, excepting the direction of the treasury, for which the second section, with three bureaux, is exclusively reserved.

There is reputed to exist, in connexion with the chancellery, a scientific committee of the ministry, composed of three members and a secretary, to discuss financial plans and institutions, and to diffuse financial instruction among the *employés*; but that committee has never met.

The Ministry of Public Instruction is composed of one direction, a chancellery, and a council of the minister, who also appoints the principal administration of the schools. The administration of the censorship is likewise included in this department.

The Direction of Public Instruction is composed of four sections, and a chancellery, having its archives, its chest, a magazine of books, an architect, a librarian, and a physician. It has annexed to it an archæological commission, and is charged with the publication of the Ministerial Journal.

The first section comprises three bureaux. The first is charged with the affairs of the districts of St. Petersburg and Dorpat, and of the Pedagogic Institution; the second, those of the districts of Kiev and White Russia; the third, of the district of Moscow, and of the Academies of Medicine and Surgery of Moscow and Wilna.

NICHOLAS THE FIRST. **145**

The second section is divided into two bureaux: the first has in its attributions the affairs of the Academy of Sciences, the observatories of Poulkov and Wilna, the Imperial Library of St. Petersburg, the Rumiantzof Museum, the district of Kasan, and the schools of Siberia. The second bureau is charged with the affairs of the district of Kharkov, of that of Odessa, of the Transcaucasian schools, and of the medical department of the universities.

The third section regulates whatever concerns the district of Warsaw, and is divided into two bureaux. The fourth is that of accounts, and comprises three bureaux.

The General Assembly of the Direction of Public Instruction is composed of the director and vice-director, of the chiefs of sections and the chief of the chancellery. In case of need, the director may summon to it scientific men and artists.

The principal object of the Journal of the Ministry is to publish the ordinances which concern this department, and to make known the state of public instruction in the different institutions. The compilation of the work is committed to an editor-in-chief and an assistant, both appointed by the minister. There are some other employés, whose number is likewise fixed by him, and the choice of whom belongs to the chief of the direction, subject to his approval.

The repair, lighting, and warming of the ministerial buildings, and the wages of servants, are defrayed out of the revenues produced by the Stschoukine-Dvor (the fruit-market), and the shops situated in the edifices belonging to the direction.

The Ministry of the Domains is composed of three directions. Between the first two are divided the domains of the empire, according to the governments in which they are situated. The third is charged to diffuse agricultural information, to effect the general survey of lands, and to inspect the surveyors. Each direction has its chancellery. The council of the ministry is formed of the directors, including the director of the chancellery, and of at least five members. The chancellery of the ministry has two sections, besides a special division for bringing the environs of St. Petersburg into cultivation.

The Ministry of Justice is composed of one direction and one chancellery. The direction has five sections: 1. the executive section; 2. that of criminal affairs; 3. that of the civil affairs of the governments of Great Russia; 4. that of the civil affairs of the other governments; and, 5. the section of accounts.

The Ministry of Foreign Affairs comprises a council, a chancellery, the direction of foreign affairs, that of internal relations, a direction of economy and of accounts, the direction of the Asiatic affairs, the archives of the State, those of St. Petersburg, and those of Moscow.

The Ministry of War has a military council composed of nine members, exclusively of the president, who is the minister himself; the general auditoriat, composed in like manner the chancellery of the ministry; that of the Emperor, called the field chancellery, and nine directions: 1. that of the staff, which has three sections and a military topographical depôt; 2. that of the inspections, having five sections; 3. that of the artillery, composed of seven sections; 4. that of engineers, having three sections; 5. that of the commissariat of war, which includes six sections; 6. that of provisions and supplies; 7. that of the military colonies; 8. that of the service of health; 9. that of the auditoriat.

This ministry has in its department the military academy; the medico-chirurgical academy; the scientific military committee, composed of nine members and a director; the committee of military censorship, formed of six members and a president; the scientific committee of military medicine; the publication of the Invalid, &c.

The Ministry of the Marine is under the orders of the chief of the staff of the marine. It comprises a council, called the Council of the Admiralty, a scientific committee, a chancellery of the ministry, and another of the Emperor, called the Campaign Chancellery, a general auditoriat, that of buildings, the general administration of the hospitals, the administration of the general intendance of the navy, the directions of the artillery, of the commissariat, of naval works, and of the forests of the marine.

The Ministry of the Court comprises the chapter of the orders, with its bureaux of dispatch; the direction of appanages, which has four sections and nineteen offices in the provinces, has been, ever since the appointment of its chief, M. Perovsky, to the ministry of the interior, united with that department. The ministry of the court has, moreover, in its attributions, the cabinet of his Majesty, the chancellery, which is divided into three sections, the control of the ministry, the counting-house of the Court, that of the intendance of the Crown, that of the stables, the school of monumental architecture at Moscow, the counting-house of the hunting establishment, the direction of the theatres of St. Petersburg and Moscow, the counting-house of the palaces of Moscow, with the *chamber of arms*, the administration of the palaces of Tsarskoie-Selo, Peterhof, and Gatschina, the Academy of Arts, and the Botanical Garden.

We pass over in silence the organization of the administrations having the rank of ministry, to notice the chancellery of the Emperor, and the commission of requests, which are of higher importance.

The Chancellery of the Emperor owes its origin to Nicholas, and may serve for an exact measure of his administrative and organizing genius. It is composed of six sections, each of which has a secretary of state for its chief. The first section is charged with the correspondence with the ministries, and with the preparation of the rescripts which accompany the donations of the Emperor and grants of orders, as well as the mere expression of the imperial gratitude. These papers might some day form a curious collection of proofs serving to establish the nullity of the men and the acts of this reign. Bulletins of this sort, as pompous as they are empty, record none but vulgar services, which, in other countries are not the object of any remuneration beyond the ordinary appointments. What particularly exercises the ingenuity of the inditers of these rescripts, is to decide whether they are to make the Emperor say to this or that person, "your benevolent," quite short, and to another, "your ever benevolent."

The second section is occupied with the *framing of the laws*, as if it was the province of the chancellery of the Emperor, and of one of its sections only, to make laws. Accordingly, the codes of Nicholas are not new-made laws, or laws borrowed from foreign countries and adapted to Russia; but a crude mass of superannuated ukases, hunted out and botched up agreeably to the commands of power.

The third section is that of the *secret police*.

The fourth is charged with the beneficent institutions founded by the Empress-mother.

The fifth is the *ministry of the domains,* which has straggled thither by accident.

The sixth and last is the Emperor's field chancellery.

The commission of the requests was instituted to do justice to the complaints and petitions addressed to his Majesty, and is composed of a president and some members appointed by the Emperor: the most important of them is the secretary of state charged to receive petitions. He has under him a particular chancellery, which enjoys the prerogatives of an imperial chancellery.

Petitions must be addressed to the secretary of state or to the Emperor, signed by the petitioner, with an indication of his condition and place of abode. They mey be written on loose paper.

The term during which complaints may be preferred against the decisions of the tribunals, is limited to a year for persons residing in the interior of the empire, or two for those living abroad, unless such complaints are founded on new documents, or on evidence that those before furnished were false.

The commission does not pay attention to matters decided in full Senate, in the council of the empire, or in the committee of the ministers, excepting, however, the cases in which serfs claim their liberty, or which relate to the rights of nobles and minors, affairs referred to the commission by the special command of the Emperor, and lastly, such in which, independently of the sentence, the statement of facts is contested.

The denunciations which have not a close connexion with the subject of the petition are not taken into consideration by the commission, which sends them to the authority to whose province they belong, or to the secret police. Applications for decorations, and complaints against superiors, are referred to the chiefs whom they concern. Requests for audiences of the Emperor are not presented to him, unless there is a question about important revelations. Petitions for donations and pecuniary grants, when they emanate from high functionaries, must be submitted to the Emperor. Solicitations that the Emperor will stand sponsor for infants are not delivered to his Majesty, unless when the services of the petitioners appear to the commission to give them a right to prefer such a request.

All the decisions of the commission must be submitted to the Emperor, as well as all matters which cannot be decided unanimously in its bosom.

The commission addresses the plans which it receives from individuals to the competent ministries; when these reject proposals which the commission judges of importance, it may then apply for the Emperor's authorization to refer them to the council of the empire.

CHAPTER VI.

OF THE PROVINCIAL ADMINISTRATION.

RUSSIA is divided into fifty-three governments, forty-three of which are administered
after one and the same general fashion, while
the others have a particular administration,
such as Siberia and the Caucasus, with their
sub-divisions, Bessarabia, the countries of the
Cossacks, and those of the roving tribes. As
for the rights of certain provinces incorporated with the Russian empire, on the express
condition of the preservation of their privileges, Nicholas swept them all away. When,
on his accession to the throne, it was proposed
to remould the laws of the empire into a single

body of legislation, M. Speransky was charged
with this operation, and a deputy from each
province enjoying particular rights was summoned to St. Petersburg, in order to concert
with them the new collection of the laws.

M. Speransky, an upright and able man,
himself a native of Kiev, had the intention to
maintain the provincial rights, discovering in
them nothing incompatible with autocracy,
nothing contrary to the interests of the Russian
government. Bearing in mind the differences
of origin and civilization, he purposed to per-
petuate in the legislation the varieties to which
they had given rise. Poland, the eldest of the
European nations in the work of liberty, had
endowed Lithuania and White Russia, while
those two countries formed part of the kingdom, with liberal institutions, such as the
publicity of judicial proceedings, and those
provinces had continued to enjoy them till the
end of the reign of Alexander.

Subsequently, when Poland had paid with
her independence for her glory and her faults

on the subject of liberty, a reaction was felt
in the countries which had belonged to her.
M. Khavransky, governor-general of Witebsk,
a man of narrow mind and unbounded devotedness, found means to persuade M. Chadour-
sky, marshal of the nobility, to solicit the
complete annexation of that government to
Russia. The supreme power hailed this proposal with ecstacy, as if it had been the expression of the general wish of the nobility;
and the same stratagem was soon repeated
with the government of Mohilev. All that
country was tricked out of its particular rights;
the Russian laws were substituted for the
Polish, and, as the former differ from the
latter, even to the very dispositions that regulate inheritance, a great perturbation in all
transactions was the consequence. M. Bibikof,
governor-general of Kiev, used still less ceremony. Without having recourse to a marshal of
the nobility, he applied direct to the Emperor,
praying that the provinces committed to his
administration might be admitted to the en-

joyment of the *blessings* of Russian legislation.
An imperial decree fulfilled this request; and,
when the governor-general was boasting one
day in his own house of this measure, the
Count de B., a landed proprietor of the province, told him to his face that there was
nothing to brag of so mightily ; "for," said he,
"it is rather for the Russians to borrow the
Polish legislation than for Poland to submit to
theirs."

It was not long before the governments of
Kharkov, Poltawa, and Tschernigov experienced the same fate. Oral proceedings at law
were superseded by written ones; the *posovs*,
or the right belonging to the meanest subject
to bring the highest functionary into court,
was abolished. Speransky was grieved to the
heart, and the deputies were sent back to
their homes, excepting those of the Baltic
provinces, who had powerful protectors at
court: but their turn seems likely to come
soon. M. Ouvarof, the minister of public
instruction, is labouring for that purpose with

all his might, and the Emperor lends him a
willing ear on this subject. The Russian
element, language, and laws, are daily gaining
there more and more ascendency over the
German element, language, and laws; and,
how worthy soever may be the attitude of the
patriots of those countries, they are anything
but easy about the futurity that awaits them.
Finland alone has retained its rights intact,
and has even a senate of its own, while the
provinces of the Baltic have none but that of
St. Petersburg to appeal to. It is worthy of
remark, however, that the *ésprit de corps* and
the distrust of the Russian judges are so great
among the Germans, that very few cases are
cited in which they have appealed to the
Russian senate, so much do they prefer settling
their differences among themselves.

In regard to the administration, Russia is
divided into governments-general and simple
governments. The first are those which have
governors-general for chiefs, to whom the civil
governors are subordinate, while, in the simple

governments, the latter are dependent on the ministry of the interior alone. The governments-general are composed sometimes of a single government, at others of several. Thus the two capitals, Moscow and St. Petersburg, and likewise Orenburg, form each a distinct government-general, while Little Russia, New Russia, White Russsia, East Siberia, West Siberia, the German provinces, Finland, compose three or four governments. The governor-general of Kharkov has in his dependence the governments of Kharkov, Tschernigov, and Poltawa; that of Kiev, in Podolia, has Kiovia, and Wolhynia; that of Witebsk has Mohilev, Smolensk, and Witebsk. Wilna, Minsk, Grodno, and Covno, form a separate province.

One would seek in vain to explain the necessity for governors-general*. The bor-

---

* Their uselessness has been pointed out in a remarkable work, recently published in Paris, by the title of *Système de Legislation, d'Administration, et de Politique de la Russie en* 1844, *par un homme d'Etat Russe.*

dering position of some of the provinces committed to their care produces many conflicts with foreigners, and gives rise to questions of a certain importance; but the civil governors would be quite as capable of providing for their solution. These same provinces, for the most part conquered, are liable to disturbances; but the discretionary power of the governors-general increases rather than stifles them, even when those dignitaries do not get them up themselves in order to have an occasion of gaining credit. At a certain period, there was an idea of extending this institution to all Russia; but power shrunk back before the clamour excited by this project among the national Russians; and now that two-thirds of Russia can do without governors-general, people cannot discover any reason why the rest of the empire should be placed under their authority. These posts are mere sinecures, given most frequently to generals who are utter strangers to civil administration, and who are a source of infinite abuses and useless formalities. The civil governor, who finds himself dependent on a governor-general, sees his activity and his authority paralyzed, even if he can contrive to keep on good terms with his superior; which is almost impossible, thanks to the chief of the chancellery of the governor-general, a more influential personage than the general himself, whose factotum he is, and who finds in the recriminations against the civil governors an abundant source of illicit revenue: there is no end, therefore, to his complaints, and they keep increasing at the pleasure of the greedy *employés* of the chancellery. Public order, harmony between the chiefs, respect for authority, are thus grievously compromised, owing to the presence of the governors-general, absolute Padishahs, who, uniting the civil and the military power, are liable to endanger the empire itself, if the distance of the capital should ever suggest a desire to render themselves independent.

The Russian legislation thus defines the

duties of the civil governors. " The civil governors, being the immediate chiefs of the governments confided to them by the supreme will of his Majesty the Emperor, are the first guardians of the rights of *autocracy*, of the ukases of the directing senate, and of the orders emanating from the superior authorities. Charged to watch with a continual and vigilant care over the welfare of the inhabitants of all classes, and to enter into their position and their wants, they ought everywhere to maintain the public tranquillity, the security of each and all, the execution of the regulations, order, and decorum. It belongs to them to take measures to ensure plenty in their respective governments, to succour the indigent and the sick. They attend to the prompt administration of justice, and the immediate execution of all legal ordinances and prescriptions."

They can neither alter the laws nor deviate from their dispositions, nor punish any one without trial, and must submit to the approbation of the superior authority all extraordi-

nary measures which they may deem it con-
ducive to the public prosperity to adopt.

They are charged to promulgate everywhere
and without delay the laws, manifestoes, and
orders of all kinds, immediately after the
reading of them to the *goubernium*. In case
of the receipt of special orders from the Emperor, they have to inform his Majesty and
the competent minister of their having been
carried into effect.

They have to keep in the way of order,
legality, and decorum, the public authorities
which are dependent on them; they cause
an account to be rendered to them of the
management of the funds placed at the disposal of the same authorities; and they superintend the levy of the taxes and of arrears.

In extraordinary and extremely urgent
cases, the governor has a right to convoke
to the *goubernium* the chambers of finance
and of domains, civil and criminal, under
the presidency of the attorney of the government. He must then inform the senate and

the ministry in the department of which the matter in question may happen to be, of the decision to which that general assembly has come.

He is charged to collect accurate information concerning the morality and capacity of the *employés* of his government; he takes care that absences are not too long and too frequent: he presents for rewards those who have deserved them; excludes from the service, when his competence extends so far, such as have been guilty of abuses, or brings them to trial. Young men who have just left the universities, and are commencing their career of service in the provinces, are specially commended to his *paternal* care.

The civil governor has the high superintendence over the elections of the nobility, without having a right to influence them in any manner, and without being able to take a direct part in them, even though he may be a noble of the government which he is administering. He communicates to the marshal

the list of the nobles brought to trial, and who
are consequently excluded from the elections;
he administers the oath to those who come
forward to vote at them, installs the elected
in their functions, or reports to the ministers
or the senate on those whose nomination needs
to be confirmed by the Emperor. He communicates to the marshal, when the case does
happen, the obstacles which prevented the
elected from entering upon their functions,
and submits to his approval the *employés*
whom he presents for the places which the
nobility has not filled up, selecting them
in preference from among the nobles of the
government.

It is the duty of the governors to protect
religion and the church, to prevent the pro-
pagation of heresies, and to contribute to their
extirpation, to prosecute those who disturb
religious services and ceremonies, lastly, to
take care that work is suspended on holidays.

They are guardians of the rights enjoyed
by each class, and are charged to prevent any

one from usurping the prerogatives which are
not conferred on him by the laws. Thus they
take care that corporal punishments shall not
be inflicted on those who are exempt from
them; that the peasants are not ill used or
overloaded with labour and dues; that the
books of the nobility are kept in a proper
state by the deputies, and that errors are not
committed in the certificates of nobility delivered by the marshals. They see to it that
the convents and the churches enjoy the lands
and the advantages which have been granted
to them; that the ecclesiastics are exempted
from taxes, and, in case of lawsuits, represented before the tribunals by deputies of their
own profession. They have to maintain the
rights of foreigners, to cause reports to be
addressed by the local authorities to the superior authorities concerning their morality and
conduct; and they administer the oath to
those who wish to be naturalized, and inform
the superior authority of it.

Supreme heads of the police in their governments, they direct its action in all its parts, and watch over the morality of the province committed to their care: it is their duty to put a stop to all kinds of abuses; to stifle in their birth revolts and pillage; to punish debauchery and dissipation, drunkenness and prohibited games. They have to prevent vagrancy, and to repress begging; to this end, they send beggars back to the places to which they belong, procuring for them work, which produces them wherewithal to subsist on the journey; and they place such of them as have neither masters nor relations in the college of public beneficence.

They exercise particular vigilance over persons placed by the supreme order under special surveillance, and report on their conduct to the third section of the chancellery of the Emperor, as well as to the Minister of the Interior, who informs his Majesty of it.

It is their duty to prevent the formation of secret societies, and to bring the founders to justice, acquainting the Minister of the Interior,

without delay, with the nature of these societies, and the measures adopted in regard to
them.

They have to prevent the circulation of
books and prints not authorized by the censorship. They cannot permit the establishment
of any printing or lithographic press without
the consent of the minister, nor that of any
lottery for articles of a value exceeding 300
silver rubles.

They are charged to ensure the free trade
in corn; to prevent forestalling, and to settle
the price three or four times a year, according
to the market prices. They attend to the
establishment and maintenance of magazines
of corn, and, for this purpose, they are presidents of the commission of supply. They
attend also to the quality of provisions, to the
execution of the sanitary laws, to the inter-
ment of the dead, and to the state of the
hospitals.

In case of the appearance of epidemic disease, they immediately inform the Emperor of

it, through the medium of the ministry, and acquaint him with the progress of the disorder in weekly reports. In serious cases, they establish a committee of quarantine, with a military tribunal to try for offences against the sanitary precautions. They are expected to promote vaccination by all means in their power, to take care that there shall be at least one man in a thousand who knows how to vaccinate, and to this end they cause gratuitous instruction to be given.

The civil governors pay attention to the embellishment of the towns, to their paving, to the repair of the public buildings, and to the erection of churches. They are presidents of the committee of buildings, and look to it that buildings are erected in the prescribed order. They direct appropriations, and fix the compensations to be granted to proprietors; they superintend the ways and communications, cause high roads to be constructed and repaired at the expense of the Crown, and the by-roads at the charge of the communes. A particular commission is attached to them for this purpose.

They authorize the establishment of new manufactories, as well as that of fairs and markets; they take care to inform themselves of the progress of industry in their government, and report upon it to the Minister of the Finances.

They are presidents of the committee charged to draw up statistical surveys of the state of the government in every particular. These documents are published, entire or in part, in the government newspaper, and the governor is obliged to send them to the Minister of the Interior, and to submit them by extracts to the Emperor, in case the latter should choose to pass through his province.

The governors are required to pay particular attention to the raising of recruits, and to this end they preside in the committee of recruiting. They take measures that the new soldiers shall be supplied on their route.

They superintend the administration of the guardianships under which cruel proprietors, lunatics, and spendthrifts have been placed; the interdict, valuation, and sale of encumbered properties, likewise come within their province.

They direct criminal affairs, watch the proceedings, press for judgment, and ensure the execution of sentences, without having it in their power to suspend the effects of them, unless there are sufficient proofs, but with the right to cause them to be revised by a commission.

Civil matters are submitted to them only when the Crown is interested in them: but they have to redress the complaints which reach them respecting the negligence of the tribunals.

On entering and quitting office, every civil governor must address to the Minister of the Interior, and to the governor-general, if there is one, a report on the state in which he leaves his government, and another to his successor, or the vice-governor who supplies his place. This document must specify the number of affairs in hand in every department, the state of the supply of provisions, and that of the arrears of taxes: it exhibits also the ideas and plans for improvements desirable to be introduced into the different branches of the administration.

The new governor, on his installation, examines all the departments of the administration, and makes arrangements for remedying the evils which he may have discovered in any of them. He then makes one or more tours through his government, verifies on the spot the particulars which he has collected from the different authorities, and prescribes the ameliorations which he deems necessary.

He does justice to legitimate complaints and claims, and orders the competent authorities to put an end to abuses. He investigates the sufferings of the people, directs his attention to the state of the various branches of industry, and ascertains the means of making them prosper. From the observations collected in this manner, he composes a memorial, which he addresses to the Emperor in person, and a copy of which is sent to the minister, and another to the governor-general, in case there is one.

The governor repeats this visitation of the province every year or every two years, according to its extent and the importance and facility of the undertaking; and he records his observations in the report which he makes annually, about the 1st of March, to the Emperor, and which is, as it were, the annual statistical *exposé* of the government. He addresses, besides, special reports to his Majesty, at different periods, that is to say, relative to the expenses occasioned by the levy of the recruits, in the six weeks subsequent to the recruiting; on the ordinary taxes, at the end of the year; and of the extraordinary taxes, after they are collected. Every fortnight, he informs the third section of the chancellery of the Emperor of all particular events. Every

four months, he acquaints the ministry with
the progress made in fulfilling the orders of
the Emperor and of the Senate; every six
months he furnishes it with a statement of
the prisoners confined for above a year, and at
the end of the year, he sends a table of the
business that has been transacted.

Such are the immense attributions of the
governors: their mission, if duly executed,
might be of great benefit to the country; but,
unfortunately, these functions are most frequently conferred on incapable men, whether
it be that intrigue or patronage preside at
their distribution, or that in Russia there is a
complete dearth of upright and enlightened
men. It is a fact, that the most flagrant
abuses are daily committed within the jurisdiction of the internal administration; the
governors are not more incorrupt and disinterested than the other Russian functionaries,
but they are quite as ignorant and negligent.
It would be too long to specify the numberless
proofs of their unheard-of double-dealing; and,

as one cannot denounce them all, it would not
be just to call down punishment on some and
to spare the others. Suffice it to say, that
one borrows money, never to return it, from a
man whom he has it in his power to serve;
that another makes the dealers whom he
tacitly authorizes to sell a drug supply him
gratis; that a third receives money from a
farmer of spirituous liquors, to allow him to
put water into his wine; that a fourth has
buildings adjudged to him at inadequate
prices; that a fifth puts up to auction the
properties of minors, without giving notice to
the public, that he may buy them a bargain
by means of his emissaries; that a sixth
employs the peasants of the Crown to con-
struct a road leading to an estate which
he has recently purchased with money
squeezed out of heretics for having set their
leader at liberty. And these are not rare
circumstances, peculiar to only a few of the
governors; but the greater number of them
are guilty of most of these extortions, or

others of a similar kind, without ever subjecting themselves to any consequences; for, if they should even be prosecuted, they find protectors who save them. This large and hideous sore of Russia, the peculation universally practised, is, we will boldly maintain, owing not less to the insecurity of the citizens than the immorality of the public functionaries. Where the caprice of absolute power alone decides the fate of all and each, where no one is sure of his life or his property; there, I say, every man thinks only of the present, and seeks only to enrich himself as soon as he can, that he may have as much as possible left at the moment when he may be suddenly stripped for acts most frequently independent of his will; while, by a rigorous consequence, real abuses pass unperceived. As for the incapacity and negligence of governors, this one expression sufficiently depicts them. When a governor complained that business was not progressing, some one objected that he himself ought to read the papers which he signed; to which he replied, that he had certainly tried to do so, but then things only went on worse.

The governors are worthily seconded by the different *employés* and agents under their orders: men without instruction and without principle, there is no abuse, no malversation, which money will not bribe them to commit. To mention but one fact among a thousand: a district tribunal, paid by an accused person, dismissed the charge preferred against him, on the ground, as it alleged, that there were no means of communication between the two banks of the river which the complainant must have crossed, or his accusation could not be sustained. The latter had no difficulty to overthrow this falsehood by the very testimony of those who advanced it. Upon pretext of a commercial transaction, he applied to the tribunal before which the complaint was brought, for a certificate, that over the river in question there was a ferry, which permitted the transport of the corn and flour required, whenever the river was not frozen. For ten assignat rubles he obtained the attestation which he solicited.

But, without anticipating, let us pause a little to consider the organization of the different provincial authorities.

Each civil governor has a chancellery, charged with the correspondence relative to the meeting of the assemblies of the nobility, the remuneration of their *employés*, the inspection of the Government by its chief, the recruiting and movement of troops, the censorship, &c.

Each government has a *goubernium* (*goubernskoie pravlénié*) under the presidency of the governor. The vice-governor of it is the first councillor. It is composed of a chancellery, a bureau of archives, a typographical department, an architect, and two surveyors. It is charged with the publication of the laws, the nomination, the promotion, and the retirement from office of the functionaries of the province. Its attributions extend also to the general movement of affairs, to the mainte-

nance of order, and to the attentions required
by the public health, to the placing of estates
under guardianship, to the verification of the
censuses, to the superintendence of runaway
peasants and deserters. It follows up the
complaints of individuals against the local
authorities, and is under the immediate dependence of the directing senate. The chancellery of the goubernium is composed of four
sections, excepting at St. Petersburg and Moscow, where there are five.

The *Criminal Court and the Civil Court* of
the government are each composed of a president, with his deputy, and a fixed number of
assessors. In some places there are five councillors besides. In the two capitals, the civil
courts are divided into two departments, each
of which has a special president and the
number of members sufficient to form a complete tribunal. In the governments of Astrakhan, Archangel, Olonetzk, Perm, and Wiatka,
the two courts form but one.

The presidents are nominated by the superior authority out of a list of candidates elected by the assemblies of the nobility.

In the eastern governments, they are appointed by the minister of justice; for those of Astrakhan, Archangel, &c., the Senate, on each vacancy, proposes two candidates to the Emperor, who chooses one of them. Their substitutes are designated by the Minister of Justice in the eastern governments, and elsewhere by the Senate, on the proposal of the minister. The assessors of the courts are chosen, two by the nobility and two by the assemblies of the towns. In the governments of Wiatka, Archangel, and Olonetzk, the assessors of the nobility are appointed by the central power; in that of Astrakhan, by the local authority, and confirmed by the Senate.

The *Tribunal of Conscience* is composed of a presiding judge and six assessors. The judge is elected by the nobility, the body of traders, and that of the peasants. In the governments of Archangel, Wiatka, and Perm, the judge and the two assessors are appointed by the Government; the first performs the functions of marshal of the nobility. Differences between parents and children are in the exclusive competence of the tribunal of conscience. Its decisions cannot be executed until confirmed by the civil governor. In case of disagreement between the tribunal and the governor, the affair is referred to the Senate. In Little Russia, the Tribunal of Conscience is represented by a court called Tribunal of the Three (*trétéiskji soud*), which the two parties voluntarily choose, and from whose sentence there is no appeal.

The local police is committed to the District Tribunal, composed of a president, called ispravnik, and some assessors. This tribunal has a chancellery, divided into two bureaux. The districts are divided into sections (*stan*), which have their special chiefs, called *stanavoï pristáv*, under whose orders are the *sotski* and the *dessiatski*. The ispravnik and the dean of the assessors are chosen by the nobility, the stanavoï by the Crown, and the assessors by the peasants of the Crown and the free farmers, from among the nobles of the government.

Let us proceed to the particular administration of certain provinces.

Siberia is divided into two parts, East and West Siberia, each of which has its distinct administration. That of the West resides at Omsk, and extends to the governments of Tobolsk and Tomsk, and to the Kirgises; that of the East resides at Irkutsk, and comprises the governments of Irkutsk and Jeniseisk, the province of Jakutsk, the circle of Okhotsk, of Kamtschatka, and of Troïtzko-Savsk.

The superior administration of each of the two parts is composed of a governor-general and his council, formed of six councillors, three of whom are presented by the governor-general, and the other three by the Ministers of the Interior, the Finances, and Justice, to the nomination of the Emperor.

In case of absence or illness, the place of the governor-general is supplied in the council by one of the civil governors, whom he nominates for this purpose. Each government is administered by a civil governor and a council, composed under his presidency of presidents of the goubernium, of the chamber of finance, of the tribunal, and the attorney of the government. Each district has a special chief, and a council, formed of the heads of the different branches of the local administration, the mayor, the judges, the ispravnik, the treasurer, and the substitute of the attorney.

The indigenous inhabitants of Siberia have a different administration, according to their mode of life and occupations. The roving tribes are governed by a *stepnaïa douma*, or chamber of the steppes, composed of *taïscha*, *saïssani*, *schoulengui*, &c., to which belongs the high administration of several united tribes. The separate tribes have strostas, with their assistants, whom they call in their language *darougua* or *taïscha*. All these chiefs are elected by the native inhabitants themselves.

The civil government of Tomsk is designated

by the Minister of the Finances, because it has also the superintendence of the mines of Altai, which are in the province of that ministry.

The Kirgises are governed by a major-general and by an administration, under the presidency of a colonel or lieutenant-colonel, and composed of four councillors, one of whom is a Kirgise, an assessor, the substitute of the attorney, and a chancellery. These authorities reside at Omsk.

The province of Jakutsk has a chief and an administration composed of three councillors and a substitute of attorney, under the presidency of the head of the province.

The administration of Okhotsk is committed to an *employé* of the navy, assisted by a council, composed of the oldest officer of the naval service after the chief, the district judge, and the ispravnik. It is dependent on the governor-general of Irkutsk, as well as Kamtschatka, which has also a district chief.

The superintendence of the cordon on the

Chinese frontier of Troïtzko-Savsk is allotted to a chief (major) assisted by a councillor and six assessors. The chief is appointed by the Minister of Foreign Affairs.

The Caucasus is divided into the Caucasian province and the Trans-caucasian country, both of which are under the commander-in-chief of the Caucasus. The chief town of the Caucasian province is Stavropol, and it is administered by a superior military *employé*, whose duties correspond with those of a military governor, and by a council composed of the civil governor, president of the goubernium, the marshal of the nobility, the presidents of the tribunals, the president of the chamber of finances and court of domains, and the attorney of the province.

The districts are governed by a military chief and a council, composed of the major of the place, the marshal of the district, the mayor, the ispravnik, &c.

The Trans-caucasian country is composed of the government of Georgia-Imeritia and of the Caspian province.   The commander of the army of the Caucasus is also the head of the administration.   He is assisted by a council, in which the military governor of Tiflis has a seat, as have also members nominated by the Emperor, and the functionaries who may be summoned to it when it is engaged with matters which concern them.   If the president cannot agree in opinion with the majority of the council, he refers the subject to the Senate or the competent ministers: he may also carry into immediate execution the opinion of the minority, or even of a single member, by taking the whole responsibility on himself, and acquainting, without delay, the minister whom the point in dispute concerns, with the reasons which have induced him to take that resolution.   Since the appointment of a lieutenant of the Caucasus, the power of the chief of this army, who unites the two titles, has been increased beyond measure.

A civil governor is at the head of the government of Georgia-Imeritia.   The Caspian province has a particular chief. The districts have each a special administrator and a substitute. They are divided into sections, which are under the management of assessors.

The Don Cossacks are administered by an ataman, who, like the governors-general, unites in his person the civil and military authority. He presides over the military government, which is composed of the chief of the staff, the dean of the members, and four assessors, and divided into four bureaux and a section of accounts and control. The military government has a right to refer to the Senate the orders which it receives from the ataman, and to which it refuses its approbation, without having the power to stay their execution. The chief of the staff supplies the place of the ataman, in case of illness, absence, or interim.

There is a civil tribunal and a criminal tribunal, each composed of an elder, two adjuncts, and three Cossack assessors, elected by the military chiefs every three years; the attorney and two substitutes are independent of the army, and appointed by the senate on the presentation of the Minister of Justice. The comptroller is also nominated by the Senate, on the presentation of the comptroller of the empire.

The country of the Don Cossacks has seven districts and as many special administrations, besides that of the Calmucks. The tribunals of the circles are each composed of a judge, a military officer, two assessors, civil officers, (at Tscherkask there are three) and two Cossacks; it has a chancellery. That of the *stanitzas* is composed of an ataman and two judges elected by the inhabitants every three years.

The Cossacks of Asov are under the rule of the governor-general of New Russia. They have at their head an ataman, and are governed, in administrative affairs, by a military chancellery.

The Cossacks of the Black Sea are under the authority of the commander-in-chief of the army of the Caucasus. Their ataman has the attributions of a general of division for military affairs, and those of a governor for civil matters.

The Cossacks of Orenburg are dependent on the commander of the army of Orenburg, those of Astrakhan on the military government of that city. Their ataman is elected by them and confirmed by the Emperor.

The Cossacks of the Ural are likewise dependent on the governor-general of Orenburg.

The Cossacks of Siberia are divided into town Cossacks and those of the line. The first are charged with the police of the towns, and are under the orders of the civil authorities. The Cossacks of the line are at the disposal of the military chancellery of Siberia, which has its seat at Omsk, and at that of the officer commanding the army of Siberia.

CHAPTER VII.

PENAL LEGISLATION.

THE penal code of Russia gives the following definition of crimes and misdemeanors: "Every action forbidden by the law under *fear* of heavy punishment is a *crime;* and every act forbidden under *fear* of slight corporal chastisement, or police correction, is a misdemeanor." This is pronouncing openly in favour of the system of intimidation, which, as Hegel said in one of his lectures on the philosophy of law in Berlin, is *a stick held up to a dog.*

Every theft and swindling act to an amount not exceeding twenty assignation rubles, drunkenness, and blows given in a quarrel, when not of consequence, are reckoned misdemeanors.

Those are accounted accomplices in a crime who have co-operated in it, or facilitated it by their acts, their words, or their writings. Moral complicity is thus established and at the same time left to the decision of the judges. Those who have provoked the crime are punished more severely than those who have participated in its accomplishment, excepting the cases in which the law has decreed equality of punishment for certain crimes.

The punishment of death was abolished by the decrees of 1753 and 1754 in all cases but for political crimes which have been carried before the *supreme penal tribunal*. This is contrary to the course pursued in the civilized world. There the penalty of death is reserved for murder and abolished for political crimes. In Russia, to love one's country and to attempt to promote its welfare in any other way than what the Government approves is a greater crime than to kill one's fellow-creature. By whom is it decided what crimes shall be carried before the supreme tribunal? By the supreme authority alone: and what is that extraordinary tribunal? It is composed, for each particular case, of members chosen by the Emperor alone, out of the council of the empire, the senate, or the other dignitaries of the Court and State. Thus it is one of the parties who is at the same time judge, and this judge cannot but be partial.

No fixed law determines the mode of execution for those condemned to capital punishment. It is left to the pleasure of the judges, for each particular case. The supreme tribunal can, if it pleases, order a man to be buried alive, quartered, or hanged. This, most assuredly is allowing too much latitude to discretionary power. Thus, on the 15th of September, 1765, the sub-lieutenant Mirovitsch was beheaded; on the 10th of November, 1771, two of the ringleaders in the insurrection which broke out at Moscow, on occasion of the plague, were hanged. On the 10th of January, 1755, Pugatschef and Perfilief were quartered, and their accomplices hanged or beheaded. On the 13th of July, 1826, five of the conspirators of the 14th of December were hanged.

It is not even necessary that a criminal should receive sentence of death before he can be put to death. The executioner can kill a man with a single stroke of the knout or *pleite*. A culprit may be suffered to perish under the gauntlet; the surgeon who attends the sufferer need only be told to shut his eyes, and he is thus dispensed from all responsibility. Again, the executioner may, either by wilful or involuntary awkwardness, break the sword of a noble, in pursuance of the sentence of condemnation, upon his head instead of breaking it above his head, and bear rather too hard, without having precisely received any express instruction on the subject. Such a circumstance occurred in 1836. M. Pavlof stabbed M. Aprelef on leaving the church where the latter had just been married to Mademoiselle K., after having promised to marry the sister of M. Pavlof, whom he had seduced. By command of the Emperor, the latter was tried within twenty-four hours, and sentenced to degradation: the executioner fractured his skull in breaking his sword.

Every man who, in whatever manner it may be, has the knowledge of a political plot, is bound to give information of it, upon pain of being reckoned an accomplice and treated as such. The ukase of the 25th of January, 1715, says: "Whoever is a true Christian and a faithful servant of his Sovereign, may, without doubt, denounce verbally or in writing *necessary and important affairs*, and especially the following: 1. Every wicked plot against the person of his Majesty, and treason; 2. Rebellion or insurrection." Hence the crimes called crimes of *the two points*. In 1730, slander against his Majesty and the Imperial House was added to the first.

Relationship exempts in no degree from

this obligation. Serfs receive their liberty
for denouncing their masters, if they conspire
against the Sovereign. Any other denunciation on their part against their lord cannot
be received. Children are in the same predicament in regard to their fathers. Neither
has religion found any more favour from this
law, which pays no respect to the sacredness
of confession, but enjoins every priest to denounce any man who acknowledges himself
guilty of conspiracy.

The punishment of death is applied indis-
criminately to rebellion in arms or with violence; to treason, a crime which consists in
having lent assistance or co-operation to the
enemy, or kept up an understanding with him;
to the surrender by an officer of forts or ships
entrusted to him, unless in case of absolute
necessity; and lastly, to those who, by out-
cries, have diffused a panic terror in the ranks
of the army.

Sentence of death may also be pronounced
by the military tribunals before which citizens

may be brought for infraction of the quarantines.

Offensive words against the members of the Imperial family, either written or uttered *vivâ voce*, constitute the crime of lese-majesty, which is punished with death whenever it is carried before the supreme tribunal; but, before the ordinary tribunals, it incurs only those punishments which are substituted for the penalty of death, such as the knout and compulsory labour. The same is the case in regard to all crimes against the *two points*.

Political death entails the privation of all the rights of citizenship. He who is condemned to it, is laid down on the scaffold, or placed under the gallows, and then sent off to compulsory labour. The decrees of 1753 and 1754 have limited these symbols of capital punishment to the purely political crimes carried before the supreme tribunal.

The *confiscation of property*, for the benefit of the Crown, was abolished by Article 23 of the Charter granted to the nobility on the

21st of April, 1785; it was thenceforth to take place only for the benefit of the heirs of the condemned. On the 6th of May, 1802, this arrangement was extended to the other classes of the people. The property of criminals condemned to death and executed passes to their heirs as if they had died a natural death. It is the same in cases of civil death.

The decrees of 1809, 1810, and 1820, have re-established the confiscation of immoveable property for the benefit of the Crown against the nobles of border provinces, who, during an insurrection, retire without permission to a foreign country.

The law of the 2nd of April, 1722, says that Russian seamen, who, without the permission of the Government, enter foreign service, and engage to reside abroad, shall be considered as deserters; and it adds that those who, after entering into the service of a foreign country, with the consent of the Government, do not return on the first summons sent to them, shall be treated without mercy. Lastly, the law of 1762 purports, that all Russians, not returning to Russia, when publication is made that the good of the State requires it, shall have their property sequestrated. Nicholas, by his ukase of the 15th of September, 1836, has decreed that, " in case the Government shall deem it necessary to put the laws before cited in execution, a regular order of recall shall be addressed to the individual in question, and *whether he returns or does not return, judgment shall be pronounced upon him, and the matter shall be followed up according to the laws.*"—Draco was clearer in his sanguinary decrees.

The ukase of the 17th of April, 1834, decrees the sequestration of the property of those who remain abroad beyond the terms allowed by the laws.

All this complication in the laws is but the consequence of the blindest arbitrary caprice. Thus, while the murderers of Peter III. and Paul I., the Orlofs, the Pahlens, the Bennigsens, the Ouvarofs, the Zubofs, have found nothing but honours as the reward of their murders, the conspirators of 1825, who were unsuccessful in their attempt, atoned for it on the gallows. Thus too the Russian government has always treated emigrant foreigners with extraordinary hospitality, nay even loaded with favours such as have deserted the ranks of their army; while it dares to brand as high treason the mere emigration of Russian subjects, and proceeds with the utmost rigour against those whose interests oblige them to settle abroad, while the Russian legislation naturalizes with the greatest facility all those who wish to fix their abode in Russia. The law says, in fact, that every foreigner, if he is not a Jew or a Dervise, may immediately make himself a Russian subject, by taking the required oath of fidelity. Nine months after his declaration, he must be admitted to the rights of citizenship; and, even after he is naturalized, he may renounce his title of Russian, on the payment of three years' taxes.

The deprivation of nobility entails the sequestration of property till the pardon of the condemned, which enables them to recover their property, or till their death, after which their fortune is restored to their family. This law does not extend to property, moveable and immoveable, for the possession of which it is not necessary to have a title of nobility; this remains at the disposal of the condemned, who may even acquire more in these conditions.

The marriage of the man who is deprived of his civil rights is dissolved, and his wife is at liberty to contract a new one. If the criminal obtains his pardon before his wife has formed another alliance, the husband recovers his rights. The children born before the condemnation of the father continue in the class to which he belonged, and those that are born afterwards follow his new condition. This circumstance occurred, among others, with the sons of General Rosen, condemned to Siberia for the insurrection of 1825; his eldest son remained a baron, and those borne him in

Siberia were colonists there; then, when the father went as a common soldier to the Caucasus, they, by the particular favour of the Emperor, were made cantonists, or soldier-boys.

The wife and children of a convict retain their rights of property, even if they accompany him into exile; but, in this case, they cannot return to Russia till his re-instatement or his death: thus affection is punished equally with crime.

The knout is the punishment that comes immediately after the penalty of death, and which is reckoned to have superseded it. It is inflicted for the political crimes of the *two points*, which it was not thought fit to send to the supreme tribunal, and which, in that case, would have incurred capital punishment; for sacrilege, violation of tombs, stealing articles belonging to a church in the church itself; for injurious words against the Trinity and the sacred books; and for non-revelation of such expressions. Jews, Mahometans, and Pagans who convert a Christian to their faith by force or fraud, are punished with the lash. The same punishment is applied to murder with premeditation, to the abduction and sale of a free man for a serf, to child-stealing, to the forgery of decrees of the Emperor or of the Senate, or to the use that may have been made of such papers by heirs acquainted with their illicit origin, to the fabrication of false national or foreign coins, to the forgery of Russian assignats and papers of credit, to the introduction of false Russian assignats fabricated abroad, to the melting down of Russian coins, excepting that of platina. The knout is the punishment adjudged for rape perpetrated on a young girl, a married woman, a widow, or a man; it is likewise inflicted on the serfs of the violated person who did not oppose the accomplishment of the crime, or defend their mistress. The law inflicts it also on pirates, negro slave traders, on those who secrete malefactors, on incendiaries, and on the non-revealers of all these crimes.

The murder of a relation or of a chief is not punished more severely than ordinary murders, (law of January 1, 1835). The murderer who delivers himself up to justice obtains the commutation of the knout for the *pleite*, or cat-of-nine-tails.

The number of lashes of the knout is fixed by the judges specially for each culprit. They are, however, prohibited from adding to their sentences the terms formerly usual, " to flog without mercy or with cruelty." Since the decree of the 25th December, 1817, the practice of tearing out the nostrils of criminals has ceased; but those who have undergone the punishment of the knout, robbers, and murderers, without distinction, are branded on the forehead and cheeks with the Russian letters, B. O. P., (V. O. R.,) which signify thief.

Next to the judge, the executioner has it in his power to aggravate or to lighten the punishment; indeed his power in this respect exceeds that of the magistrate, for it depends upon him, if not to kill the sufferer, at least to put him to infinite torture, as he can also, if he pleases, do him but little harm; and this is usually the case when he finds in the mouth of the culprit a piece of money which makes it worth his while to be merciful. Charitable persons never fail to fill the hands of a man led forth to punishment, and he takes good care to slip the most valuable piece into his mouth.

The punishment of the knout always entails that of compulsory labour, which the culprit undergoes in Siberia, in the mines, or in the manufactories. The Tartars of the governments of Kasan, Simbirsk, and Orenburg, are sent in such cases to the fortresses of Finland.

The whip or knout is made of leather, platted in a triangular form, which, as it is well known, produces the most dangerous wounds.

The *pleite*, or cat-of-nine-tails, is composed of very thick leather thongs, loose and of immoderate length; it cuts out with ease a piece of flesh at every stroke. The punishment is inflicted publicly or merely at the police. In the first case it is called *execution*, in the second *correction*. When administered publicly, it is followed by exile to Siberia, where the culprit is treated as a colonist.

This punishment is incurred by striking some one in a public place, by tearing or destroying the decrees of the Government*, by opposing the action of the legal authorities†, or the public execution of a condemned criminal‡.

Whoever deprives a man of a member, is punished with the *pleite;* and so is he who mutilates himself to escape the recruiting. The number of stripes is fixed for this case from twenty-five to fifty; and if the person recovers from his wounds, he is made a soldier.

For stealing articles of the estimated value of more than thirty silver rubles, culprits are

---

* Aggravated cases incur the knout.

† If the offender is armed, he receives the knout.

‡ Breaking open the prisons and setting the prisoners at liberty is punished with the knout.

punished with the *pleite* at the police, made
soldiers, or exiled to Siberia. For thefts to
the value of from six to thirty rubles, the culprits receive the *pleite*, but are not exiled.
Under six rubles, theft is punished with confinement in a house of correction.

Perjury and false testimony are punished
with the *pleite*.

All these punishments, equally barbarous
and ridiculous, neither intimidate malefactors
nor correct even those who have suffered them.
The lash leaves no mark, say the criminals
themselves; whereas the tearing out of the
nostrils left upon the condemned an everlast-
ing mark of infamy, which they strove to
efface by their good conduct; and hence they
were reputed to be the most honest men in
the mines as well as in the colonies. Far be
it from us, however, to desire the re-establishment of this barbarous mutilation; we should
rejoice, on the contrary, in the abolition of
the knout and the *pleite*, and wish, if not for
the re-establishment of the punishment of

death, at least for the organization of a better
combined penitentiary system for the amelioration of criminals. It is long since people
recovered from the horror that was once excited by labour in the mines. The mere exile
to Siberia does not frighten persons without
profession and without property. The colonists
there have lands in abundance granted to them,
and the country is not everywhere uninhabit-
able. The ill usage attending and following
the despatch of the convicts excites horror only
in men who are more or less highly educated.
But it is time to say a few words concerning
Siberia, that country of exile and of punishment.

Persons condemned to transportation travel
thither on foot, carts not being allowed excepting for the sick: murderers and great
criminals are chained. Every attempt at flight
is punished with corporal chastisement, even
in nobles. Instead of numbers, proper names
are given to the exiles, but different from those
which they bore before their condemnation.
If they were to change them among them-

selves, they would be punished with five years' compulsory labour, over and above their sentence.

At Kasan, the exiles coming from most of the governments are collected. That city has, in fact, a bureau of dispatch for exiles, which is authorized to retain, for the salt-works of Iletz, an indeterminate number of convicts condemned to compulsory labour or merely to exile: at Perm, the authorities may keep a number for the fabrication of wine, and even for the college of public beneficence.

At Tobolsk sits the committee of the exiles, composed of a chief, his assessors, and a chancellery having two sections. It depends on the civil governor of Tobolsk, and has bureaux of dispatch in several towns.

On their arrival in Siberia, the criminals are set about different kinds of labour, according to their faculties. Some are employed in the mines, either because they have been specially condemned to them, or, having undergone the punishment of the *pleite*, they are deemed fit

VOL. II. P

for that sort of labour, or simply because there is a want of labourers there: but, in this case, they are not confined to the mines for more than a year, which counts for two years of exile, and with double pay. If they commit any new crime, they remain there two years longer, even though the tribunal has not sentenced them to compulsory labour.

Those who have learned a trade are set to work at it; others become colonists, and others again domestic servants. Those destined for the latter station are divided among the inhabitants who apply for them. These are obliged to feed them and to pay them wages, at the rate of at least a silver ruble and a half per month in advance. The term of this punishment is eight years, at the expiration of which these compulsory valets can turn peasants, serfs of the Crown.

The usual duration of compulsory labour is twenty years, after which the condemned may establish themselves freely in the mines where they worked, or in other occupations. Those employed in the cloth manufactories remain there but ten years. Labour in the fortifications is considered as the most severe.

Cripples and incurables form a particular class.

The colonists are not exempt from taxes for more than three years : for the other seven, they pay half of the personal contribution. At the expiration of their punishment, they pay the whole of the tax. After an abode of twenty years in Siberia, they become subject to the recruiting.

The serfs sent to Siberia on the application of their masters, are forwarded at the expense of the latter, and distributed in the villages as agricultural labourers.

The exiles are at liberty to marry in Siberia either free persons or condemned culprits. The free woman who marries an exile for her first husband, receives a donation of fifty silver rubles, and the free man who takes to wife an exiled woman receives fifteen.

Persons condemned for political offences remain in Siberia under the special surveillance of the third section of the chancellery of the Emperor.

Running the gauntlet is a military punishment not applicable to other individuals, unless they become amenable to the military tribunals, as for the infraction of the quarantines, or for the rebellion of serfs against their masters. A whole battalion, armed with switches, is drawn up in line: the culprit, with his hands tied before to the but-end of a musket, is led along the line preceded by a drum to drown his cries, till he has received the number of stripes specified in the sentence, which, indeed, scarcely ever happens; for few men can bear more than four or five hundred, and a greater number is most frequently allotted to a criminal. When the sufferer becomes unable to walk, he is carried upon a hand-barrow, if his life is not yet in danger. Most commonly he is carried, to all appearance dying, to the hospital, where he remains till his recovery, after which the punishment is repeated, and so on till he has received the full number of lashes fixed by the sentence. The Russian penal law gives to this punishment the German appellation of *Spitzruthen,* in memory of its Austrian origin, but it is usually designated " driving along the ranks."

A man is made a soldier for ever or for a time. In the latter case even, it is forbidden by law, to fix a term for his punishment, its operation depending upon the conduct of the culprit, the disposition of his chiefs, and the favour which he enjoys. He is thus deprived of his last consolation, the prospect of expiating his crimes, and at the same time that first rule of law, the proportioning of punishments to offences, is overthrown. That the good conduct of the culprit should be capable of abridging his punishment, and his misconduct of lengthening it, is perfectly natural ; but, at least, let the judge who pronounces it fix its duration! As for the punishment itself, we will not say a word about that : its absurdity is glaring; but it is consistent with the whole spirit of Russian penal legislation, which sometimes deprives criminals of nobility, as if all the other classes of the people ought to deem themselves too happy to receive a criminal into their bosom; sometimes for the slightest offence transfers soldiers of the guard into regiments of the line, as if the latter had not honourable men in their ranks. In imposing military service as a disgrace, the law does not stop to consider that it is striking at the honour of the colours; and, in substituting flogging for the punishment of death, it does nothing but crown its work of barbarity.

The civil *employés* are made soldiers for crimes committed in the service, such as peculation, insubordination, and abuse of power. Heretics who strive to make proselytes, or mutilate themselves, incur the same punishment; but they can deliver themselves from it by embracing the Greek religion. Every man exempt from corporal punishment, and condemned to exile in Siberia, may be made a soldier, if he is not more than thirty-five years old. On the other hand, every man unfit for military service, and who has been condemned for a crime, is exiled to Siberia.

The Imperial will, in short, is the supreme arbiter of this punishment. It frequently happens that the Emperor Nicholas, when visiting the prisons, meets with men confined there who please him by their height, and whom he immediately points out to be made soldiers, without inquiring the cause of their imprisonment, without knowing whether it is for murder, or merely for prevention, or perhaps for an offence of little importance. The law leaves to the Government the faculty of making soldiers of the peasants condemned to exile by their communes or their masters.

In the prisons, the women must be separated from the men; the nobles, the *employés*, the citizens, and foreigners, from the prisoners of low class. Accused must not be mixed with condemned persons, nor even those who are merely objects of suspicion with those whose guilt is more probable. Important criminals are separated from those who are less so. Children, persons confined for debt, and, lastly, the co-accused, must be shut up apart. Ecclesiastics liable to imprisonment are sent to the consistory.

Prisoners are, as a general rule, supported at the expense of the State; nobles and *employés* are not, unless they are destitute of the means of existence. In this case, they are allowed seven silver copecks per day, and even twenty in Georgia. Children under the age of ten years receive half the ordinary pay; and prisoners for debt double, at the expense of their creditors, who must pay in advance for any term they please; but, if they omit to do so, the prisoners are liberated on the very next day.

To prevent the escape of prisoners, as well as to punish any attempt of that kind, the gaoler is allowed to put irons on their arms and legs. Women must never have them but on their arms. These chains must not exceed the weight of five pounds and a half, and they must be lined with leather at the part which encompasses the ancles. Persons exempt from corporal punishments and minors are likewise dispensed from chains. It is prescribed that, to prevent escapes, the prisoners shall every month have half the head shaved, excepting prisoners for debt, females, persons exempt from corporal punishments, and those who are merely under arrest for a certain time.

Vagabonds and men without profession, persons condemned to exile without the addition of any disgraceful punishment, when they have not been exempted from it by their condition, and individuals sentenced to labour in a fortress, or to confinement in houses of correction, are dispatched in *labour companies* as well as those who have been specially sent for misconduct, on the part of their commune or their masters.

There are twenty-seven of these companies in twenty-seven government towns. The prisoners who are incorporated with them are subject to discipline, and wear military uniforms of two kinds, either for vagabonds or criminals. They are employed on the public works, or, for want of occupation of that kind, in work that is bespoken, at the rate of six silver copecks per day.

Duelling in Russia is punished as murder, if death ensues from it; as a mutilation, if wounds only are the consequence. Whoever has gone to the ground and prepared his weapon is deprived of his civic rights, and exiled to Siberia. Seconds are punished as accomplices of the crimes which have been the result of a duel.

Attempts at suicide are punished in the same manner as attempts at murder.

Blows on the head, face, or any other dangerous part, constitute a grievous offence, amenable to the criminal tribunals. Offences by words or by writing are called simple. The punishments for grievous offences are, begging pardon, fine, damages, imprisonment, removal from the service, or corporal punishment, according to the class to which the offender belongs; simple offences are visited with damages only.

Any offence against a citizen is punished with a fine equal to the amount of his annual tax. Blows are rated double, as well as offences committed against the wives of citizens; and in case these pay any tax themselves, the fine is increased by so much. Daughters receive in the like case a compensation four times the amount of that which would be awarded to their parents; for sons of tender age, the compensation is reduced to half.

Grievous offences committed against the clergy are punished with double the fine fixed for the citizens. For offences against nobles, the damages are regulated according to the salary which they receive in the service, or which they would receive in it according to their rank.

Prosecutions for simple offences are limited to a year; for grievous offences to two years.

Every slanderer must retract his words, and is liable, besides, to two years' imprisonment. The author of a libel is punished as if he had committed the crime with which he has reproached his adversary, and his publication is burned in the public place.

Offenders, instead of being sent to Siberia and the colonies, may be merely restricted to a specified residence; as there is likewise exile in the provinces of the interior, or that of a lord to his estates. The law says very innocently that banishments of this kind only take place after trial, or rather according to a disposition of the Government. It is the same with the dispatch of foreigners to the frontiers, which depends solely upon the secret police.

The nobles, as well hereditary as personal, the traders of the first two guilds, and such of the third as have filled posts in the municipal administration equivalent to any class whatever in the public service, the clergy, both secular and regular, with their wives

and children, are exempt from corporal punishments, for which is substituted military degradation, whenever the culprit has not been
condemned to exile or to compulsory labour.
All those persons as well as their wives, are
exempted from ignominious marks.

In case of the illness of a convict, the
infliction of corporal punishment is deferred
till his recovery; and if his health does not
admit of his undergoing it at all, he may be
dispensed from it with the assent of the authorities. Pregnant women do not suffer punishment till forty days after their delivery, and
women with children at the breast enjoy a
reprieve of a year and a half.

Children under the age of ten years are
not liable to any punishment, and the crimes
which they may commit cannot affect their
future condition. Children from ten to fourteen years old cannot be condemned either to
compulsory labour or to the knout, or to
flogging publicly inflicted. From fourteen to
seventeen, they are liable to compulsory

labour, but not to undergo ignominious corporal punishments. From eleven to fifteen, they incur, for offences of little consequence, the rod, and from fifteen to seventeen the *pleite* at the police.

Aged men of seventy years and upwards are exempt from corporal punishments and ignominious marks. Lunatics and persons who have committed offences in a state of somnambulism are not punishable; they are merely shut up in madhouses, the former for two years, the latter for six weeks, after their cure.

Every murderer without premeditation is punished with confinement in a convent.

The right of legitimate defence extends to him who sees the life of another in danger, or who defends a woman threatened with violence. Crimes committed upon compulsion are not punishable in the person of him who has been only the instrument of them.

Offenders cannot be prosecuted for crimes after the expiration of ten years from the time of their perpetration, excepting in cases of religious apostacy and military desertion.

Whoever denounces forgers and smugglers is, from that very circumstance, screened from the prosecution which he would have incurred as their accomplice; but the criminal whose guilt is averred obtains no alleviation of his punishment.

Drunkenness is an aggravating circumstance in every sort of crime committed with pre-meditation, and is never an extenuating con-sideration.

Anonymous denunciations remain without effect, but no oath is required of the informer. Children are not permitted to denounce their fathers for private crimes.   In 1822, the council of the empire exempted wives from the obligation to denounce their husbands for theft.   Magistrates who instigate false accusations with bad intentions are punished with the penalties decreed for the crimes with which they have charged innocent persons.

The declarations of the accused before the

tribunal, if conformable to the facts established, are considered as the best evidence of his guilt. But these confessions are not indispensable for conviction and condemnation.

Children under the age of fifteen years, lunatics, persons deaf and dumb, men deprived of civil rights and of honour, those who have never received the sacrament, foreigners whose conduct is unknown, the relations, the friends, and the declared enemies of accused persons, are not admitted as witnesses. Parents, however, can depose against their children.

Any judge interested in the cause may be rejected and obliged to refrain from acting, at the request of the parties.

Criminal proceedings are gratuitous, and are drawn upon loose paper; but the travelling expenses of the magistrates who conduct them, and of the witnesses, must be paid by the accused.

When the facts of a case are of such a nature as to entail severe punishment, the cause, after it has been tried by the tribunal of first instance, (*zemskii soud*,) must be submitted to the revision of the criminal court established in the chief town of the government, in all cases, whether condemnation or acquittal has been pronounced. Sentences which award merely correctional punishments are not referred to the superior tribunals, unless by appeal of the condemned.

The decision of the criminal court must be submitted to the civil governor of the province; if it is sanctioned by him, it is carried into execution immediately; in the contrary case it is submitted to the revision of the Senate.

The Senate cannot interfere in any affair when the sentence has been confirmed by the governor, unless there has been some violation of the laws or regulations of the proceedings, or by virtue of a special order of the Emperor; and, in this case, it can do no more than lighten the punishment.

Sentences which condemn nobles to deprivation of their rights must always be revised by the Senate. Trials of noble persons for mur-

der must also be submitted to it, even when
the criminal court has acquitted the accused.
Capital accusations, in which *honorary citizens*
and *employés* who have not yet attained the
fourteenth class are implicated, must likewise
be referred to it.

As for the condemned commoner, he can
carry to the Senate his complaint against the
criminal court; but the sentence of the latter
is put into execution as soon as it is passed.
From that day, the convict belongs to the
authority of the exiled at Tobolsk.

The Senate takes cognizance of every affair
in which nobles are implicated with serfs, and
of all those in which nine persons at once have
been condemned to corporal punishment.

The titles of nobility, orders, and kaftans of
honour, cannot be taken from any man, unless
the sentence has been confirmed by the Emperor.

If the titles of accused nobles are contest-
able, but yet there are no proofs of their
nullity, the application of corporal punishments is remitted.

The following anecdote will serve to show, better than any reasoning, the absurdity of the system of criminal procedure pursued in Russia. The circumstance occurred in the government of Twer.

A peasant quarrelled with another about a matter of interest. He suffered him to depart quietly for his own home, then, summoning his man to his assistance, he ran across the fields overtook, and killed him on the high road. It was dark. A woman passing that way recognized one of the murderers at the moment when they began to run away, but without having seen them commit the crime. The two culprits were apprehended, and, besides them, three young men who were absent that day from the village.

Agreeably to the practice usual in such cases, the accused were required to lay hold of the corpse by the feet, that their countenances might be watched at that moment. The faces of the three young men betrayed no emotion, while the actual murderer turned pale and trembled at the slightest contact with the body of the victim. But he was rich; he made considerable presents to the judges and the clerks, and, contrary to custom and the law, he had been confined in the same cell with his accomplice. One day he told him that it was ridiculous for them both to throw themselves away, and that, if he would take the guilt upon himself alone, he would give him 100 rubles. To this his man consented. Meanwhile M. B***, the civil governor, came to inspect the prison, and entering the cell of the murderers in question, he upbraided them severely for not confessing their crime. The master replied that he was innocent, and that his man alone had committed the murder for which they were imprisoned. The latter, on being questioned in his turn, confessed that he was the only criminal. The *employés* who accompanied the governor, quite prepossessed in favour of the generous peasant, laid hold of this confession, and asked their chief if they should draw up a minute of it. The governor assented, and, when he was gone, the man claimed the reward of his devotedness; but the master told him that, since he had been stupid enough to confess before receiving the money, he should not have it. The man lost no time in denouncing the whole affair to the tribunal, and to retract his confession; but he was condemned for *contradictory depositions,* knouted, and sent to Siberia, while the principal author of the crime still enjoys his liberty.

The law forbids a corpse to be touched till the cause of death has been ascertained. A female peasant thrust her head into the stove of a Russian bath, and there lay apparently lifeless. Her husband came in, drew her out by the legs, and, seeing that she was dead, went to seek the officers of justice, who began with dragging the man off to prison, saying that it was forbidden to move a corpse before the arrival of the magistrates.

An ispravnik, charged to cause a peasant convicted of an offence to be flogged, seized

another person of the same name, who suffered
himself to be beaten, without correcting the
mistake till he had received the stripes. The
grave magistrate, without suffering such a trifle
to perplex him, sent in quest of the real
culprit, and ordered a repetition of the punishment.

It is, for the most part, men utterly igno-
sant, peasants who have no notion whatever of
law, who prepare the first proceedings in criminal affairs. The *procès-verbal* must be
signed by the accused; and when he can
neither read nor write, which is very often
the case, he is required to make three crosses,
which he generally does without knowing the
contents; for no time is left him for re-
flection, and he is enjoined to sign somehow
or other. As all these crosses are like one
another, substitutions are rendered easy; and,
owing to these ridiculous signatures, innocent
persons have been seen wandering to Siberia
instead of the guilty. Luckily, by the way,
the governors, on inspecting the convoys of

the criminals, ask them if they are the persons mentioned in the lists; and when these furnish data tending to prove the contrary, they keep them back, and cause their cases to be revised. In this manner it happens that justice is sometimes rendered to the innocent.

With closed doors there cannot be any justice; and, while there is no publicity in Russia, the judges alone will be the gainers by suits.

At Klemovitschi, the secretary of the tribunal of the town and liberties was charged, in the absence of the judges, to commence the proceedings in a case in which a young female was concerned. He had reason to believe that she was a virgin, and offered to save her at the price of her honour. The crime was consummated in court; but it was betrayed by certain indications on her dress. The attorney of the place followed up the affair, and the secretary was turned out of his post. But how many other facts of the like nature, or worse, must pass unperceived!

CHAPTER VIII.

OF RUSSIAN LITERATURE.

Is there a Russian literature or not? Such is the question that one frequently hears asked, and not merely by men who can tell you nothing more about Russia than the perpetual phrase, " It is very cold there," nor by those who carry their simplicity so far as to inquire if it is really true that the Russians are Christians.

Persons of superior understanding and extensive knowledge make no scruple to solve the question in a negative manner. " As to Slavonian literature," said a celebrated Frenchman one day, " it has nothing to boast of but

a translation of La Fontaine's fables." The
honourable peer was somewhat mistaken .
Russia has had her La Fontaine in Kryloff,
whom distinguished poets have been pleased
to translate into French, as well as into
Italian.

We must take leave to be more reserved,
and not to answer in so evasive a manner.
We shall therefore assert that there are at
least as many, if not more, reasons for ad-
mitting than for denying the existence of a
Russian literature.   If literary productions, be
their value what it may, are capable of con-
stituting a literature, Russia incontestibly has
one; if, on the contrary, we would give the
name of literature only to a series of compositions which defy time and the revolutions of
taste, and which are proof against the progress of knowledge, we must confess that she
has very few and scarcely any of these.

Literature in Russia is very nearly what
the Romance literature formerly was in France.
In like manner as this was intermediate be-

tween Latin literature and French literature,
so, in Russia, the literature at present existing
may be considered as intermediate between
the Slavonian literature and that which Russia will probably have some time hence. It
will perhaps seem strange that we should
speak of a Slavonian literature in opposition
to a Russian literature, when the first is composed, in Russia, almost exclusively of religious
books; but, there, as in other countries, the
monks were long the only depositaries of
knowledge, the only literary men; their language, or that of the Church, which originated
among the Slavonians of the Danube, was the
first written language, and still retains over
the spoken language, or the Russian language
properly so called, an influence as prejudicial
as at first it was beneficent, by initiating the
Russians all at once into the beauties of the
sacred Scriptures. The profane language has
at this day great difficulty to make its way
through this ecclesiastical slang.

The Russian language is far from being

formed, and it cannot have a literature without a well elaborated idiom. In France, in England, in Germany, one may create new words, introduce new expressions, but the authors of a century back will be read for centuries to come; while it is not probable that the Russian authors now read will be read a hundred years hence. They will be thrust aside among historical curiosities, consulted, perchance even relished, for the originality or the substance of their ideas, but assuredly not for the form in which they have been clothed. This fate has already overtaken the most ancient of them.

The Russian language has not yet received its definitive stamp: a medley of Slavonian, foreign, and Russian words, use has not consecrated some, definitively rejected others, created new or national terms enough for the new or foreign ideas. Hence, among other things, the Russian authors are divided into two camps, which are engaged in implacable hostility on the question whether to prefer *sei* or *eto*, two words meaning precisely the same thing (equivalent to *this*), and both of which are equally destitute of harmony, the first being more Slavonian and the second more Russian. These are the watchwords of two parties and two schools, the Slavonian school, and the Russian school. This division is met with even in politics: the Slavonians are on all points devoted to ancient usages, enemies of Peter the Great and of European civilization.

The rules of Russian grammar are far from fixed, tolerably arbitrary, and confused; in consequence there are not, perhaps, in the country a hundred persons who write their language correctly; authors themselves vary more or less in their orthography. Several Greek letters were excluded from the Russian language by an ordinance of Peter the Great; the letter *jate* (*e* derived from the *i*,) is still a source of infinite difficulties to every body, and, its utility being almost null, there is reason to believe that some influential person will

banish it, to gratify those whom it embarrasses. There are still two *i* 's in the Russian
alphabet, the *i of ten* and the *i of eight*, names
which they received from the circumstance that
the Slavonians used the letters for figures; the
first must be strictly put before vowels, and
will certainly have the fate of the *epsilon*,
which was banished from use by Peter I.
The Greek *f* and *y* are likewise almost superfluous

The Russian language is inaccessible to foreigners, because it presents no conformity
with the other languages. It is of doubtful
harmony and of equivocal richness, but easily
managed, and susceptible of becoming very ex-
pressive. It is not sonorous for many reasons
—the multiplicity of discordant sounds of the
stscha, of *y*, of *kh;* then again the predomi-
nance of the consonants over the vowels, and
of hard syllables over the soft syllables. Its
copiousness consists only in double uses, or in
the use of words perfectly equivalent, which
by no means constitutes richness. A language

cannot be called rich unless it is capable of
expressing, in different words, all the shades of
ideas, all the variations of feelings, and the
Russian is too little cultivated to vie in this
respect with foreign languages. Its synonyms
are distinguished for the most part only by the
kind of style in which they are employed.
The Slavonian words belong to a higher order
of composition, as to the elevated line of
poetry, while their equivalents in Russian are
reserved for prose. Most frequently it is the
very same word, to which the Russians have
added a vowel, which forms precisely the distinctive character of the genius of their language. Thus, *breg* in Slavonian, the bank, is
called *bereg* in Russian; *vlas*, hair, is in Russian *volos:* the two former are used only in
poetry. The exigences of rhythm frequently
cause Slavonian words to be preferred to those
of the modern idiom, and thus oppose the unity
of the language.

The Russian language has, however, one
advantage, which consists in the facility of the

constructions which it possesses, like the Greek and the Latin, and which it owes more especially to the existence of the declensions; this freedom permits the distribution of words in the sentence, according to the importance of the expressions and the force of the ideas.

So much is certain, that Russian literature is in its infancy; for it has nothing to boast of but poets, and poetry has always been the first step of a nation in the career of letters. There is not a single Russian philosopher. Karamsin is the only historian of his country, and he himself, in the opinion of many persons, is rather an agreeable story-teller than a profound historian. To this opinion I by no means subscribe; for I think that, if Karamsin is not the Niebuhr of Russia, he has more than one claim to be called its Gibbon, if it is absolutely necessary to judge by comparison of the known from the unknown. The other Russian historians are but annalists or compilers.

Karamsin is generally considered, and with

good right, as the reformer of the Russian language. It was he who first had the courage to introduce into it the turns of foreign but totally indispensable phrases. Superior in style to Lomonossof, he is frequently inferior to him in the logical concatenation of ideas; though the historical subtilties of Lomonossof bear at times the impress of parodox.

Karamsin's history exhibits a strange medley of liberalism and servilism, equally dissembled and disguised. What more honest than that maxim professed by him, that savage nations are fond of liberty and independence, and civilized nations of order and peace! Elsewhere, in relating the cruelties of Ivan IV., whose reign inspired some of his finest pages, we find him exclaiming, that the Russians perished for absolutism, as the Spartans did at Thermopylæ.

The novel has scarcely sprung up in Russia, and it cannot yet claim a single classic work. Still some distinguished productions of that class are enumerated, such as "Jurii," "Miloslavsky," and "Roslavlef," by Zagoskine; "the Icehouse," by Lajeschnikof; "The Family of the Kholmskis;" " The Dead Souls," by Gogol. To make amends, there is a whole host of tale-writers, at the head of whom must be placed, M. Pavlof, whose " Yatagan" and "The Demon" are productions of sufficient merit to grace the literature of any country; M. Dahl, more national than his name; Count Sallohub, the gentleman of Russian authors; the fertile Marlinski, who is no other than Alexander Bestouchef, exiled to Siberia in consequence of the revolt of 1825, and killed in the Caucasus; the patriotic Glinka, &c. In the class of science, there is a complete penury. Kaïda-nof's " Universal History" is not even a good school-book. M. Arsenief's "Statistics of Russia" and his " History of Greece" only prove what he could have done had he dared to write; his "Geography" does not prove even that. In politics there is absolutely nothing. As for jurisprudence, M. Nevoline's " Ency-clopædia" is mentioned with commendation.

M. Mouravief has made himself singular by his
theological works. M. Norof has published
"Travels" in Sicily, to Jerusalem, and in
Egypt, where biblical observations are agreeably mingled with archæology. M. Levchine
has produced a description of the steppes of
the Kirghise Kaïssacks, which has been translated into French. Father Hyacinth has
studied China under all its aspects; thanks to
his long residence in the Celestial Empire as
a Russian missionary. He has consequently
become an authority on every subject relative
to the Chinese language, literature, and manners.

Journalism is in a state of the deepest
degradation. "The Northern Bee," the only
daily journal, not official, which assumes the
title of political journal, cannot get or dares
not publish any domestic news, and is more
than circumspect in regard to foreign news.
It flounders in a slough of vulgar, low polemics,
feasts itself upon the vile flatteries addressed
to the Russian government, and torments itself

to bar the road against all intelligence which deviates from its own ruts, against every free spirit, and against every heart that has the least independence. Messrs. Gretsch and Boulgarine are at the head of this publication. The first has the character of being an excellent *purist*, but a worse than middling novelist; the second is a tale-writer, who aims at the piquant without rising above the trivial. They are neither of them Russians, which does not prevent them from being the stanchest patriots in Russia: the one is of German origin, the other of Polish; without prejudice to Germany or Poland be this said. Genius and baseness are of all countries.

If Russia has but one daily journal that is not official, on the other hand, the number of monthly "Reviews" is considerable; they frequently contain valuable articles, among others which are insignificant, worthless, or bad. The "Reading Library," edited by M. Sinkovsky; the "Patriotic Annals," by the indefatigable M. Kräfsky; and the "Moscovite," which has been recently transferred by M. Pogodine to M. Kiréïevsky, are the most estimable of these publications; but their encyclopædic and voluminous form bears witness to the infancy of this species of literature. M. Polevoï's "Moscow Telegraph" has nobly distinguished itself in the history of Russian journalism, and been suppressed for its liberal spirit. The "Son of the Country" and the "Russian Courier" have closed their melancholy career. M. Korsakof's "Pharos" is a subject of raillery for M. Boulgarine himself; it darkens rather than enlightens. The "Contemporary," by M. Pletnef, does not answer the legitimate hopes given by Pouschkine, the founder of that quarterly review, and has ceased to agree with its name. The "Literary Gazette," which reminds one by its title of that founded by Pouschkine and Baron Delweg, appears three times a week, keeps itself aloof from the obscurantism of a Gretsch and a Boulgarine, and in its spirit resembles the "Patriotic Annals."

Beside Messrs. Gretsch and Boulgarine are placed at the head of Russian journalism, Messrs. Polévoï and Sinkovsky, who represent a less dark and more consolatory shade. M. Sinkovsky is not deficient either in science or acuteness of understanding. M. Polevoï has made himself a study for the mass of Russian readers. He has published a "History of Russia," unfinished and imperfect, and a great quantity of tales and dramatic pieces, in which patriotism is coupled with a courtier-like obsequiousness that descends to servility. Such are "Pauline, the Siberian," the "Grandfather of the Russian Navy," "Igolkine," &c. His drama of "Death or Honour" forms an exception to this sad rule, and is liberal without being national. For the rest, M. Polevoï is a writer more deserving of indulgence than any other, on account of his circumstances. We must also do him the justice to admit that, whenever he has had leisure to take pains with his articles of criticism, he has risen above mediocrity.

But let us return to poetry, which alone has attained a tolerably high degree of development in Russia. I shall not treat here either of Lomonossof, not less profound than universal, who, on the same day, made astronomical observations, and wrote pages of history or philosophy, fruits of his studies in Germany, or even bespoken odes; nor of Soumarakof, as insipid as he was old; nor of Trediakovski, not less ridiculous than dull; nor of Fon-Visine, that pamphleteer of the age of Catherine, equally witty and sarcastic. His "Court Grammar," several comedies, and his "Letters from France," defy time and the revolution which the Russian language has undergone since he wrote. Neither will I pause at Dimitrief, whose fables are better than his odes; nor even at Derjavine, who wanted nothing but science to be the Russian Göthe; nor at Kniajuine, the father of Russian comedy; nor at Ozerof, the real creator of tragedy in his country, and whose "Dmitri Donskoi," "Fingal," and "Œdipus," are meri-

torious imitations of foreign dramas. Unfortunately, these pieces no more exhibit the
stamp of originality than that of genius, and
are not remarkable either for the plot or the
characters.

All these authors belong to by-gone ages,
and their language has become so antiquated,
that it excites regret to see so many fine ideas
and happy sentiments doomed to oblivion.

Pouschkine, Krylof, and Griboïédof, are the
three worthy representatives of modern Russian literature; all three died during the present reign.   Griboïédof was assassinated in
Persia, where he performed the functions of
chargé d'affaires.   Pouschkine fell in a duel in
1836; and Krylof expired peacefully, as he
lived, amidst the general esteem. The court
bestowed a splendid funeral on this man, who
gave it no umbrage.

Krylof is the Russian La Fontaine, in all
the glory and splendour of that name; he is
the good-natured and the pure, the profound
and the humorous fabulist, whose imitations

are equalled only by his original productions, and who leaves far behind him the fables of Khemnitzer and Ismaïlof.

Griboïédof has left a master-piece, "The Misfortune of Genius." One might say, in one sense, that he has opened, but it would be more correct to say, that he has closed, the arena of comedy, inasmuch as he has attained a height to which no writer either before or since has arrived. By his master-piece he has, as it were, exhausted Russian comedy, and rendered it impossible for time at least, or manners, to be such as he has depicted them. So cleverly has he seized and delineated the defects of his countrymen, that he has left nothing to do even for genius, which is obliged to wait till time, remodelling characters, has destroyed the resemblance of Griboïédof's portraits. This resemblance is already beginning to be effaced for some, the originals of which are becoming more rare, but the principal hero of the comedy has lost none of the interest that he ever excited. If Famoussof, the

boyar, and Scalosoub, the military officer,
have grown rather old under the influence of
civilization; the Tschatskis have only multi-
plied, and you meet with but too many of
those young Russians, who, on returning from
abroad, find their own country unendurable,
and leave it again, if not for ever at least for
as long a time as possible. Moltschaline is
the worthy representative of the Russian *employés;* his very name, which signifies to *hold
one's tongue,* admirably expresses the quality
which must distinguish every *employé* in Russia, and which Griboïédof has so cleverly
portrayed in these words:—" You must not
have an opinion of your own." His dialogue
with Tschatski reveals a distinguished painter
of manners.

" *Tschatski.* Now that we have an opportunity to say a word to one another, Dmitri
Alexandrowitsch, what is now your kind of
life?"

" *Moltschaline.* The same as it used to be."

" *Tschat.* And, formerly, how did you live?

To-day as yesterday; from the pen to cards, from cards to the pen; ebb and flood have their fixed hour."

"*Molt.* Since I have been in the archives, I have had three rewards."

"*Tschat.* Ranks and grandeur tempted you, I suppose?"

"*Molt.* Every one to his talent."

"*Tschat.* What is your's?"

"*Molt.* I have two—sobriety and regularity."

"*Tschat.* Magnificent ones, forsooth, and worth all ours put together."

"*Molt.* The ranks have not smiled upon you; you have not prospered in the service."

"*Tschat.* Ranks are given by men, and men are liable to make mistakes."

The Russian young ladies are cleverly hit off in these few words.

"Our young ladies understand how to prank themselves in taffeta and crape; they cannot utter a word with simplicity, but only in a charmingly mincing manner; they sing French ballads, taking the highest notes; they attach themselves to military officers because they are themselves *patriots*.

"And what of our old ones? When once they perk up their heads, and clap themselves down to the table to talk over matters, every word is a verdict, for they are all thoroughbred; and sometimes they run on about government in such a way, that, if any spy were to overhear what they say, woe betide them!"

The indignant imagination of Tschatski attacks all the abuses of Russia; it lashes them unmercifully, and without the authorization of the censorship.

"I should have devoted myself to fable; I am passionately fond of fable; nothing but satires on lions and eagles. People may call them animals, but they are tzars for all that."

Tschatski reviews his old Moscow acquaintances, ridiculing them all, and while he stigmatizes the vices of Russia one after another, Famoussof incessantly interrupts him with the exhortation—

"Give up your liberal ideas; pay attention

to the management of your estates; and above all, go and serve." "I am ready to serve," he replies, "but I have a great objection to be subservient."

The "Misfortune of Genius" has been found fault with for having no plot, but such a vein of wit and sarcastic humour runs through the whole piece that this defect is scarcely perceived.

To find anything to rival Griboïédof, we must turn to another sphere, and other characters. Of this M. Gogol was duly sensible, and he has done it with success. In Little Russia, his native country, and in his southern imagination, he has found an abundant source of inspiration. His "Reviser" is rich in grotesque characters and in comic scenes. Nature is there exhibited in all her prominent traits, unvarnished and unadorned—a burlesque Nature, which the author is at no pains to disguise or to embellish, in any of her freaks, however unamiable.

Pouschkine is the representative of Russian

genius, the head of the literature of his country. Highly educated, noble, hot, persecuted, he united in himself all the requisites for success, and death carried him off amidst his most glorious triumphs, at the moment when, after having been the ornament of Russia, he became her prop and beacon.

Banished three times from the capital, wandering in those parts to which Ovid was exiled, his Muse conversed worthily with the Latin poet, and exhaled her sorrows in a touching epistle which he addressed

"To Jasykof.

" A tender tie has in all ages bound poets together: they are priests of the Muses; the same flame thrills them. Strangers to one another from accident, they are akin by inspiration. I swear, Jasykof, by the shade of Ovid, that I am related to thee.

" It is long since I went, one morning, along the Dorpat road, to carry my clumsy staff to thine hospitable abode, and came back with a heart full of the picture of thy life exempt from care, of thy free and animated converse, and of the strains of thy sonorous lyre. But Fate plays maliciously with me: long have I been wandering without home at the behest of despotism. When I fall asleep, I know not where I may wake. At this time, alone in gloomy exile, my days drag on in misery. Hearken, poet, to my call: disappoint not my hopes. In the village where lay concealed the pupil of Peter, the loved slave of tzars and tzarinas, and their forgotten guest, my Arabian ancestor, on the spot where, thinking no more of the court and the splendid promises of Elisabeth, he mused in the cold summers, in the shade of lime-tree alleys, on his distant Africa, I await thee!"

"Russlan and Ludmila," was the first poem of Pouschkine's; "The Prisoner in the Caucasus," "The Gipsies," "Pultava," "The Fountain of Bakhschissarai," "The Two Robber Brothers," and "Count Nouline" followed.

"The Prisoner in the Caucasus" is one of his best productions, though he himself always considered it as the work of a raw youth. The different translations of it which have been made give but a faint idea of the original. Nature—one of the most beautiful natures in the world, that of the Caucasus, has been copied most exquisitely; and the noble and virgin love of the daughter of the mountains admirably embellishes this picture. Only listen to her language, at once passionate and tender, voluptuous and chaste ; see her hand the milk to the Russian prisoner, saw asunder his fetters, give him liberty, and stay without him.

The warlike manners of the Circassians are also admirably depicted in this poem.

"He watched for whole hours how at times the agile Circassian, in a vast desert, in a long-haired cap and black bourka, inclining over the pommel of the saddle, supporting himself with neat foot in the stirrup, flew along at the will of his courser, and accustomed himself beforehand to war.

" He admired the beauty of his simple and martial dress. The Tscherkess is covered with armour, of which he is both proud and fond. He wears a coat of mail, and carries a musket, the Cuban bow and quiver, the dagger, and the sabre, the trusty associate of his toils and his leisure. Nothing fatigues him; no sound betrays his presence. On foot or on horseback, he is always the same, invincible and indomitable. A terror to the careless Cossacks, his wealth is a mettlesome horse, bred in the mountains, his faithful and patient companion.

" What art thou musing on, Cossack? Thou art calling to mind past years, thy bivouac in a tumultuous camp, the conquering shouts of the regiments, and thy country. Perfidious reverie! Farewell to the free *stanitza*, the paternal hearth, the silent Don, war, and cherry-cheeked damsels! A secret foe steals to the bank, the arrow is drawn from the quiver, away it flies, and the Cossack falls upon the blood-stained hill."

"Pultava" pictures the ambition and the perfidy of Mazeppa, and the love of the septuagenarian for his god-daughter, the Princess Maria Kotschoubeï, who forgot the gray hair of the veteran in the splendour of the grand-hetman. In opposition, the poet shows us the magnificence and power of Kotschoubeï, his thirst of revenge against the man who had stolen his daughter—the man who had imparted to him all the secrets of his rancorous and haughty spirit, and even his recollections of that entertainment, at which Peter had seized him by the beard, an insult which Mazeppa had sworn to wash away in the blood of the Tzar, and also his plot with the King of Sweden. Kotschoubeï denounces the whole to Peter, and an aspirant to the hand of his daughter, a young and noble Cossack, carries to the Tzar his letter concealed in his schako, that schako which will not fall but with his head. The chivalrous Peter sends the denunciation to Mazeppa himself, and leaves him to decide the fate of Kotschoubeï. The prince is thrown into a dungeon; and the hetman strives to wring from him, in his turn, his secret, the secret of his treasures. " Three treasures have been the comfort of my life," replies Kotschoubeï to Orlik, the confidant of Mazeppa; "my first treasure was my honour, that the torture took from me; my second treasure, the honour of my beloved daughter, I watched over with trembling, day and night, Mazeppa has robbed me of that; but I have preserved my third treasure, my sacred revenge, and that I am preparing to carry to my God."

Kotschoubeï's head is struck off; Mazeppa triumphs, but the battle of Pultawa overthrows his plans, and he flees in the track of the pugnacious King, "who would fain force Fate to turn like a regiment at the sound of the drum." After the execution of her father, Maria forsakes the house of her husband, as she had fled from that of her father to ally herself with the ferocious hetman. In the night following the battle of Pultawa, she appears to him in a dream, pale, in rags, and a maniac.

"Eugene Onéguine" is a novel in verse, full
of nature and a charming gaiety, and a picture
of provincial manners, the heroes of which
please as much as they interest.   The account
of Lenski's duel with Onéguine has more
especially been dictated by inspiration : one
would say that Pouschkine foresaw his own
fate when delineating that of the poet
Lenski; hence, those verses will not die, but
be for ever treasured in the hearts of the
Russians.   The double interest which attaches
to this curious piece induces us to translate it
entire.

"The pistols have glistened; the hammer
strikes with a sound against the ramrod, the
balls drop into the fluted barrel, and the cock
has clicked for the first time.   The powder in
gray streaks is spread over the cover of the
pan.   The jagged flint, firmly fixed, is re-set.
Behind a post, neighbour Guillot, confused,
takes his place.   The two adversaries throw off
their cloaks.   Zaretski has measured thirty-
two paces, with wonderful accuracy; he has

placed the friends at the two extremities, and each has taken his pistol.

"'Now, approach one another'. Coolly, without yet taking aim, the combatants, with firm step, slowly, both at once, advanced four steps —four steps towards death. Then Eugene, without ceasing to advance, began first to raise his pistol slightly. They took five more steps, and Lenski, closing the left eye, began also take aim; but at that moment Onéguine fired . . . . . The poet's last hour has struck; he drops his weapon in silence.

"He gently raises his hand to his breast. His dim eye expresses death, not pain. Thus it is, that, on the declivity of the mountains, glistening and sparkling in the sun, slowly descends the avalanche of snow. Seized with a sudden chill, Onéguine ran to his antagonist looked at him, called him . . . . . to no purpose. He is no more! The young bard has found a premature end. The tempest has raged; a charming flower has withered since morning. The fire is extinguished upon the altar.

"He was lying motionless, and the dull rigidity of his brow had in it something awful. He was wounded in the breast; the ball had passed through and through, and the blood issued reeking from the wound. But a moment ago that heart throbbed with inspiration, hate, hope, and love. Life played in that body; the blood boiled. Now, as in a forsaken house, all is dark and quiet: silence reigns there for ever. The shutters are closed; the windows are whitened with chalk. The mistress of the house has disappeared; she is gone, but whither? God knows. All traces of her are lost.

"It is agreeable to enrage by an impudent epigram an improvident enemy, to see how, lowering his horns in fury; he cannot help recognizing himself in it with shame. It is more delightful still, my friends, if he stupidly bellows, 'It is I!' it is more delightful still to prepare for him in silence an honourable grave, and to take aim slowly at his pale brow at a noble distance—and yet to send him to his fathers cannot make you happy.

"And if before your pistol there falls a young friend, who, glass in hand, may have offended you by a saucy look, or by an inconsiderate answer, or by any other nothing, or who, in a sudden fit of anger, has even fiercely challenged you, say what feeling will overwhelm your soul, when, stretched motionless on the ground before you, with death on his brow, he stiffens by degrees, and remains deaf and silent to your agonizing call!

"Filled with the anguish of remorse, tightly grasping the pistol, Eugene gazed at Lenski. He is dead,' cried the second—' dead! Horror-stricken at that terrible exclamation, Onéguine retired trembling and called his servants. Zaretski gently laid the cold corpse upon a sledge, and took home with him the funereal treasure. The horses, scenting death, neighed, capered, champed the steel bit till it was covered with white foam, and flew like an arrow.

" You grieve my friends for the poet. In the brightness of joyous hopes, disappointing the world, scarcely out of the garb of boyhood, he is extinguished. Where is the burning agitation, where the noble fire of lofty, tender, and courageous thoughts and feelings! Where are the stormy desires of love, the thirst of knowledge and study, the dread of vice and disgrace, and you, traditional dreams, fore-taste of a celestial life, ye dreams of sacred poesy!

"Perhaps he was born for the happiness of mankind, or at least for glory. His lyre, now silent, might have rung to distant ages by sonorous and endless accents. Perhaps the poet's place was marked high on the ladder of the world; perhaps his martyr-shade has car-ried with it a sacred mystery; for us is lost a creative voice, and, beyond the tomb, the hymn of time, the blessings of nations cannot reach him.

"But it may be too that a common fate awaited the poet. The years of youth would have passed; the fire of the soul would have cooled within him; he would have altered much, forsaken by the Muses; he would have married; then, living in the country, happy and deceived, he would have worn a gown of *tricot*, and would have become acquainted with the realities of life; he would have had the gout at forty; eating, drinking, yawning, becoming fat, growing old, he would have died at last in his bed, amidst children, crying women, and physicians."

The last moments of Pouschkine were poisoned by the impression of a domestic misfortune, a misfortune whether real or imaginary, it has been impossible to ascertain. We know not whether we have to accuse his imagination, his enemies, or his wife, of having hurried him to the grave. All of them perhaps contributed to do so. Anonymous letters, sent to him concerning the real or alleged infidelity of his wife, urged him to challenge his rival, his own brother-in-law, who had the misfortune to wound him mortally.

Pouschkine had African blood in his veins: his great grandfather was a negro in the ser-

vice of Peter I., General Hannibal.   Hence,
perhaps, that susceptibility, which was one of
the secrets of his genius, and to which sufficient indulgence was not shown.   He was as
liberal as it is possible to be under the iron rod
of the Russian government; but he was still
more patriotic than liberal.   His post of gentleman has not effaced the remembrance of
his persecution, any more than his verses
addressed "To the Calumniators of Russia"
have destroyed the effect of his liberal poems.
His ode on "Liberty," and his "Genealogy,"
are the most curious of his unpublished pieces.
Neither has his satire on Ouvarof, the Minister
of Public Instruction, been introduced into the
collection of his complete works.   To make it
pass the censorship, he had recourse to a stratagem: entitling it, "The Death of Lucullus,
translated from the Latin," he sent it to a
Moscow review, by which it was eagerly accepted and published.   Being summoned before the minister of the police, and required to
tell on whom he had made these verses, "On

yourself, Count," he replied. As the latter burst into a laugh, he asked why M. Ouvarof had not done the same when he was told that the satire was directed against him. Count Benkendorf reported the whole to the Emperor, saying that, after such a witty reply, he had not the courage to reproach the poet.

His tales in verse are read and read again with ever new delight; his epistles are as beautiful as they are numerous; but his prose does not appear to me equal to his poetry: I am aware, nevertheless, that every body is not of this opinion. His prose tales, I think, have not the particular stamp of his genius; though "The Captain's Daughter," "The Queen of Spades,," and some others, occupy a distinguished place in Russian literature. His "History of Peter the Great," went no further than the plan, and that of the "Rebellion of Pugatschef," remarkable as it is, has not revealed a Tacitus in the author. Pouschkine made an attempt at tragedy in "Boris Goudonof," in which sublime verses are found mixed up with prose.

All his lyrical productions are so many titles to renown. His elegy on the death of Chenier is full of profound lessons to despots.

" Be proud and rejoice thee, poet; thou hast not bowed the obedient head before the disgrace of thy days; thou hast despised the mighty tyrant. Thy torch, flashing terror, has thrown a cruel light on the council of the chiefs without glory. . . . . . Thy verse has whizzed past their ears.

" 'Be proud, O Bard! . . . And thou, ferocious beast, play with my head: it is in thy claws. But listen, know this, atheist—my cry, my furious laugh, pursue thee! Drink our blood, live upon murders: thou art but a pigmy, a cowardly pigmy. And the hour will come, and it is not far off. The tyrant will fall. Indignation will at length burst forth. The sighs of the country will awaken wearied Fate. I am going; it is high time; but thou shalt follow me: I wait for thee."

In a preceding passage, Pouschkine makes Chenier say :—

" ' I shall not see you, O days of glory and happiness! the axe awaits me. My last hour approaches. To-morrow, the execution! With solemn hand, the executioner will lift my head by the hair above an indifferent crowd. Farewell, my friends. My ashes, deprived of a home, shall not repose in the garden where we passed days free from care, amidst sciences and feasts, and where we chose beforehand the place for our urns. But, my friends, if my memory is sacred to you, fulfil my last request : · weep my fate in silence. Beware of exciting suspicions by tears. In our days, you know, tears are a crime. A brother now dares not mourn for a brother.

" 'One more request! You have heard a hundred times these verses, neglected creations, fugitive thoughts, scattered traditions of my youth. My friends, those pages contain my whole life, hopes and dreams, tears and loves. Recognize them, I beg of you, in Abel and Fanni; collect these tributes offered to an innocent Muse. The rigid world and proud

renown will know nothing of them.   Alas!
my head will fall before the time; my unripe
genius has not created works lofty enough for
glory: I shall soon die all.   But, pious
towards my shade, preserve my manuscript.
When the storm has passed away, meet sometimes in religious circle, to read my faithful
scroll, and, after listening long, say, It is he,
it is his own discourse.   And I, forgetting my
sepulchral sleep, will enter unseen, and take my
place among you; I shall forget myself while
listening to you: I will quench my thirst with
your tears, and perhaps I shall be cheered by
affection; perhaps my sad and pale *captive*,
listening to my songs of love.' . . . . . . But
suddenly breaking off his sweet song, the poet
bowed down his pensive head."

   " The Drowned," " The Copper Chevalier,"
and " The Nymph," one of Pouschkine's last
pieces, approach perfection.   If, in his poems,
he may pass for an imitator of Lord Byron, his
" Nymph" reminds us of Göthe by the profun-
dity of the ideas and the finish of the versifica-

tion.   Ill-informed critics have said of Pouschkine, that he had taken upon himself an easy
task, that of transferring into his own language the ideas of other nations.   Those who
have thus spoken had not to overcome the
same difficulty as the Russian poet; they wrote
in a language ready made, and have not risen
above mediocrity.   Pouschkine is, in every
respect, a national poet; in his verses you feel
that you are living in Russia, that you are
breathing a Russian air; whether he praises or
lashes his country, a flattering friend or a
severe counsellor, the Russians are equally
fond of him, and honour in him their greatest
glory. It is likewise he who, next to Karamsin,
has contributed most to the formation of the
Russian language.

In fulfilment, however, of our critical duty,
we must admit that his verses are encumbered
with Slavonisms; and this is a fault with
which he frequently reproached himself towards
the end of his career, and which he strove to
avoid in his last compositions.   Having neither

rival to excite his zeal, nor master who might have served him for a model, nor critic whose strictures were worthy of attention*, he has at times neglected his style, and indulged in licences which detract from classic purity. That indolence of mind so common in the Russians has also contributed its share to this result. Whenever the subject kept his mind in exercise, he could give an exquisite polish to his compositions, and, according to his own admission, it was these that cost him most trouble. In him feeling and judgment are superior to imagination; happy reflexions mingle with a strong and warm but not romantic sensibility. He also passed too frequently from one idea to another without any transition.

Ryléïéf was the poet and martyr of liberty; a poet circumspect by compulsion, it is true, but not less dear to the friends of that noble

* The blind animosity of M. Boulgarine against him served only to dishonour himself and to disgust Pousch kine.

cause ; for it is admirable to see poetry in open conflict with power, it is not less curious to see it breathing freely in its fetters. Ryléïéf was, moreover, a man of action; he displayed courage under all circumstances, and, though his unhappy end* should not cause his literary merit to be estimated above its real value, the latter is sufficient to overpower the voices of servile courtiers, who make it a duty to depreciate the talent of every man condemned by power, and so impose silence on slaves, who cannot be grateful for sacrifices of which they are not worthy. If it is a fault to exaggerate one's own merit, not to acknowledge that of others is the surest sign of ignorance.

Ryléïéf's poetry always breathes a sacred love of liberty and a profound contempt for tyranny. The subject is taken in preference from the cause of independence. Vaïnarovsky was the champion of it in Little Russia,

---

* He was hanged, as one of the ringleaders in the conspiracy of 1825.

and the confession of Nalivaïko is that of the poet himself.

"'Tell me not, O holy father,' said the conspirator to the priest, 'that it is a heinous sin . . . . . I know what fate awaits him who first rises against the oppressors of the people. But where and when has liberty been purchased without sacrifices! . . . . My mother and my sister have sung to me an immortal past.

"'Well, my son, I will fulfil the desire of thy soul,' said Rogneda to Isiaslav; 'may my story breathe into thee the spirit of Rogovold; may it inflame thy blood with ardour for great actions, love for thy native land, and contempt of oppressors!'"

Kazlof, an elegant gentleman in his youth, blind for the greater part of his life, dictated, like Milton, his verses to his daughters. His mind and heart had gained in energy and beauty all that his body had lost on the day that he was struck with paralysis.

Dead for this world, he had exiled him-

self to the regions of thought; there concen-
trating his recollections, and recalling his past
sensations, he has often risen in poetry to a
great elevation; whether he has retraced scenes
of nature, or depicted the situations of active
life, or, lastly, sung the dreams of his imagination. In him sorrow is always mingled with
pleasure, regret with love, hatred with resignation, and these contrasts form a medley interesting by its originality. " Tschernetz" (the
Black Penitent,) and the " Princess Dolgo-
rouky," are two of his poems, which will de-
servedly escape oblivion.

Joukovsky is a correct translator, a colour-
less poet, and a prose-writer of little celebrity.
His " Bard in the Russian Camp" has gained
him great popularity since 1812. His translations of Schiller and Byron are better. He is
at this moment completing a translation of the
" Odyssey." It was he who directed the education of the Grand Duke, heir to the Crown.

Jasykof has sung, with extraordinary talent,
the pleasures of Bacchus and the manners of

the German students, among whom he contracted estimable principles, which have governed his life as well as his poetry. He has always adhered to the maxim which he has so well expressed in these beautiful verses:—

" Does the purple smile cheerily upon thee? is the sentence of arbitrary power terrible to thee? be thou innocent as a dove, bold and impetuous as the eagle; then will sweet and mysterious sounds rise from thine harmonious chords: charmed by these strains, the slave will forget his sufferings, and King Saul will lend an ear unto them."

It is no slender merit to have never flattered power; but this is not Jasykof's only one, and his songs will live as long as the recollections of university life.

It has often been remarked how close a correspondence there seems to exist between the life and the capacity of a man and the literal signification of his name. The proper names of Russians have in general a signification of some kind. Pouschkine means cannon;

Jasykof, tongue; Joukovsky, drone. In this manner, Pouschkine might pass for the alarm-gun, for from him dates a new era in Russian literature; and Joukovsky has said of Jasykof that his name was given to him on account of the purity of his language.

' Baratynski is the most celebrated of Pousch-kine's disciples. His youth was as unfortunate as his after-life was resigned. After he had been nine years a soldier in Finland, he passed the rest of his days in a peaceful re-treat, and died at Naples. He has enriched the Russian language with several apt words, and literature with a great number of remark-able poems. "Edda the Gipsy" and his verses "On the Death of Göthe" will long survive him.

ON THE DEATH OF GÖTHE.

"HE appeared, and the aged bard closed his eagle eyes in peace. He died calmly, after having accomplished in this world all that is of this world. Weep not over his sublime tomb; grieve not that the scull of genius is the heritage of worms.

" He is extinguished; but nothing under the sun of the living escaped his attention, and his heart had an echo for all that speaks to the heart. He traversed the universe on the wings of thought, and found limits only in that which has no bounds.

"Every thing supplied food for his mind: the works of sages, the creations of the inspired arts, the traditions of past ages, and the hopes of ages to come. By means of thought he could penetrate at pleasure into the cottage of the pauper as into the palace of the king.

" He lived a like life with all Nature. He listened to the rippling of the brook, he understood the rustling of the leaves, and felt the plants grow. For him the book of the stars had no secret, and the waves of the sea conversed with him.

" He observed and analyzed the entire man.

And, if the Creator has limited our transient existence to this terrestrial life, if nothing awaits us beyond the grave after the world of facts, his tomb will justify the Creator.

But, if it is given to us to live after death, he, who has lived out life here below, and who has, in sounds deep and sonorous, rendered to earth all that belongs to earth, he will arise with soul serene before the Eternal, and nothing terrestrial will trouble him in heaven."

The qualities of heart gained M. Baratynsky the love of all who approached him, and the severity which the Emperor Alexander displayed towards him only increased the interest felt for him by estimable men.

He was eleven years old, when the cadets of the corps of pages, seduced by Schiller's famous drama, formed a band of robbers, the eldest of whom, the captain, was but fourteen years of age. These silly youths amused themselves with stripping passengers and stowing away their booty intact in the loft of

their hotel. They continued these pranks for
six months, during which the persons entrusted
with their superintendence and education had
not the slightest suspicion of the matter. At
length, being taken in the fact, they were all
expelled from the corps of pages. Baratynsky
was one of them. When eighteen years of
age, he solicited service, and, not obtaining it,
he offered to enter a regiment as a private
soldier. The Emperor had the cruelty to keep
him in this situation for nine successive years.

In vain Russia rang with the fame of the
young poet; in vain the highest functionaries
interceded for him: the Tzar was inflexible.
Prince Galitzine, Minister of Public Instruction,
solicited his pardon every year on Good Fri-
day; and at last he applied for it singly, to
the exclusion of every other. Alexander's
constant reply was, "How can you expect me
to wear the epaulette with a man who has
been a robber?" Baratynski was not a man
at that time; he had not robbed; and he had
voluntarily atoned for a juvenile fault. These

considerations could not convince the Emperor; till, at length, yielding to the entreaties of Diebitsch, he made Baratynsky an officer. The latter never wore the epaulette and immediately sent in his resignation. Men who raise themselves above the crowd, distinguish themselves from it even in their aberrations; and if I have paused to record this fact, it is because the advocates of power have at times thought fit to distort it.

Venevitinof had a presentiment of his end, when he wrote these lines:—

"Oh no, my friend, thy words are useless: presentiments are not liars, and it is long since I accustomed myself to comprehend their language. My soul said to me long ago: 'Thou shalt traverse the world like lightning: it is given to thee to feel all that can be felt; but thou shalt not enjoy life.'"

Lermontof, for a poem on the death of Pouschkine, was banished to the Caucasus, where he fell in a duel, like his illustrious master.

Prince Viazemsky and Baron Delweg have published several poems of merit.

Khomïakof has written two rather remarkable tragedies, "The False Demetrius," and "Jermak."

Tepliakof has left behind him two volumes of poetry, admired by many readers.

Madame Rostopchine has attempted light poetry, with the grace which characterizes her.

M. Venedictof relinquished his lyre as soon as he had drawn from it a few harmonious strains.

The number of young poets is considerable, and futurity reserves, without doubt, for some of them, a distinguished place in literature.

The principal obstacle to its development is the censorship. To the rigour of the laws which govern it, must be added the arbitrary system prevailing in that as in all the departments of Russian administration. As the heavy responsibility which rests upon the generals frequently prevents them from adopt-

ing useful decisions and gaining battles, so
that to which the censors are subject checks all
intellectual activity; for they often think it
better to suppress a work than to let it pass,
lest they may afterwards have reason to repent
it. Their line of conduct is marked out only
in a vague manner, and in general terms.
They have to protect the interests of God and
of his representative on earth: the monks
watch over the first, and all have an eye upon
the second. M. Delarue having translated
into Russian Victor Hugo's lines (A une Belle)
" Were I King, and were I God," was denounced by the metropolitan of St. Petersburg, and persecuted in the service. The
Ambassador of Saxony directed the attention
of the Emperor to an article by M. Tschedaef,
who was forbidden to write anything more.
One of the Emperor's daughters laid before
her father a feuilleton of " The Invalid," de-
scribing the debut of a female Italian per-
former, though it had been postponed ; and
the poor author, who had written his article to

order, and beforehand, passed more than a month in the guard-house.

Messrs. Gretsch, Boulgarine, and Voiéïkof themselves have not escaped similar severity, and they have been shut up for having engaged in too virulent a controversy. Count Klein-michel caused an author to be arrested for having made himself merry at the expense of the cravat of an officer of ways and communi-cations. The censors themselves are frequently subjected to the same penalty or a still worse: he who allowed M. Tschedaef's article to pass was confined in a convent. Hence they are cautious even to absurdity. In that verse of Pouschkine's, which we have quoted, " Long have I been wandering at the behest of despo-tism," the word despotism was struck out, and the poet substituted for it inclemency, though not forming a rhyme. In the verse of Jasykof, " The purple smiles cheerily upon thee," the word Aurora was substituted for the purple.

The Russian censorship, as we see, is not only preventive, it is likewise repressive ; and

responsibility reaches the writer, even when
his work has been authorized. A man com-
promises himself more by his writings than by
words, and in Russia a compromised man is a
ruined man, for he cannot raise himself again
but by abasement. The melancholy fate of
most of the Russian authors is fit only to disgust with that career those who are most
capable of shining in it. One does not like to
follow in the track of martyrs, and their
laurels have not charms for every body. When
we see men ruin themselves by their talent,
those who possess one hasten to bury it, or
cross their arms in desperate inactivity. If
tranquillity and repose are essential to the
prosperity of literature, it requires also
liberty. One groans and complains under the
yoke, but one neither sings nor dreams, and
one can scarcely think. Literature requires
also an enlightened protection, and crowned
philosophers become very rare in our days;
the hand that wields the sword is seldom light
enough for the pen. If literary productions

enlighten a nation, it is requisite also that the people should be enlightened in its turn, in order to promote the progress of literature, to encourage authors by distinguishing merit, and by appreciating it at its just value ; and in this respect the Russians are at once too severe and too indulgent. Some have no taste but for foreign literature; others are content with very inferior productions. In short: *Tempora si fuerint nubila, solus eris.*

———

CHAPTER IX.

STATE OF INDUSTRY.

In Russia, agriculture is in the primitive state, a state of alarming backwardness. Dearths occur periodically: more or less general, they happen regularly every five or six years, and each time bring the country to the brink of ruin.

The fault of this is not, as one would be tempted to believe, in the severity and the inconstancy of the climate, but in the deplorable state of agriculture, which in Russia has not yet profited by the progress which it has made in other countries; it is likewise owing to the insufficiency of the ways of communication, in consequence of which certain parts of the empire are sometimes glutted with corn, while others are suffering famine, without any possibility for the former to afford assistance to the latter. To this cause must be likewise attributed in a great measure the enormous differences that are remarked in the prices of grain; they are sometimes at 1 to 10, not only according to years, but even according to localities.

Pasturage, that teat of agriculture, is an object of no attention. Artificial meadows are generally unknown, and irrigation and draining still more so. The cattle spoil the grass, and the hay that is made is ill dried and badly preserved.

A simple routine presides over all the operations of agriculture. People sow, cut, and harvest, not at suitable seasons, but at such times as their forefathers were accustomed to do, reckoning from certain holidays, which are more or less moveable, according to the ancient calendar in force in this country.

Next to serfage, the practice of fallows, which prevails in Russia, is the principal cause of the wretched condition of agriculture. With this system, forage never can prosper, and consequently the cattle can neither attain the quantity nor acquire the quality desirable. Accidents of temperature have a different influence on the different agricultural crops, and there, where they are not varied, there is no remedy for those dearths which affect all productions at once. The want of hands is not an obstacle to the introduction of a better system of fallows; for it is more profitable to cultivate less land, but well, than to cultivate a great deal, but ill.

The cattle are in a state of incredible inferiority. For the most part, the Russian cows are like goats, and the horses employed in agriculture are of the size of asses. In the government of Archangel alone is still kept up the Kholmogor breed of cattle, which is of Dutch and English origin. In the south we meet with Hungarian horses; but those two superior breeds of horned cattle have remained confined to the localities into which they were imported. The Russian sheep consumes quite as much as it brings in; the sheep of the Kirgises and of the Crimea serve exclusively for food, and their skins for making pelisses; their fleece is fit only for the fabrication of felt. Merinos are not to be found unless on the estates of some wealthy proprietors, and the Sicilian and Saxon breeds exist only in certain provinces.

The greater part of the cattle are raised in the steppes, where they are of no use for agriculture. It is from that quarter that Russia derives nearly the whole of the tallow and hides which she exports. It is likewise among the pastoral tribes that horses are most numerous: they constitute the whole wealth of the Kirgises and the Calmucks. There are Kirgises who keep herds of 10,000 horses, pasturing in bands according to their age, and guarded by stallions instead of herdsmen. The provinces of the Caucasus and of the Don have likewise numerous and capital studs. The governments of Perm and Wiatka possess draught horses renowned for their agility, which were originally brought from the island of Oesel. The Crown keeps well furnished studs for the supply of the court and army; and, in this respect, private industry has not been backward. There are horse-fairs at Moscow, Lebedeine, Kharkov, Koursk, &c., and the German cavalries come to Russia to purchase remounts. Races have not yet acquired all the importance that is desirable.

The forests occupy an area of twenty-three millions and a half of dessiatines, half a million of which are in timber fit for the navy. It is in Siberia, along the river Ob, that this timber is preserved intact. That country is equally rich in cedars. The Russian colonies in America furnish for the construction of certain parts of ships, particularly bowsprits, a sort of wood that is in request, and is called odoriferous. In the south of Russia, the forests are gradually disappearing, and the

high price of wood begins already to be felt
in the countries contiguous to the great canal
lines, where a vast quantity is used in boat-
building. Hence it were earnestly to be wished
that the boats may speedily be superseded by
steam-vessels. They have already been established on the Wolga, from Nijni to Astrakhan, on the Ural, and the Dnieper above the
cataracts; and there is talk of constructing
them for the Kour and the whole of the Mary
canals. But the inveterate habits of the
people, and the little importance of internal
commerce, will long be powerful obstacles to
the desirable development of steam navigation.

It is but a few years since the Government
opened its eyes to the calamities impending
over the country in consequence of the destruction of the forests; but the measures
which it has adopted are insufficient, ill-
planned, and still worse executed. Besides,
they do not extend to the forests of private
individuals, which are mostly joint property,
and where each of the proprietors is desirous

to fell as much as possible. The stealing of wood is practised openly everywhere, and on a large scale. No economy is used in the employment of the trees, either for the extraction of the tar and pitch or in stripping off the bark, which serves for making the shoes generally used by the common people. Conflagrations also are very frequent, and often no pains are taken to extinguish them till they approach habitations. The use of turf, coal, or any other substance that might serve to spare the wood, is not common. Some dispositions, however, have been made for promoting the education of foresters, which promise to be useful: to this end, schools have been erected at Petersburg and Tzarskoïe-Selo, as well as two special courses at Mittau.

The breeding of bees is diffused throughout the whole empire, and is practised with success even in Siberia, where, however, the honey has not the perfume which distinguishes it in other countries. There are provinces which derive millions from this single branch of industry, for the consumption is prodigious; honey is superseding sugar among the less wealthy classes; hydromel has ever been the favourite beverage of the Slavonians, and is becoming that of the Mahometans. The churches consume a great quantity of tapers, and, besides, Russia exports wax to foreign countries.

The culture of silk, on the contrary, has hitherto not prospered; and Government, after having exclusively devoted its attention to it, has relinquished it to private industry, which has no hopes of obtaining satisfactory results but in the Caucasus. The attempts made in the governments of Astrakhan, Ekaterinoslav, Kiev, &c., have not been crowned with success. The want of knowledge and of taste for this occupation, has been an obstacle at least quite as powerful as the climate.

The vine is cultivated and wine made with quite as much negligence as ignorance. The Caucasus, the Crimea, the Don, have vineyards which, under the management of skilful hands, might be capable of yielding satisfactory results.

Hunting and the fisheries are sources of considerable wealth for Russia, but the produce of which it would be rash to pretend to estimate, even in an approximative manner. Hunting is particularly important in Siberia, where it constitutes the exclusive occupation of several tribes, some of which pay their taxes in furs. The islanders are free from all tax, but on condition of hunting for the account of the American Company, which supplies them with the necessary utensils, and buys the animals of them at a fixed rate. All these countries abound in fallow-deer, and the species of animals most renowned for their furs; but this abundance is liable to great fluctuations, and is moreover suffering a diminution which is more and more perceptible. The interference of the Government is become absolutely necessary, as well to prevent the complete destruction of the animals, as to regulate the business of destroying them.

The most considerable fishery is carried on in the Caspian Sea and the rivers which discharge themselves into it, particularly the Wolga, that mother of the Russian rivers. The fishery, after being monopolized by the Government, is become in a great measure free; but the curing of the fish needs great improvement.

The mines are destined to fill an important place in the resources of Russia, and are already a great profit to the Crown, as well as to some private persons. The Ural is rich in gold, platina, a metal which is the exclusive produce of Russia, iron, and copper. There too are found silver, malachite, and precious stones. In Siberia, the mines of Altai and Nertchinsk are particularly rich in silver; as are also the former in copper, and the latter in quicksilver. In Finland, there is found little silver, but so much the more copper and iron: there are sixteen mines of the latter metal. In Georgia, the silver mines are closed, but those of copper are of considerable importance. The province of Baku, recently acquired from Persia, abounds in sulphur and naphtha. The total produce of the mines is estimated at about one hundred and sixty-five million francs per annum. From 1823 to 1836, there had been obtained five hundred thousand and fifty poods* of gold, and one thousand two hundred and fifty-five poods of platina. The extraction of salt is about thirty million poods per annum.

Notwithstanding all the efforts of the Government and the illusions of patriots, Russian industry is still in its infancy. Ancient processes, antiquated routines, are followed in preference in the manufactories. Those who are engaged in them are deficient in taste and technical knowledge, because they receive no special instruction, and the general civilization sets them at fault. The Government does not pay sufficient attention to the diffusion of normal schools of arts and trades, nor take pains to place information useful to the pursuits of industry within the reach of workmen, as is done in civilized countries.

* A pood is 36 lbs. avoirdupois.

The efforts which have been made for this purpose, either by the creation of new establishments, or by the introduction of courses of chemistry, mechanics, and drawing, into the existing schools, address themselves to children, and not to grown men; thus, among others, the foundlings of Moscow have masters for all these sciences, and it is but the smaller number of them that follow the career of industrial occupations.

The Russian government merely confines itself to securing manufacturers against all foreign competition, which causes them to persevere in their apathy and incapacity. To protect three or four thousand Russian manufacturers, it imposes annoying privations and excessive expense on millions of consumers; and, in spite of this factitious protection, the Russian manufacturers cannot compete with those of other countries. The raw materials, workmanship, living, are five times as cheap in Russia as in England, and, notwithstanding this immense advantage, Russian manufactured goods are fifty and one hundred per cent. dearer than those of English production. Foreign manufacturers are not easily tempted to settle in Russia, though capitals there yield double and treble what they produce in other countries. The cause of this is the insecurity of property, the deplorable state of legislation and the judicial system, and the little consideration which persons engaged in the pursuits of industry enjoy either with the Government or in the public opinion.

So long as foreign competition does not excite the Russian manufacturers to produce goods of better quality, and so long as instruction shall not have descended to them, one cannot expect to see industry prosper, nor even those branches of it which are, in some measure, the exclusive property of Russia. Thus the hemp, the leather, the metals, which Russia produces in quantity or in quality superior to other countries, have not yet become objects of perfect elaboration. The Russians have still to learn the art of producing varnished leather and leather for carriages; and if their sail-cloth is of good quality, the fine cloths must be imported from abroad. Their imitations in bronze are all servile copies, and cannot sustain a comparison with those of France. The bad taste of the silks surpasses anything that can be conceived, and their quality is notoriously very inferior. In woollen cloths they succeed only with the most ordinary qualities, and nothing but the excessive cheapness of these enables them to compete with foreign woollens. These goods are chiefly exported to China, but for the superior qualities they are obliged to help themselves out with foreign cloths. In 1839 there were already five hundred and fifty manufactories of woollens. The cotton manufacture has made great progress since the year 1825; in fourteen years the importation and fabrication have increased six-fold: the first has risen to a million poods, and the second to the estimated value of one hundred millions of assignat rubles. The national silk manu-

factures require four million rubles' worth of
raw silk, and the foreign silks consumed
amount to fourteen million assignat rubles.
There are more than two thousand leather
manufactories, and nearly two hundred of
beet-root sugar, a number surpassing that of
the other sugar manufactories. The productions derived from flax represent the sum of
twenty-five million assignat rubles.

Roads for the most part wretched and im-
passable, middling only in certain places, seas
inaccessible for a full half of the year, inveterate principles of dishonesty among the traders,
laws elastic and injudicious in regard to bank-
ruptcies, the want of instruction, the want of
credit, the want of all consideration for the
trading class, strictly confined in a caste, like
the castes of India—here is a thousand
times more than is necessary to paralyze every
sort of commerce. The existence of fairs, the
colossal operations of which people delight to
boast of, are another proof of the instability
and the insufficiency of commercial operations.

The whole external commerce of Russia is in the hands of foreigners. The navigation is principally performed by their ships; foreigners are at the head of the first commercial houses, and in Petersburg alone there are three thousand of them. Even in Asia, commerce is carried on only through the medium of the natives, who attend the fair of Nijni to buy Russian goods; and it is they too who conduct the caravans. The Russian merchants are so poor in capital, that foreign traders are obliged not only to give them a year's credit for what they sell them, but even to advance by so much the price agreed to be paid for the goods which they buy of them.

The prohibitive system shackles all the movements of foreign commerce. A state sells only in proportion to what it buys, and Russia, in refusing her productions to foreigners, thereby contracts her own exportation, money being frequently no more in demand than any other commodity. English competition is supplanting the Russian com-

merce more and more in all the markets of
Asia, and Russia finds herself limited to the
sale of raw productions only in those markets.
In China, England is preparing to strike her a
blow from which she will perhaps never recover. The Aleutian Islands and the Russian
colonies in America impoverish more than
they enrich the Company which monopolizes
them.

CHAPTER X.

OF THE ARMY.

RUSSIA believes that she has resolved this problem: that in the army the cane can and ought to supply the place of honour. "The cane," said a Russian professor of tactics, "gives ardour to the soldier." It is considered as the best means for leading troops into fire. One day, in the Caucasus, the Russians, attacked with grape-shot, refused to advance. General Wiliaminof seated himself upon a drum in the first line, and called out of the ranks several soldiers, whom he ordered to be flogged. He then commanded the battalion to advance, and the Russians drove back the Circassians. Ever after this affair, Wiliaminof was reputed a master in Russian tactics. This is one instance out of a thousand, and Prince Schakhovskoy had recourse to the same expedient with his grenadiers at the bridge of Ostrolenka. "How can it be otherwise?" say the Russian officers; "the stick is a sure and positive thing; there is no escaping it, and its effect is terrible; while the enemy's ball is uncertain; besides, a man may resist the latter, but not his commander."—"It is the flesh that rebels in man, it is therefore the flesh that must be quelled," said the professor mentioned above. It was apparently in accordance with this maxim, that he one day persuaded a Russian officer to make a report to his superiors, charging himself with drunkenness, and they actually put him under arrest for six months. What is more barbarous than to beat a man? Nothing, unless it be to set one's self up for the apologist of such a proceeding, to erect it into a system.

We will take leave to ask the learned pro-

fessor how it happens that, in the Russian
guard, where the stick is less and less used,
and cannot, or at least ought not, to be inflicted without judgment, the *ésprit de corps*
and moral courage of the soldier are so much
improved? Why was the Russian soldier, in
the time of Catherine, when the stick was
very little used, renowned for his valour?
Why, in short, has the army which has
gained most victories, the French army, never
known so unworthy a practice? How is it,
again, that in general, in war time, officers are
obliged to change their treatment of the soldier,
and to be much less cruel in all that relates to
discipline? It is because in the day of battle
their own balls are not to be distinguished from
the enemy's, and more than one outrage has
been revenged in the blood of an officer too
unjust or too severe, without the possibility of
discovering the hand by which it was spilt.

It is impossible to conceive all the ill usage
to which the Russian soldier is exposed on the
part of his superiors, high and low. Without

pay, without suitable food, overwhelmed with oppression and stripes, he is destined beforehand to the hospital and a premature death. Hence the Russian army loses nearly as many men in time of peace as in time of war, and during the reign of Nicholas the recruitings have been continued without intermission.

Next to the want of instruction in the officers, the weak side of the Russian army is in the want of intelligence in its soldiers; and the superiority of the French army is owing precisely to the combination of these two means of success. Those days are past when physical strength alone decided the victory; and intelligent bayonets have now an incontestable preponderance. It is the intelligence of the French soldiers that has metamorphosed the military art. Guided by that, the French soldiers, during the great revolution, unable to withstand the numerous legions of their coalesced enemies, broke out of the ranks and dispersed themselves as tirailleurs; the courage of the masses was paralyzed by this innovation.

At Tilsit, Napoleon betrayed to Alexander this grand secret of French tactics. It was first imitated by the Prussians; the Russians afterwards adopted it: but that intelligence which had invented this method, and which can invent something else every day, that intelligence which teaches the soldier how to extricate himself from all dangers, and which assists him in all difficulties, is not to be borrowed; it is naturally developed and has not yet been successfully counterbalanced by that savage instinct of the Russians, the instinct of self-preservation and divination, which the enemy has often had occasion to admire in them. Neither are they destitute of intelligence; every courageous man is intelligent, and nobody denies the courage of the Russian soldier. His spirit is merely bowed down beneath the stick; and if he were ever to have officers capable of appreciating him, he would be the first soldier in the world. In this respect, the army and the whole nation are in the same predicament.

A Russian officer residing in Paris made a report concerning the spirit of the French army which highly pleased the Emperor. His Majesty decorated him, and, wishing his army to profit, at least in part, by this so highly vaunted spirit, he introduced into it the *free step*, which, in fact, forms a singular contrast with its name. Nothing was ever seen more stiff and awkward than this step and the jerk of the arm with which it is accompanied.

It is the officers that make the army. The best army in the world was the Prussian army under Frederick II., the French army under Napoleon, the Russian army under Souvorof. Now, that which the Russian army at present wants is precisely good officers and able generals. In Russia, genius needs to be noble in order to raise itself above the obscure ranks of the army, and to place itself at its head; and military nobles, even when they seriously pursue their profession, are not so liberally endowed by genius as by the social organization.

If we consider separately the different arms of which the Russian army is composed, we shall find that its artillery is excellent, manœuvring with celerity but with more resolution than precision: it fires well enough for a battle, ill enough in a siege. The Russian cavalry is one of the best mounted, and is surpassed by the Hungarian cavalry alone: it particularly excels in the alignement; but the soldiers are too much cramped in their uniforms, all made to one size, to be at ease on horseback. The Cossacks are a cavalry peculiar to Russia, and which attempts have been made in vain to imitate elsewhere, in Austria, for example, and in France, under Napoleon. It is a whole nation on horseback; every individual acquires the habit of riding from his childhood, and makes, in fact, but one with his steed. The Cossacks are of great utility for the service of the advanced posts, for reconnoitring and harassing the enemy; but in mass they are of no value: a company of regular infantry easily repulses the attack of a whole regiment

of Cossacks.   The Russian infantry is justly
famed for its firmness and perseverance.   In
general, in a body, the Russian soldier is excellent; but taken separately, he loses himself.
It is requisite for him, more than any other,
to feel the contact of his neighbour, and to
hear the voice of his officer.   He is a machine,
inured to fatigue, obedient to the least sign,
unique in its kind for the precision of its
movements, but which is good for nothing
when its spring is deranged.   Every Russian
corps without officers is a body without soul.
"Kill the blacks," said the Turks, meaning the
Russian officers, "and it will be all up with
the grays (the soldiers.)"

The Russians have a system of tactics of
their own.   They are too stanch *Romans* to
acknowledge the superiority of other nations
in this point, or to adopt all their principles.
Accordingly, they disapprove Napoleon's system of marching into the heart of a country
and disregarding the fortresses.   The capital,
according to them, is but   strategical point;

and in proof of this they adduce Moscow, the fall of which did not entail that of the empire. The capture of that city was, nevertheless, a thunderbolt for Russia; besides, every nation cannot sacrifice its capital, neither has it at its service a severe winter, which ensures the disorganization of a hostile army that is scantily provisioned. Of what service were the sieges of the Russian fortresses in 1828, but to prolong the war and to increase its disasters?

On another equally important point in tactics, the concentration of masses, the Russian generals are mostly ignorant. Paskevitsch alone practised it in a trifling degree at the commencement of the campaign in Poland. It is to Souvorof that the Russians incessantly refer on every point relating to the military art; and it is to him that they attribute the honour of having best comprehended the character of the Russian soldier. He made the priming of his cannon of human flesh, never spared the troops, marched to victory

over piles of dead, and fought on the day
of battle as fiercely as the meanest of his
soldiers; thus making the fate of a campaign,
of a war, of a country, dependent on a single
shot. Such tactics are too cruel or too rash
to deserve commendation; yet this is the only
thing that the partisans of Souvorof borrow
from him, incapable of copying him in his
best points—that principle, for example, that
it is necessary to destroy in its origin every
assemblage of the enemy, by bearing down
upon the spot where it is forming with great
celerity, and before it has become dangerous.

Men are still held so cheap in Russia that
more than once, at Leipsic, at Varna, in the
Caucasus, when a Russian detachment, on the
point of succumbing, has been liable to occasion the loss of an entire corps, volleys of
grape-shot have been poured on Russians and
enemies, mowing down both alike.

Nowhere has the mania of parades and
exercises of all kinds and denominations been
carried to such a length as in Russia.   Excess

in what is good is itself an evil, and the good alluded to here is extremely doubtful; for practical utility is not what is kept most in view in these sorts of manœuvres. One ought to have seen the Russian foot-soldier lifting his leg for a quarter of an hour to set it down again on the ground with the same formality and the same slowness; to have witnessed the complicated exercises which the heaviest horse-soldiers perform on foot; to have seen the Russian officer at the head of his platoon twist himself like a litter-horse, in order to be convinced that a man of any other nation would not submit to such a manœuvre, which is frequently akin to degradation and tends to brutalize. This it is that forms *par excellence*, the favourite amusement as well as the most assiduous occupation of Nicholas, and likewise of all the princes of the Imperial family. It is the art, and the only art, in which they excel. A corps of nearly a hundred thousand men is specially reserved for the diversion of the Emperor, and this diversion is most expensive, for the guard absorbs the greater part of the material and moral force of Russia. There it is that the sons of the wealthiest families ruin themselves, and each regiment of the guard costs twice as much as a regiment of the line. If the Emperor would at least divide his favours among the different corps of the army, and call them by turns into garrison in his residence, they would all improve in bearing and elegance, and the country would be a gainer by it.

The recruiting takes place annually; the levies are of five recruits to a thousand souls; there are also extraordinary recruitings at such times and in such proportions as the supreme power thinks fit to assign to them.

All individuals subject to personal impost are subject also to the recruiting, such as the peasants of all kinds and the bourgeois properly so called. The following are exempt from it: the traders of the three guilds, the carriers who inscribe themselves as traders, the citizens who hold the elective functions, or who are engaged in the trade to the Caucasus, beyond the line of the quarantines; the peasants of the Crown who have filled public offices for nine years, the pupils of the orphan-houses and of the foundling hospitals, unless they are condemned to be soldiers; those of the agricultural farm of the ministry of the domains, if they have become overseers, during the whole time that they are in office; and the sons of the mayor of the *voloste,* so long as they are not separated from their father. The native inhabitants of Siberia, the Samoyedes in the government of Archangel, and the colonists of certain classes, are likewise exempt from the recruiting.

The inhabitants of Archangel, those of the countries bordering on Austria and Prussia for an extent of a hundred wersts, the free agriculturists of the government of Mohilev, the Tartars of the government of Astrakhan, foreigners settled in the Tauride, the workmen of Narva and certain thinly peopled districts, enjoy the privilege of liberating themselves on paying three hundred silver rubles for each recruit. The Lopares of the district of Kola, and the pupils who have completed their courses at the technological institution, may ransom themselves for one hundred and fifty silver rubles.

The age required for being a soldier is fixed at from twenty to thirty-five years. The nobles who wish to make soldiers of some of their serfs in addition to their contribution, can get them admitted from eighteen to forty.

In the same family, the bachelor passes before the married son, the elder before the youngest, one who has no children before another who has. Between those who are married and have children the parents decide, and, in default of them, the lot determines. Exceptions may be made to these rules by general consent. The family which has but one working member furnishes no recruits, unless one-third of the families are in this predicament, and then one recruit is levied out of all these families together.

In each government, there is a committee which specifies the places where recruiting offices *(rékroutskoié pritsoutstvié)* are to be established. There are as many as four in the most populous governments, and there must always be one in the chief town. The latter is composed of the president of the chamber of finances, the marshal of the district, the councillor of the chamber of finances, who directs the section of revision, a military *employé*, and a medical *employé*.

The citizens of each town, the peasants of the Crown in each union of villages, the properties of each lord in the same government, form separate recruiting districts. If a district of citizens has not the required number of inhabitants for furnishing a recruit, it remains debtor to the State for a fraction proportional to its population, and it pays at the next recruiting, or whenever it happens to owe an entire man. If the district is composed of peasants of the Crown, it pays in money; and if the share coming to it is above one-fourth of a recruit, it is obliged to furnish a man, who is accounted for at the next recruiting.

The Russian villages of the Caucasus, which have suffered from the insurrection of the mountaineers, and have had men killed, wounded, or carried off, are authorized to substitute Tscherkessian prisoners for their recruits, at the rate of two for one.

Each recruit must measure two arschines three verschoks. Certain districts of Wologda, Archangel, and Perm, enjoy a remission of one verschok. The recruits admitted have the front, and those who are rejected the back of the head shaved. The peasants of the same district may become substitutes for one another, and any free man may make himself a substitute for money.

Chapter XI.

THE CAUCASUS.

THE Caucasus has several points of resemblance with Algeria. In one, as in the other, Christianity is struggling with Islamism, civilation with barbarism. The climate of both these uncultivated countries is equally fatal to Europeans: heat and fever decimate their ranks in both. This resemblance is partially found even in the habits and manners of the two countries, and in the arms and stuffs, which indicate the same tastes. The East, Islamism, the Turkish character, have every where stamped their seal. Abdel-Kader, the Arab chieftain, has a worthy and fortunate rival in

Schamile, the chief of the Circassians, and
the moral power which these two extraordinary
men exercise over their people, excites respect
even in their foes; but there ends the resemblance. The Circassian is terrible in a different
way from the Arab, and the Caucasus is mountainous otherwise than Algeria. Hence, while
the French troops in Africa have suffered
very little from the enemy, there is not a crest,
a defile, a stream, in the Caucasus that has
not been drenched and dyed with Russian
blood. The Circassians defend most obstinately every foot of ground, and they are still
far from acknowledging the superiority of the
Russian arms and civilization. In consequence,
while Algiers is merely a means of occupying
the French army, an occasion of distinction
and promotion for its officers, the Caucasus is
for the Russian army an ever-yawning grave,
which swallows up its officers, and wears out
its generals; and we much fear that all the
courage and energy which the Russians display in this warfare, will be absolutely thrown
away.

Nothing excites such pity as to see the Russian soldier, the fair-complexioned child of the snowy desert, battling with the son of the mountains, nimble as the deer, hard as the rock, rapid as lightning. Nothing is more melancholy than to see Russian tactics pitted against the wild bravery of the Circassians. The most skilful dispositions are frequently frustrated by the abrupt movements of the Tscherkesses, who have no tactics but their courage and cunning. The invaders have not, neither can they have, any topographical map of the Caucasus, which defies every sort of appreciation, or at least the means which the Russians employ for taking plans; and the interior of the country is totally unknown in every respect. Nobody has yet penetrated into the gorges of the mountains; the natives themselves are acquainted with only part of them, and have but confused ideas of the general whole. The most enterprizing emissaries have as yet explored but a few localities. The Russian troops, therefore, march in the dark,

and at random; while the Circassians act
with a perfect knowledge of what they are
about. They fall like lightning upon the Russian columns, even when these have number
and ground in their favour, and like lightning
they instantly vanish in the clefts of their
rocks. Frequently, too, they conceal themselves among the rushes which cover the banks
of their rivers, and form, as it were, impenetrable forests; thence they attack sometimes
the head of the Russian columns, sometimes
the rear, which they contrive to destroy, or
merely send a few balls, which never fail to
hit their mark, and seek the officers in preference; they then bury themselves among the
reeds, and all attempts to find them are fruitless. At other times they hide in the thick,
gloomy forests, which Nature has planted for
their defence. The Russians, before they venture to penetrate into them, pour forth a tempest of cannon-balls, and then send tirailleurs
thither.. Nothing indicates the presence of
the enemy; the column enters the wood; in-

stantly the trees become instinct with life; the balls shower upon the Russian soldiers, who either fall in mass, or are forced to betake themselves to flight.

The Circassians rarely venture into the plain, their attempts of this kind having cost them very dear. In 1828 they crossed the Cuban to the number of 12,000. The Cossacks of the Black Sea, forewarned of their attack, received them on this occasion with a murderous discharge of grape-shot, and, having cut off their retreat, made a horrible carnage among them. Such as escaped the slaughter were drowned in the Cuban or buried in the marshes on the other side of that river. The number of cuirassed horsemen who perished in this affair was remarkably considerable. It is related that, on this occasion, the Circassians had hurried to the combat hugging their sabres to their sides, with shouts of "Come, Mary beyond the Cuban!" meaning by that name the Cossack women, who tempt them more than their own, though so renowned for

their beauty. This singularity is met with, it
is true, among the polished nations; the foreign
type, owing to the attraction of novelty, frequently gaining the preference before real
beauty.

In the month of September, 1838, the Circassians fell unawares upon Kislovodsk, still
full of visitors who had come to use the mineral baths. They sacked the two houses
which stood most forward in the plain, killed
the inhabitants, slaughtered the small body of
guards which happened to be at hand, and
retired delighted with this bold enterprize; but
the piquets had already apprized General Sass
of this attack. Swift as lightning, he cut off
their retreat with a handful of Cossacks of
the line, and four hundred Tscherkesses paid
with their lives for this rash incursion.

It is only when the Russians have gone into
winter-quarters that the Circassians venture
upon the attack of forts in considerable bands.
The courage of the Russian garrisons has frequently, in such cases, been required to make

amends for the smallness of their number. By this time too the mountaineers have learned to make a better use of cannon; formerly, the Russian pieces which fell into their hands were retaken in the very first affair, and turned against themselves.

The Circassians deserve the character of excellent marksmen, and the Russian officers are the first victims of their skill. These perish in very considerable number, a number, indeed, quite disproportionate to that of the soldiers. It has frequently been found necessary to make them wear the great coat of the latter to save them from the enemy's balls; but this precaution is repugnant to their valour; and, while it is but optional, they not only disdain it, but even make an ostentatious display in their dress. The white cap is the one which they prefer, and a close coat of damask of the country is their habitual costume. Discipline allows them full latitude on this point.

The Circassian fusii is of extraordinary

length, and is adapted to a support, or even to
the hilt of the sword, the point of which is
thrust into the ground; it is very true; the
ball is small and of copper. Lead and powder
are scarce, so that it is not uncommon to see
the natives give an ox for two or three pounds
of powder, and they will confront the greatest
dangers in the attack of forts where the
magazines of ammunition promise them a valuable booty. The Circassian sword is of
wonderful temper, rounded like a half-sword,
and without hilt to guard the hand. The
Russians have conceived that they could not
do better than to adopt it for certain corps of
their cavalry, and in the Caucasus their officers use it in preference.

In the Russian army, the Cossacks of the
Line, as they are called, are the troops most
capable of coping with the Circassians.
Living close to them, they have adopted their
customs. their dress, and their arms, and rival
them in dexterity as well as speed. The
Cossacks of the Black Sea, though less useful,

have made themselves respected, which is by
no means the case with their brethren of the
Don, who have become a theme for raillery to
the Tscherkesses, as well on account of their
red vests as for their absolutely feminine ti-
morousness: the mountaineers slaughter them
like sheep. The Russian foot-soldier is indeed
to be pitied in this war so unsuited to his nature.
When he does not feel his neighbour's elbow, he
is done up; and where he is not engaged in
breaking or in repelling masses by masses, he is
of no use. Partisan warfare, the war of tiraïl-
leurs, takes him at unawares. His havresack
at his back, armed with a wretched musket,
which he fires quite at random, with a sword
which does not deserve the name, the bayonet
is of little use to him, and more than one soldier has been seen despatched by the sword of
a Circassian, whom he had pierced with his
bayonet, because he could not draw it out
quickly enough. Opposed to such an adversary, the Circassian is a hero of fable; rarely
missing his man, using the pistol after dis-

charging his fusil, playing with the dagger as
well as with the sword; born and bred to war,
and for war, he is also a ferocious beast,
revelling in carnage, indomitable and intractable. Brave as his blade, nimble as his steed,
subsisting on a handful of rice, fanatic as the
Mussulman, blood-thirsty as a pagan, fighting
for his independence amidst inaccessible mountains, he may flatter himself that he shall
make any one repent who attempts to subdue
him. Violence can effect nothing with him;
he delights in the sight of blood: on the grave
of every brother slain by a christian he places
a mark, which he does not remove till he has
revenged his death by that of an enemy.
Civilization with all its seductions has no
charms for these men, and they shut their
hearts against every feeling that might endanger their independence. The Circassians
enrolled among the Russian troops retain all
their nationality and the warmest love of their
country. The very boys, who, carried to St.
Petersburg, brought up in the Greek religion,

were afterwards sent to their own country as
missionaries, flung their books into the first
Circassian river, and returned to their homes
with the sentiments which they had carried
away with them, and frequently with increased
hatred of the Russians; at other times their
brethren have made cartridges with the bibles
of the Russian emissaries. Hence people are
convinced that it is better to tolerate their
religion, and the Circassian cadets at Petersburg have a moullah who comes to instruct
them in their faith.

Divided into tribes independent of each
other, at times obeying merely the commands
of a prophet or a moullah whom they believe
to be inspired, or a prince who finds means
to gain an influence over them, if they could
ever forget their intestine quarrels and range
themselves under one and the same banner,
no power in the world could conquer them.
The best thing, therefore, that the Russians
could do is not to suffer the influence of
Schamile to increase, in hopes that the severity

which he exercises to keep the different tribes
that obey him under his authority, will urge
them to shake off his yoke and to rid themselves of him, but to foment and take advantage in every possible way, of the dissensions
of these tribes and their chiefs; for hatred
among these savages is so fierce that Circassians have been known to join the ranks of
the Russians and fight their old friends, their
brothers, their uncles, with a rancour that
nothing can equal.

Every Circassian carries arms, and among
the slain have frequently been found women,
who had astonished the Russians by their intrepidity.   Hence it is no more possible to
ascertain the number of their combatants than
that of the inhabitants in general.   Though
the latter is computed at a million only, that
is assuredly more than is needed to paralyze,
in so mountainous a country, all the enterprizes of the Russian army, even though it
were increased to double or treble the force at
present employed in the Caucasus.

In this war no quarter is given; the harshest
slavery is the lot of the Russian prisoners; and
to withhold from the Circassians the pecuniary
means of prolonging the war, the Government
has adopted the principle of not ransoming
them. If the Russians were to treat their
Tscherkessian prisoners better than they now
do—for they rarely fail to beat them cruelly
as soon as they are taken—they might hope
to see their number increase. Meanwhile the
courage and the fanaticism of the Circassian
cause him very often to put an end to his life
rather than surrender to the Russians. One
day a Circassian, after his horse had been
killed under him, found himself surrounded by
about twenty officers of the Russian guard.
Resolutely presenting his fusil, he manifested
a determination to dispatch the first who
should approach him. The officers consulted
whether one of them should encounter the
danger, or whether they should all rush upon
him at once, and leave to their gallant adversary the choice of his victim. They adopted

the latter course; but, on the first forward movement, the Circassian flung his piece on the ground, and stabbed himself with his dagger. On examining the fusil, they found that it was not even charged.

The Circassians employ the fusil in the same manner as Europeans use the sword or sabre, with extraordinary address. The Cossacks of the line imitate them in this, as in everything else, and a hill is still pointed out on which both parties fought with the fusil with equal desperation. At the moment when three hundred Cossacks of the line had reached the summit, they perceived several thousand Circassians advancing towards them. The officer would have fled, but his brother detained him; and this handful of brave fellows sustained the attack with courage. All perished; and when the field of battle was inspected, it was found that the Cossacks had sold their lives dearly, for they had made a circular mound of carcases around them. The oldest of the Cossacks, and at the same time

the most expert in the management of the
fusil, had fallen furthest advanced in the
enemy's ranks, after breaking his weapon in
several places; and, when dead, his hand still
grasped the beard of a Tscherkess. The Russian soldier, on his part, uses the but of his
piece almost as cleverly as the Circassian does
the barrel; he prefers it to the bayonet, with
which, he says, you can kill but one man at a
time, whereas with the but you may knock
down two or three at a single blow. Hence,
on a day of battle, most of the Russian buts
are broken, and the soldier frequently applies
to his officer for permission to return his
musket. The Poles had the same predilection
for fighting with the but, which has thus become a favourite practice with the Slavonians;
and it certainly requires some strength to wield
the weapon in this way with facility.

Since the annexation of Georgia and the
cession of the Persian provinces, the Russians
occupy the two faces of the chain of the Caucasus, which they thus coop up on both sides.

The interior of the mountains is composed of
arid rocks, fit at most, for pasturing the flocks
which supply the wants of the poor Tscherkessian tribes.   Is this really sufficient to
tempt the conquerors, especially when war in
this country demands such sacrifices in men
and money?   I have no doubt that, if the
mountaineers were left to themselves, they
would remain quiet, and would be glad to live
on peaceful terms with the Russians, and to
cultivate an intercourse profitable for both
parties.   The truces, short and transient as
they have been, confirm me in this opinion.
It is always the vexations and rapacity of the
Russian *employés* that have provoked the insurrections of the natives ; and the abuses must
have been atrocious to urge the Circassians to
prefer the calamities of war to the repose of
peace.   It is owing to this cause that Dag-
hestan, from being a tranquil province, has
become the haunt of the most implacable
enemies of Russia ; that the Tschetschenzes
have risen more than seven times in ten

years; and that the place where Schamile resides has been more than five times in the possession of the Russians, without their being able to keep it. The Circassians dwelling at the foot of the mountains ostensibly recognize the power of Russia, but, in the intervals between the campaigns, they lend a helping hand to the mountaineers, and assist them in the attack of the forts. If no cause of complaint were given them, they would not expose themselves to danger by attempts which the Russians have the power to punish severely. Hitherto, capitulations have been too easily granted, whereas the energetic repression of insurrections would have the infallible effect of abridging the calamities of war.

With the means and the men at present employed, the war in the Caucasus is a sterile war, and the obstinacy with which the Russian government persists in its continuance, will only serve to produce bloodshed, to embitter animosities, and to render reconciliation impossible. The war that it ought above all

things to wage, is with its own *employés,* who
are its greatest enemies, and who, after pro-
voking the conflict, render it so fatal by plun-
dering and robbing without mercy. They sell
the very powder to the enemy. They conceal
the number of the dead, and the army of the
Caucasus is so wretchedly supplied, that there
is not a single surgery deserving of that name.
The generals, on their part, protract the war,
to retain a source of emolument and promotion ; and, while there are no soldiers who
understand how to fire, the loss will always be
on the side of the Russians, their artillery
being of no use to them in this wholly irre-
gular warfare.

At the commencement of the present reign,
there was in the Caucasus General Yermolov,
whose name alone was a terror to the Circassians, while it is still held in veneration by the
Russians. Intrigue occasioned his recall. His
pupil, General Wiliaminof, could have continued his system and caused his removal to
be less sensibly felt, if he had been free in his

actions; but, fettered by the General-in-Chief, Baron Rosen, and by the ministry, he was obliged to confine himself to the execution of their orders. The negligence and the abuses laid to the charge of General Rosen, led to his dismissal. General Golovine, who succeeded him, managed, during his command in the Caucasus, to maintain the superiority of the Russian arms, and to erect some advanced forts, among which that named after him is of great utility. Being soon disgusted with a post more toilsome than glorious, he gave it up to Baron Neidhardt, whose German pedantry fixed his attention upon trifles and endangered important points. The hopes of the country have been revived by the appointment of Count Worontzof, who, invested with a discretionary power, has an immense advantage over all his predecessors. Having displayed some military ability in the campaign in France, and some administrative skill in his post of Governor-General of New Russia, he appears to justify the choice which has been

made of him. But one failing, peculiar to him,
is that of being as unfortunate in the choice
of his agents as he is obstinate in keeping
them. Now, all the calamities of the Caucasus
spring precisely from the knavery of the functionaries who have hitherto been employed
there; and, as much more is expected from
the administrative measures than from the
military enterprizes of Count Worontzof, there
is reason to fear that his efforts will not
always be crowned with success. His entry
upon his functions was marked by a measure
which cannot be censured too severely. Long
before his appointment, some Circassian chiefs
had solicited permission to carry on the slave-
trade in the Black Sea. Not so much out of
humanity as not to afford them the means of
enriching themselves, their application was
refused. By complying with it, Count Worontzof conceives that he has disposed them in
favour of Russia; but Tscherkessian gratitude
is not a thing upon which the Russians can
rely; and it is to be regretted that a civilized

man has deemed it right to yield to considerations far from courageous for authorizing the violation of a law of humanity and re-establishing the white slave-trade, at the same time that the Russian Government is protesting against the traffic in blacks.

Schamile appears to be one of those superior men whom the wars of independence have frequently produced. He has already more than once made the Russians severely repent having suffered him to return to his mountains. Being taken prisoner in 1828, with Kasi-Moullah, his master and predecessor, he was long confined in a Russian fort, and liberated with other prisoners solely because they were all believed to be inoffensive. His son has since fallen into the hands of the Russians, who are educating him with the cadets at St. Petersburg. This chief exercises a magic influence over his countrymen, by force and by money, as much as by his moral ascendency. Chaste, like all men, who have a high mission to fulfil, he disdains the law of the Prophet, which authorizes the keeping of a numerous harem, and devotes his wealth to the maintenance of his life-guards, whom he makes use of to excite the Circassian tribes against the Russians.

THE END.

DATE DUE